Dimensions M
Home Instruc
Guide 3B

Author

Jenny Kempe

Singapore Math Inc.

Published by Singapore Math Inc.

19535 SW 129th Avenue
Tualatin, OR 97062
www.singaporemath.com

Dimensions Math® Home Instructor's Guide 3B
ISBN 978-1-947226-63-0

First published 2022
Reprinted 2022

Printed in China

Acknowledgments

Design and illustration by Cameron Wray with Carli Bartlett.

Preface

This book is a guide for a parent or tutor teaching a student in a home or private setting. Its purpose is to help you understand the way mathematical concepts are presented in the Dimensions Math® curriculum, to gain an understanding of how these concepts fit in with the program as a whole, and to provide suggestions on how to introduce the concepts and use the textbook effectively. It will also offer suggestions for additional activities for reinforcement and practice. This guide does assume that you will be spending some time teaching or working with your student directly.

The relevant word for this book is **guide**. These are not detailed lesson plans telling you what to do or say, step-by-step through the whole lesson. Instead, there are background notes, some suggestions on how to help your student with a challenging problem, and things to watch out for as your student works through the problems.

Be flexible and use your judgment in what activities you use in order to meet your student's needs. A guide cannot predict what your student already knows, finds easy, finds challenging, how much time needs to be spent using manipulatives, or how long a lesson might take.

Study the textbook, along with this guide, before you teach, and then preferably teach without referring to the guide. The textbook is the basis of the curriculum. Although it is written to the student, it is meant as a tool for the teacher. If you spend time ahead of the lesson familiarizing yourself with the textbook contents, in conjunction with reading this guide, and even doing some of the problems yourself, you will be able to more effectively guide your student and address any difficulties. Look at the problems in the workbook as well.

Scheme of Work

Week		TB	WB	Guide
	Chapter 8 Multiplying and Dividing by 6, 7, 8, and 9			1–7
1	Chapter Opener	1		8–9
	1 The Multiplication Table of 6	2–6	1–3	10–11
	2 The Multiplication Table of 7	7–11	4–6	12
	3 Multiplying by 6 and 7	12–13	7–9	13
	4 Dividing by 6 and 7	14–16	10–12	14
2	5 Practice A	17	13–16	15
	6 The Multiplication Table of 8	18–22	17–19	16
	7 The Multiplication Table of 9	23–26	20–22	17
	8 Multiplying by 8 and 9	27–28	23–25	18
	9 Dividing by 8 and 9	29–30	26–28	19
3	10 Practice B	31–32	29–32	20
	Workbook Chapter 8 Answers			21–30
	Dimensions Math® Tests 3B, Chapter 8, pp. 1–12			
	Chapter 9 Fractions — Part 1			31–34
	Chapter Opener	33		35
	1 Fractions of a Whole	34–38	33–36	36–37
4	2 Fractions on a Number Line	39–42	37–39	38
	3 Comparing Fractions with Like Denominators	43–46	40–42	39
	4 Comparing Fractions with Like Numerators	47–50	43–46	40
	5 Practice	51–52	47–50	41

Week		TB	WB	Guide
8	5 Liters and Milliliters	102–106	94–96	86–87
	6 Kilograms and Grams	107–110	97–100	88
	7 Word Problems	111–115	101–104	89
	8 Practice	116–118	105–108	90–91
9	Dimensions Math® Tests 3B, Chapter 11, pp. 37–48			
	Review 3	119–122	109–114	92–93
	Workbook Chapter 11 Answers			94–102
	Dimensions Math® Tests 3B, Continual Assessment 3, pp. 49–68			
10	**Chapter 12 Geometry**			103–106
	Chapter Opener	123		107
	1 Circles	124–127	115–118	108
	2 Angles	128–131	119–120	109
	3 Right Angles	132–136	121–124	110
	4 Triangles	137–139	125–126	111
	5 Properties of Triangles	140–142	127–129	112–113
11	6 Properties of Quadrilaterals	143–146	130–133	114–115
	7 Using a Compass	147–150	134–138	116–117
	8 Practice	151–154	139–142	118
	Workbook Chapter 12 Answers			119–126
	Dimensions Math® Tests 3B, Chapter 12, pp. 69–80			

Week		TB	WB	Guide
12	**Chapter 13 Area and Perimeter**			127–130
	Chapter Opener	155		131
	1 Area	156–159	143–145	132
	2 Units of Area	160–162	146–149	133
	3 Area of Rectangles	163–165	150–152	134
	4 Area of Composite Figures	166–169	153–156	135
	5 Practice A	170–171	157–160	136
13	6 Perimeter	172–174	161–163	137
	7 Perimeter of Rectangles	175–176	164–166	138
	8 Area and Perimeter	177–179	167–169	139–140
	9 Practice B	180–182	170–172	141
	Workbook Chapter 13 Answers			142–148
	Dimensions Math® Tests 3B, Chapter 13, pp. 81–92			
14	**Chapter 14 Time**			149–152
	Chapter Opener	183		153
	1 Units of Time	184–189	173–176	154–155
	2 Calculating Time — Part 1	190–193	177–179	156–157
	3 Practice A	194–195	180–182	158
	4 Calculating Time — Part 2	196–199	183–186	159–160
	5 Calculating Time — Part 3	200–203	187–190	161

Week		TB	WB	Guide
15	6 Calculating Time — Part 4	204–206	191–194	162–163
	7 Practice B	207–208	195–198	164
	Workbook Chapter 14 Answers			165–170
	Dimensions Math® Tests 3B, Chapter 14, pp. 93–100			
	Chapter 15 Money			171–174
	Chapter Opener	209		175
	1 Dollars and Cents	210–213	199–201	176
	2 Making $10	214–215	202–203	177
16	3 Adding Money	216–219	204–206	178
	4 Subtracting Money	220–223	207–209	179
	5 Word Problems	224–226	210–212	180–181
	6 Practice	227–228	213–216	182
	Dimensions Math® Tests 3B, Chapter 15, pp. 101–112			
17	Review 4	229–232	217–221	183–184
	Review 5	233–236	222–226	185–187
	Workbook Chapter 15 Answers			188–194
	Dimensions Math® Tests 3B, Year-End Assessment 4, pp. 113–136			

Materials

Materials

- 1-L beaker
- Analog demonstration clock with geared hands
- Base-ten blocks (or centimeter cubes)
- Bills ($1, $5, $10, $20)
- Cardboard strips and brad fastener
- Coins (100 pennies, 50 dimes, 50 nickels, and 20 quarters)
- Compass
- Containers (cups, bottles)
- Dry-erase board (Individual)
- Geoboard and rubber bands
- Index cards
- Meter stick
- Paper strip or ribbon 1 meter long
- Platform scale (in kilograms)
- Ruler
- Set squares (both 90°-45°-45° and 90°- 30°-60° triangles)
- Stopwatch or timer
- Tape measure
- Toothpicks

Optional

- 100-mL beaker
- 500-mL beaker
- Balance
- Centimeter cubes
- Counters
- Fact cards (purchased)
- Fraction tiles
- Laminated hundred chart
- Metric weight set
- Number cubes (or dice), which can be labeled with numbers
- One-inch square tiles
- Playing cards
- Straws
- Short lengths of pipe cleaner or thin wire
- Store cards (20 of them): pictures of objects on index cards, with a cost between $1.00 and $25.00
- Tangrams
- Teaspoon

Printouts

Available for free download at singaporemath.com/higprintouts. Also available for purchase in ready-to-use packs at singaporemath.com.

- Alternate Set Squares
- Area of Figures
- Blank Multiplication Chart
- Centimeter Graph Paper
- Chapter 10 Opener
- Circle
- Circle Dot Paper
- Equivalent Fractions Puzzle
- Fraction Bars
- Fraction Bars to Twentieths
- Fraction Number Lines for Chapter 9
- Geoboard
- Graph paper
- Inch Graph Paper
- Lesson 10-2
- Lesson 10-3
- Lesson 12-4
- Lesson 12-5
- Lesson 13-1
- Multiplication Chart
- Multiplication Chart — 6
- Multiplication Chart — 7
- Multiplication Chart — 8
- Multiplication Chart — 9
- Number Cards 0–100
- Pentominoes
- Set Squares
- Square Dot Paper
- Tangram Pieces
- Triangle Sides

Mental Math Sheets

Available for free download at singaporemath.com/higprintouts. Also available for purchase in ready-to-use packs at singaporemath.com.

Notes

Textbook

Use the textbook as a resource to teach the concepts and to provide your student with some practice. The A book is for the first half of the year, and the B book is for the second half of the year.

Let your student write in the textbook! Blue boxes and blank lines are meant to elicit a student response, and can be filled in by your student. By letting students write in the textbook, they can see the written answer or numeral in context without having to write out the entire equation. If you decide to omit some problems during the lesson time, you will know which ones you can come back to for review later. In addition, by letting them own their textbook, you let them "own" their work, and the textbook becomes a reference to their own learning in the future. In later levels, there is less room and some problems will have to be worked out on a separate piece of paper or white board, but the responses in the blue boxes and blanks are still valuable resources for reference. Students can even make notes to themselves in the margins.

Each chapter starts with the Chapter Opener. Most of the lessons are organized into Think, Learn, and Do sections. Some lessons are designated as Practice or Review.

Chapter Opener

Generally, the Chapter Opener will ask students to recall material they have already learned, so that you can assess if they need some review. Sometimes the opener will introduce students to what they will be learning in the chapter. The Chapter Opener does not need to be an entire lesson, but can be used as an entire lesson if you feel you need to provide more review of earlier material. It might be done the same day as a test on the previous chapter.

Think

Most of the lessons in the textbook start with this section, which provides an initial problem or activity for the student to think about. Generally, you will have your student look at the problem and do the activity or answer the questions, covering up Learn, which comes next and often starts on the same page as Think.

In some cases, especially at this level, it will be easier to precede Think with a similar activity using objects, and then look at both Think and Learn at the same time.

Learn

This section consolidates what was learned in Think, adds explanation, and introduces new vocabulary. It may include several methods students could have used to solve the problem in Think. You should discuss the contents of Learn with your student, including all the possible methods or strategies, and have your student fill in blue boxes and blank lines.

Do

This section includes activities or problems that build and expand on the material in Learn. Generally, the progression of problems moves from concrete activities or pictorial representations to more abstract problems. You should guide your student in working through the initial problems. You can then usually let your student work independently on the final few problems, but should be available to answer questions and should check answers immediately.

Be flexible in meeting your student's needs. Exactly which problems and how many you have your student do independently depends on your student and how well they understand the concepts. If they understand the concepts well, they should have no problem doing all the problems, but if the problems seem repetitive, only assign some of them or omit the easier ones. If your student is struggling and the lesson is taking them a long time, have them do the easier problems and fewer of them, and omit the more challenging problems for now. You could start the next day's lesson by asking your student to do one or two of the omitted problems as a review. You could return to omitted problems for extra practice later, or if your student needs more continuous practice.

Practice

These are separate lessons that allow students to practice the concepts from the preceding lessons in the chapter. They often include more challenging problems towards the end. Although your student should be able to do these independently, you may have to help with some of the problems.

Review

There are five total cumulative reviews in the A and B textbooks. There is one halfway through each A and B, one at the end of A, and two at the end of B.

Workbook

The workbook has an exercise for each lesson, including the reviews. Each exercise has one or more sections called Basics, Practice, Challenge, or Check. The purpose of each of these is described below.

Be flexible with the workbook as well. There is often an excess of problems you can choose from. Your student may not need to do Basics if the lesson was easy. You may want to assign only some of the problems in Practice when there are too many. You may need to be present and guide them through Challenge.

Basics

These problems cover the concepts taught in the lesson. They guide students through the steps in solving the problems in a way that is meant to review all the concepts from the entire lesson (not just those from Learn). Some of the problems in this section may not necessarily be "basic" or the easiest problems of the exercise if they cover a concept introduced later in the lesson.

Practice

These problems provide practice. They generally progress in difficulty.

Challenge

These are optional enrichment problems. They either build on the material in the lesson to introduce some additional concepts, or require different problem solving strategies, like working backwards or drawing a picture. Use them in any way that best fits your student's abilities. Some students may be able to work on them independently, some will need a lot of guidance, and some might skip Challenge, or return to it at a later time.

Check

This section is only in exercises that correlate to a Practice or Review in the textbook.

Tests

The optional test book has two differentiated tests for each chapter. There are also two cumulative tests which correspond to each of the reviews in the textbook. Test B is a bit more challenging than Test A.

Tests are used for assessing a student's understanding and for assigning a grade. In a school situation it could signal whether a student needs some remedial help. Since you are in a home-education environment, and working directly with your student, you will have a more immediate sense of how well your student has mastered the concepts.

You can have your student do a test as an assessment, or use the test book as a source of additional problems. You could also save the tests for summer review.

Scheduling

The Scheme of Work at the beginning of this guide offers a suggested weekly schedule. You can use it simply to be sure you are on track to finish in however many weeks you have alloted for the semester. Any provided schedule is arbitrary, since some lessons may take your student a shorter time or a longer time.

Solutions

This guide provides solutions to many of the problems, not just the answers. As problems become more complex, particularly word problems, more than one method of solution is possible. While this guide sometimes offers several possible methods, it will not provide every possible method of solution. It might even provide one that may be less common for your benefit. Your student may solve the problem with a different method. If your student's method is less efficient than the one in this guide, you might want to discuss the method in the guide.

Mental Math Sheets

Available for free download at singaporemath.com/higprintouts. Also available for purchase in ready-to-use packs at singaporemath.com.

These are optional resources for your student to practice mental calculations. The notes for each chapter in this guide will list which ones can be done after a specific lesson. Use them however you wish and repeat them as many times as you wish. They can be used for practice and review during a later chapter.

For the sheets that practice the math facts, you could record the time it takes your student to do them, then have your student try to beat their previous times in future rounds. There is no rule for how fast a student needs to be able to answer a certain number of these math facts.

Some students simply do not like worksheets or timed drills and do not benefit from them, in which case, skip them. There are many websites with games for practicing addition and subtraction facts that offer an enjoyable and beneficial way to build proficiency.

For the sheets that practice other mental math strategies, if your student struggles with mental math strategies and is better off just doing the algorithm, you might want to skip them.

Chapter 8 Multiplying and Dividing 6, 7, 8, and 9

	Lesson	Page	Objectives
	Chapter Opener	8	
1	The Multiplication Table of 6	10	Use previously learned multiplication facts to learn the remaining four multiplication fact for 6. Learn the division facts for 6.
2	The Multiplication Table of 7	12	Use previously learned multiplication facts to learn the remaining four multiplication fact for 7. Learn the division facts for 7.
3	Multiplying by 6 and 7	13	Multiply a two-digit or three-digit number by 6 or 7.
4	Dividing by 6 and 7	14	Divide a two-digit or three-digit number by 6 or 7.
5	Practice A	15	
6	The Multiplication Table of 8	16	Use previously learned multiplication facts to learn the remaining four multiplication fact for 8. Learn the division facts for 8.
7	The Multiplication Table of 9	17	Use previously learned multiplication facts to learn the remaining four multiplication fact for 8. Learn the division facts for 8.
8	Multiplying by 8 and 9	18	Multiply a two-digit or three-digit number by 8 or 9.
9	Dividing by 8 and 9	19	Divide a two-digit or three-digit number by 8 or 9.
10	Practice B	20	

Materials

Materials

Optional

- Counters
- Fact cards
- Laminated hundred chart (use the back to create a multiplication table)
- Number cube
- Playing cards

Printouts

(singaporemath.com/higprintouts)

- Blank Multiplication Chart
- Graph paper
- Multiplication Chart
- Multiplication Chart — 6
- Multiplication Chart — 7
- Multiplication Chart — 8
- Multiplication Chart — 9
- Number Cards 0–100

Mental Math Sheets

(singaporemath.com/higprintouts)

Mental Math		After Lesson
1	Doubling a two-digit number	Chapter Opener
2	Multiplying a two-digit number by 2, 3, 4, or 5	Chapter Opener
3	Multiplication facts for 6	1
4	Division facts for 6	1
5	Multiplication facts for 7	2
6	Division facts for 7	2
7	Division by 6 and 7 with remainders	2
8	Multiplication facts for 8	6
9	Division facts for 8	6
10	Multiplication facts for 9	7
11	Division fact for 9	7
12	Division by 8 or 9 with remainders	7
13	Multiplication and division facts for 6, 7, 8, 9	7
14	Multiplication and division facts for 6, 7, 8, 9	7
15	Multiplication and division	9 (enrichment)

Notes

Multiplication

In Dimensions Math® 2A and 2B, students learned the concepts of multiplication and division and the multiplication and division facts for 2, 3, 4, 5, and 10.

In Dimensions Math® 3A, students learned that the "×" symbol can be interpreted as "times" or as "multiplied by." So 3×4 can mean either 3 groups of 4, or 3 in 4 groups. Students learned that for any whole number a or b, $a \times b = b \times a$. This is true for either interpretation of the symbol.

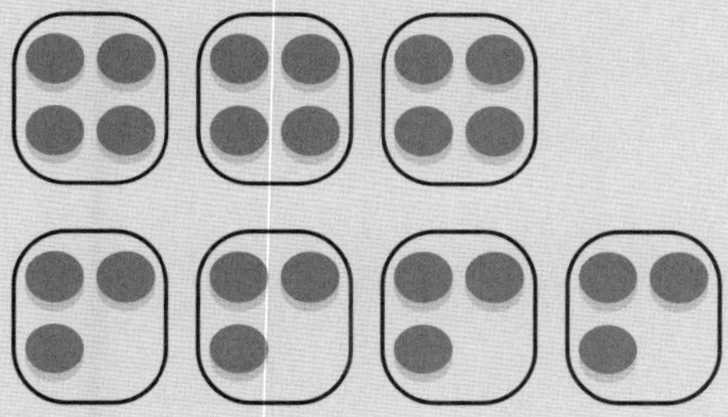

$3 \times 4 = 4 \times 3$

3 times 4 = 4 times 3

3 groups of 4 = 4 groups of 3

$4 \times 3 = 3 \times 4$

4 multiplied by 3 = 3 multiplied by 4

4 in 3 groups = 3 in 4 groups

By the end of Dimensions Math® 2A, and again by the end of Dimensions Math® 3A, students learned and practiced all the multiplication facts except for 16 of them, those where both factors are greater than 5. In this chapter, students will learn the remaining 16 multiplication facts.

When learning multiplication facts previously, students were taught various strategies for computing known facts from unknown facts. For example, knowing that $4 \times 5 = 20$, to find the value of 6×4 or 4×6 we can add 4 to 20. Knowing that $4 \times 10 = 40$, to find the value of 9×4 or 4×9 we can subtract 4 from 40. We can find 6×4 either by doubling twice ($6 + 6 = 12$, then $12 + 12 = 24$) or by doubling the value of 3×4. Students will continue to apply these as well as additional strategies in this chapter. They will help students quickly compute facts they have not yet memorized, or have forgotten.

These strategies make use of the distributive property of multiplication, which students will learn formally in Grade 6:

$$(a + b) \times c = (a \times c) + (b \times c)$$
$$(a - b) \times c = (a \times c) - (b \times c)$$

For example:

$$6 \times 4 = (5 + 1) \times 4 = (5 \times 4) + (1 \times 4)$$
$$9 \times 4 = (10 - 1) \times 4 = (10 \times 4) - (1 \times 4)$$

This guide will use the term "factor" to refer to the whole numbers in a multiplication expression.

Division

Students learned two interpretations for the division symbol: sharing (partitive division) or grouping (quotative division).

In a sharing situation, a given quantity is shared into a given number of groups equally to find the quantity in each group.

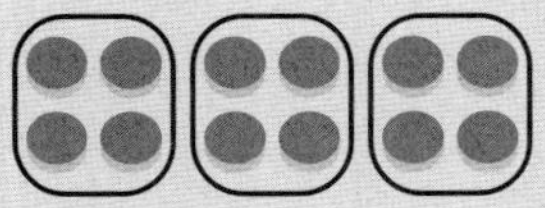

$12 \div 3 = 4$

12 shared into 3 groups is 4 in each group.

In a grouping situation, a given quantity is grouped by a given number to find the number of equal groups.

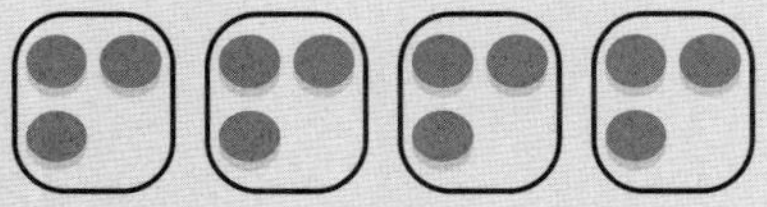

$12 \div 3 = 4$

12 grouped by 3 is 4 groups.

In each case, the equation $12 \div 3 = 4$ is read as "twelve divided by three equals four" and the numerical value of the answer is the same, even if the physical situation is different.

To learn the division facts, students learned to use the multiplication facts. For example, to find $27 \div 3$, we can think of what number ? stands for in either $? \times 3 = 27$ or $3 \times ? = 27$. Students will continue to do this to learn the division facts for 6, 7, 8, and 9.

In Dimensions Math® 3A, students learned the standard multiplication and division algorithms and multiplied or divided a number of up to three digits by 2, 3, 4, or 5. The lessons were carefully sequenced, and used place-value discs (discs with 1, 10, or 100 written on them) to concretely represent the steps of the written algorithm. Students will be multiplying and dividing numbers of up to three digits by 6, 7, 8 and 9 in this chapter, with a very brief review of the written algorithm. If your student has not learned to multiply and divide a three-digit number by a one-digit number, they should do Dimensions Math® 3A Chapters 5 and 6. Do not rely on them having a foundational understanding of the algorithm from the brief review in this chapter.

In this curriculum, R (remainder) will not be used in an equation. Students will see "$16 \div 3$ is 5 with a remainder of 1" and can write "$16 \div 3$ is 5 R 1" as a shortcut for that statement. Using R in an equation is technically incorrect. In $16 \div 3 = 5$ R 1 and $21 \div 4 = 5$ R 1, the answers appear to be the same, but $16 \div 3 \neq 21 \div 4$: $16 \div 3 = 5\frac{1}{3}$ and $21 \div 4 = 5\frac{1}{4}$.

At this level, the term "quotient" refers to the whole number part of the answer to a division expression. Students will learn to express an exact quotient as a mixed number in Dimensions Math® 4A.

Word Problems

In Dimensions Math® 3A, students learned to draw bar models to represent the information in a word problem in order to determine a method of solution. For addition and subtraction, there are two basic models.

Part-whole model for addition and subtraction:

There are 432 people at a fair. 271 of them are children and the rest are adults. How many adults are there?

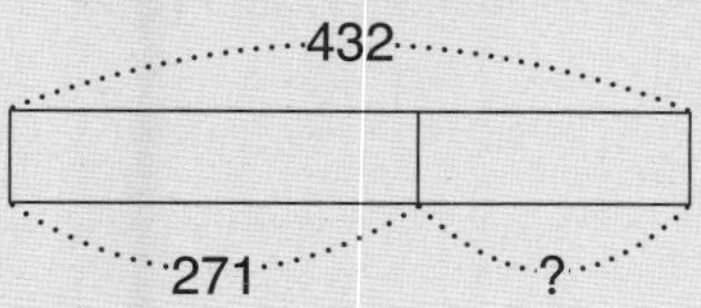

432 – 271 = 161

There are 161 adults

Comparison model for addition and subtraction:

There are 432 adults at a fair. There are 271 more adults than children. How many children are there?

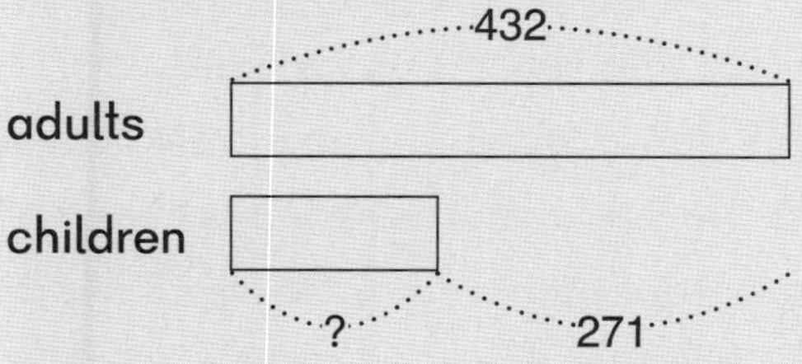

432 – 271 = 161

There are 161 children.

There are also two basic models for multiplication and division. Students learned a new notation using arrows and the term "unit" that they could use.

Part-whole model for multiplication and division (sharing):

320 jars are put equally into 5 boxes. How many jars are in each box?

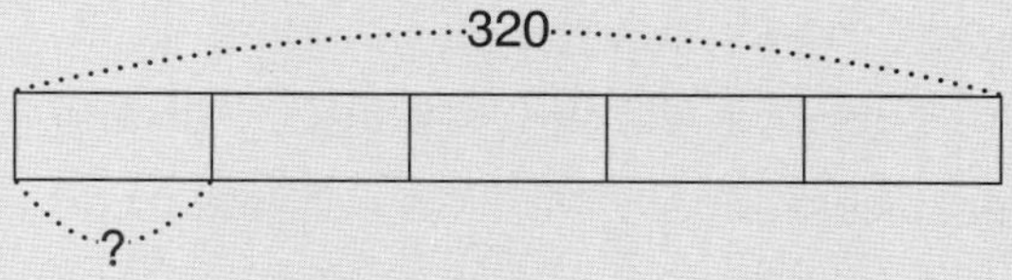

5 units ⟶ 320

1 unit ⟶ 320 ÷ 5 = 64

There are 64 jars in each box.

Comparison model for multiplication and division (sharing):

Joshua has \$135. He has 3 times as much money as Evan. How much money does Evan have?

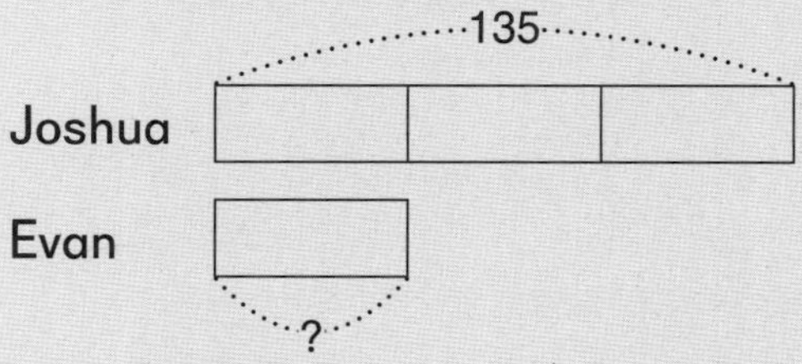

3 units ⟶ 135

1 unit ⟶ 135 ÷ 3 = 45

Evan has \$45

A grouping situation for division was also modeled, but students should not often have to draw models for grouping situations:

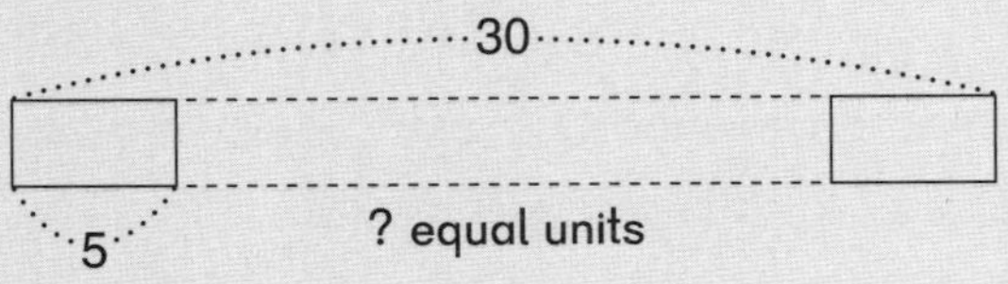

$30 \div 5 = 6$

These are examples for simple, one-step word problems. Students should generally be able to solve such problems without a model. The usefulness of bar models is more apparent in multi-step word problems, where these basic types of models can be combined. For example:

Audrey has $62 more than Bailey. Sienna has 3 times as much money as Bailey. Altogether they have $137. How much money does Audrey have?

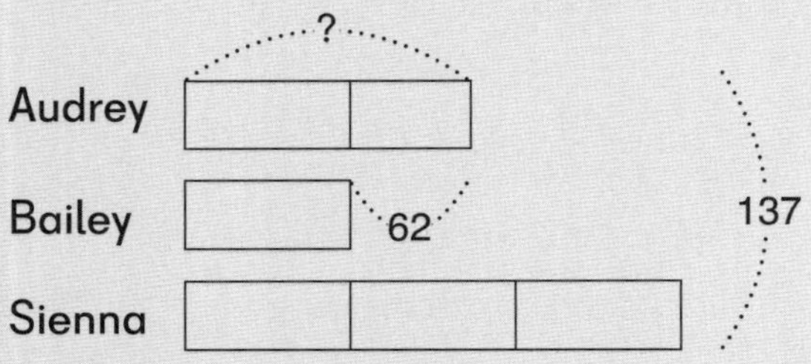

5 units ⟶ $137 - 62 = 75$
1 unit ⟶ $75 \div 5 = 15$
$15 + 62 = 77$
Audrey has $77

Bar models are a pictorial representation of the problem, and do not have to be drawn precisely like those in the textbook or in the solutions in this guide. There is not a set of rules on exactly how or what type of model to draw. The model should accurately represent the information in the problem and help in arriving at a method of solution. If your student is fine with moving directly to an abstract solution, they do not necessarily have to draw a model. However, they should be comfortable drawing bar models and will need to draw them to be able to solve some of the word problems throughout this level.

If your student is not familiar with drawing bar models, consider using Dimensions Math® 3A and doing portions of Chapter 2 and Chapter 4, as well as word problems in the reviews and practices of the rest of the chapters. Alternately, you should become familiar with them yourself, and guide your student in using bar models as you proceed.

Fact Practice

Provide opportunity for your student to practice the remaining 16 multiplication facts, as well as any other facts they do not yet recall easily.

A few general activities and games are provided here. You can also use the **Mental Math Sheets**. There are many games that you can find online that provide a fun way to practice and include a time element. Use whatever approach works best for your student. However you provide practice, be sure to keep it fun and light for your student, not frustrating and tedious.

Activity

- After Lesson 2
  Materials: Flash cards for the facts being practiced
  Purpose: Recall multiplication or division facts.
  Procedure: Mix the cards up. Show your student one card at a time and have them give the answer. If correct, place them in one pile; if incorrect, place them in a second pile. Repeat with the second pile.

Games

- After Lesson 1, 2, 6, or 7
  Materials: Four sets of number cards 1–10 (or playing cards with faces removed), a number cube labeled with factors needing practice (for example, label the number cube with 3, 4, 6, 6, 7, and 7 after Lesson 2)
  Purpose: Practice multiplication facts.
  Goal: Get the most cards.
  Procedure: Shuffle the cards and turn them face down in the middle. Each player draws a card, rolls the number cube, and multiplies the number on the card with the number on the number cube. The player with the greatest product gets all the cards that have been drawn. If there are two players with the same greatest product, the one with the card with the greatest number gets all the cards. Alternately, those two players can draw another card and throw the number cube again to see which of them wins the round.

- After Lesson 7
  Materials: Number cards 6–100; a number cube labeled with 6, 7, 8, 9, and any other two numbers; 100 counters
  Purpose: Divide when there is a remainder.
  Goal: Get the most counters.
  Procedure: Shuffle the number cards and place them face down in the middle. Players take turns turning over the top card, rolling the number cube, and dividing the number on the card by the number on the number cube. If there is a remainder, they get the same number of counters as the remainder. Play continues until there are no counters left. The player with the greatest number of counters wins.
  Variation: Instead of using counters, players write down their remainders and keep a running total. The first to reach 100 wins.

Chapter Opener (p. 1)

This Chapter Opener reminds students that they already know most of the multiplication facts for 6, 7, 8, and 9, and that they will be learning the remaining facts in this chapter. Alex is pointing out that they will learn strategies for computing these remaining facts from facts they already know.

Have your student fill out the **Blank Multiplication Chart** printout. They should be able to fill in all the facts by just adding the correct amount on the number above or to the left, even if they don't know all the facts.

Draw a diagonal as shown in the figure on this page. (If you want, you can tell your student these numbers are called square numbers. They fall at the lower right of a square with the same number of rows and columns, and are the product of two numbers that are the same.) Point out that each number on one side of the diagonal has a partner on the other side that is the same. Have your student write the equation for one such pair (using either the column or row heading as the first number in each). For example, 9 × 3 = 27 and 3 × 9 = 27. Remind them that if they know the answer to 9 × 3, they also know the answer to 3 × 9.

Ask your student to lightly shade in the squares for the facts for 1, 2, 3, 4, 5, and 10. These are the multiplication facts they already know (or should know).

×	1	2	3	4	5	6	7	8	9	10
1	1	2	3	4	5	6	7	8	9	10
2	2	4	6	8	10	12	14	16	18	20
3	3	6	9	12	15	18	21	24	27	30
4	4	8	12	16	20	24	28	32	36	40
5	5	10	15	20	25	30	35	40	45	50
6	6	12	18	24	30	36	42	48	54	60
7	7	14	21	28	35	42	49	56	63	70
8	8	16	24	32	40	48	56	64	72	80
9	9	18	27	36	45	54	63	72	81	90
10	10	20	30	40	50	60	70	80	90	100

Ask your student to mark all the answers that are odd numbers and look at the two factors. They should realize that the product is odd only when both the factors are odd, which they discovered in Dimensions Math® 3A. This idea can be used to determine if an answer makes sense: if one of the factors is even, the answer can't be odd.

Some of the strategies for calculating unknown facts involve doubling two-digit numbers. Although students had the option of using mental math when multiplying a two-digit number by a one-digit number in Dimensions Math® 3A, they were not required to. You may want to spend this time discussing and having your student mentally multiply a two-digit number by 2, and possibly also by 3, 4, and 5. You can use the following suggestions.

On the chart, point to the row for × 1 and the row for × 2. Point out that each number in the × 2 row is double the number in the × 1 row. See if your student can find a row where each number is double the one in the × 2 row (the × 4 row). Ask them to find other pairs of rows where the numbers in one row are double the numbers in the row above (× 4 and × 8, × 3 and × 6, × 5 and × 10).

Write the number 32 and ask your student to double it. They may find the answer using addition: 32 + 32 = 64. Show them that they can split 32 into 30 and 2, multiply the tens first and and then the ones (rather than multiplying the ones first, as with the multiplication algorithm), and add the partial products together.

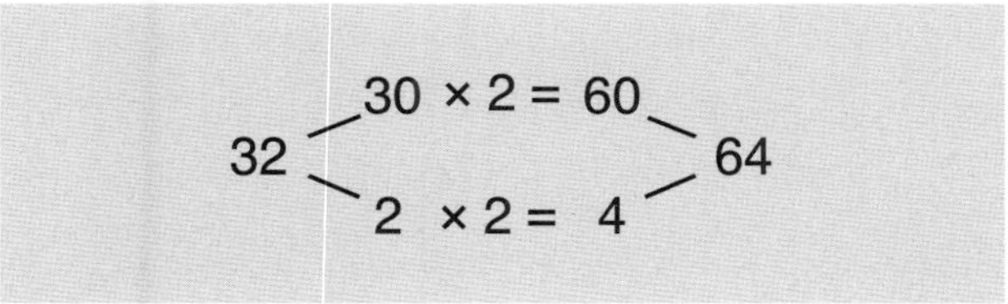

Repeat with 38, 62, and 68, illustrating the process in any way that makes sense to your student. Your student can, of course, simply use mental math strategies for addition, but if instead they understand this process as multiplication, they can apply it to multiplying by other one-digit numbers.

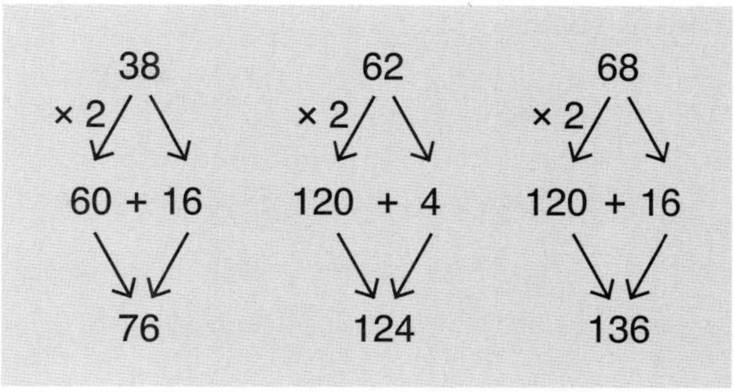

Ask your student to double some other two-digit numbers mentally (without writing each partial product). You can have them do the **Mental Math Sheet 1** for more practice.

You can optionally extend this to showing your student how to mentally multiply a two-digit number by 3, 4, and 5.

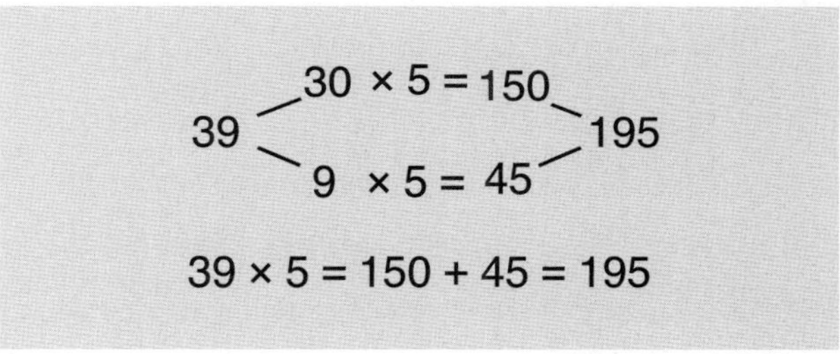

You can have your student do the **Mental Math Sheet 2** for more practice.

Lesson 1 The Multiplication Table of 6 (pp. 2–6)

Think (p. 2)

Ask your student to write an equation for each of these. You can use the **Multiplication Chart 6** printout. Your student should already realize, either from earlier levels or from having filled in a multiplication chart, that the total number of paper towels increases by 6 when the number of packs increases by 1.

Learn (p. 3)

Your student should realize that the total (the product) in each equation is all of the counters in the rows up to and including the row with the equation. You can illustrate this by covering up the rows with an index card, and then sliding the card down one row at a time. The product in the last row uncovered is the total number of uncovered counters. Doing this may also help your student fill in the blue boxes. When you uncover the row for 10 × 6 = 60, you can cover it back up to illustrate that 9 × 6 is 6 less than 10 × 6 = 60.

Ask your student to add the digits together for each of the products. Sofia is showing what they need to do. They will find that the sum of the digits is always a multiple of 3. Since it is, they could then add the digits again when the sum has more than one digit and will find that the final sum is always 3, 6, or 9. For example, for the product 48, the sum of the digits is 12, and the sum of the digits of 12 is 3. Since 6 is an even number, all products of 6 are even numbers. Students can use these two ideas to see if their answers make sense when one factor is 6. For example, 32, 51, or 56 cannot be the answer to a multiplication fact with 6 as one of the factors.

Answers

6
10

1 6
36

2 12
42

3 48

4 6
54

5 24
24
48

6 (a) 36
(b) 42 42
(c) 48 48
(d) 54 54

7 30 30
30 30

8 (a) 7 7
(b) 9 9
(c) 8 8
(d) 6 6

9 (a) 4 4 R 4
(b) 6 6 R 5
(c) 9 9 R 3

Do (pp. 4–6)

The first five problems illustrate various strategies students could use to calculate the four new facts from facts they already know. Notice that one of the factors in each equation is in bold. In the final equation, the number in bold is the sum of the two numbers in bold in the preceding two equations. Splitting one factor into two parts, multiplying each part by the other factor, and then adding the partial products together is not a new idea if students used Dimensions Math® 3A.

1. If we know that 5 × 6 = 30, we can find 6 × 6 by adding 6 to that answer. Emma is illustrating this by splitting 6 into 5 and 1. Both 5 and 1 need to be multiplied by the other factor (6) and then those partial products added. (This is different from when number bonds are used to illustrate mental math strategies for addition.)

2. If we know that 5 × 6 = 30, we can find 7 × 6 by adding 12 (6 + 6 or 2 × 6) to that answer (or mentally adding 6 twice).

3. 8 × 6 is double 4 × 6 (since 8 is double 4). You can point out that 4 × 6 is double 2 × 6, so to find 8 × 6 we can double three times: double 6 is 12, double 12 is 24, double 24 is 48. (This will be covered in Lesson 6.)

4. 9 × 6 is 6 less than 10 × 6.

5. This problem shows another way to find the value of 8 × 6: we can double 8 × 3. In this case, 6 is split into 3 and 3.

6. This problem reminds students that the answer will be the same whichever factor represents the number of groups and whichever factor represents the number in each group. If they know the products for 7 × 6, 8 × 6, and 9 × 6, they also know the products for 6 × 7, 6 × 8, and 6 × 9. Students have now learned 7 of the remaining 16 facts (or 91 out of 100 multiplication facts).

7. 8. These problems remind students that we can think of a corresponding multiplication fact to find the answer to a division problem. To find 42 ÷ 6, we can think of 7 × 6 = 42 (or 6 × 7 = 42) and know the answer is 7.

9. This problem reminds students of how to divide when there is a remainder. 28 is not a product of 6. (We know this ahead of time since, even though 28 is even, the sum of the digits is 10, which is not a product of 3, so 28 is not a product of 6.) To find the quotient, we need to think of a product of 6 closest to, but less than, 28. 4 × 6 = 24 is less than 28, and 5 × 6 = 30 is greater than 28, so the quotient is 4. To find the remainder, we subtract: 28 – 24 = 4. Have your student answer Alex's question (5). This reminds students that the remainder must be less than the number we are dividing by.

Remind your student that, if there is a remainder, the number is not fully divided, and so we will not use an equal symbol. 28 ÷ 6 is 4 with a remainder of 4. We write this as 28 ÷ 6 is 4 R 4 (not 28 ÷ 6 = 4 R 4).

Lesson 2 The Multiplication Table of 7 (pp. 7–11)

Think (p. 7)

Follow a procedure similar to the previous lesson. You can use the **Multiplication Chart 7** printout.

Learn (p. 8)

If necessary, you can cover up the rows with an index card and move the card down one row at a time. Each product is 7 more than the product before it, or 7 less than the product after it. Students do not need to know order of operations rules to understand the expressions here; they should just calculate from left to right. Mei says there are only 3 new facts, since students have already learned 6 × 7 in the previous lesson. Since they will also learn 7 × 8 and 7 × 9, they will actually learn 5 new multiplication facts in this lesson.

Do (pp. 9–11)

The first four problems show strategies similar to the ones in the previous lesson. The rest of the problems follow a similar sequence, with the addition of two word problems. For simple word problems, students are expected to read the problem, determine what operation or set of steps is needed to solve it, write the expression for each step and then solve it, completing the equation. If they do not write the answer in a sentence, they should at least write the answer on a separate line with the "unit," such as dollars, or number of pounds, or item name.

Answers

7
7
7

❶ 21
21
42

❷ 35
14
49

❸ 16
56

❹ 70
7
63

❺ (a) 42 42
(b) 49
(c) 56 56
(d) 63 63

❻ 42 42
42 42

❼ (a) 9 9
(b) 7 7
(c) 8 8

❽ **$4**
28 ÷ 7 = 4

❾ **63 pounds**
9 × 7 = 63

❿ (a) 3 3 R 3
(b) 7 7 R 1
(c) 9 9 R 6

Lesson 3 Multiplying by 6 and 7 (pp. 12–13)

Think (p. 12)

Have your student write an expression and solve it. You may want to cover up Learn or write the problem on a whiteboard.

Learn (p. 12)

This reviews the steps for the multiplication algorithm. Your student should already have a thorough understanding of this algorithm from Dimensions Math® 3A.

Do (p. 13)

Assign as many problems from here as you feel would be helpful for your student. Since they should be comfortable with the algorithm already, you could even skip this Do and proceed directly to the workbook, and instead spend some time with activities for fact recall. You could save these problems to incorporate into future lessons in other chapters, such as one problem a day at the start of lesson, as ongoing practice.

Answers

1,650

1. 414
2. 6,069
3. (a) 486 (b) 112 (c) 476
   (d) 1,456 (e) 4,690 (f) 2,808
4. **$756**
   126 × 6 = 756
5. **$1,806**
   258 × 7 = 1,806

Lesson 4 Dividing by 6 and 7 (pp. 14–16)

Think (p. 14)

Have your student write an expression and solve it. You may want to cover up Learn or write the problem on a whiteboard.

Learn (p. 14)

This reviews the steps for the division algorithm. Your student should already have a thorough understanding of this algorithm from Dimensions Math® 3A.

Do (pp. 15–16)

Assign as many problems from here as you feel would be helpful for your student before proceeding to the workbook. You may want to have your student do at least ❶ if a review of the different situations is needed. For example, in (c) there are no tens to divide and in (d) all of the hundreds need to be renamed. Be sure to remind your student how to check their answers. You might want to point out that the answer for (c) is easy to check mentally.

If your student has trouble aligning the digits when rewriting the problem in vertical format ("long division"), let them use graph paper or lined paper turned sideways.

If your student is showing their work, they do not necessarily have to write the remainder next to the quotient. Remember to check that they got a correct remainder.

Answers

159 cartons, 2 eggs left over

❶ (a)

```
   1 6
6 )9 8
   6
   3 8
   3 6
     2
```

(b)

```
   1 2 8
7 )8 9 6
   7
   1 9
   1 4
     5 6
     5 6
       0
```

(c)

```
   1 0 4
7 )7 3 2
   7
     3 2      32 ones ÷ 7
     2 8
       4
```

(d)

```
     7 9
6 )4 7 4
   4 2
     5 4
     5 4
       0
```

❷ (a) 14 (b) 13 R 4 (c) 118 R 1
(d) 130 R 6 (e) 83 R 2 (f) 114 R 2

❸ **125 miles** $750 \div 6 = 125$

❹ **92 pots** $644 \div 7 = 92$

Lesson 5 Practice A (p. 17)

Since much of this chapter is review, and the workbook exercise provides practice as well, you might want to spend this lesson helping your student with the multiplication and division facts, and save some of these problems for later ongoing practice.

The word problems are multi-step problems, but they are fairly easy and should not be a challenge, nor require a bar model if your student has done earlier levels. If they are a challenge, guide your student in determining what they need to find first. If your student is not familiar with bar models, you might want to show how a bar model could represent the problem for ❸, since they will need to draw bar models for some of the word problems in the workbook. A possible model is given here.

If your student is not comfortable yet with drawing bar models, or has not yet seen the notation using arrows and the term "unit," you may want to spend some time discussing the solutions given in this guide for the word problems in the workbook exercise. Using this notation is not essential for all word problems involving multiplication or division, but can be helpful for problems involving comparison, such as ❻ in the workbook exercise.

Answers

❶ (a) 42 (b) 56 (c) 48
(d) 9 (e) 7 (f) 9

❷ (a) 448 (b) 3,378 (c) 4,230
(d) 15 R 2 (e) 131 R 3 (f) 43 R 1

❸ **$4**

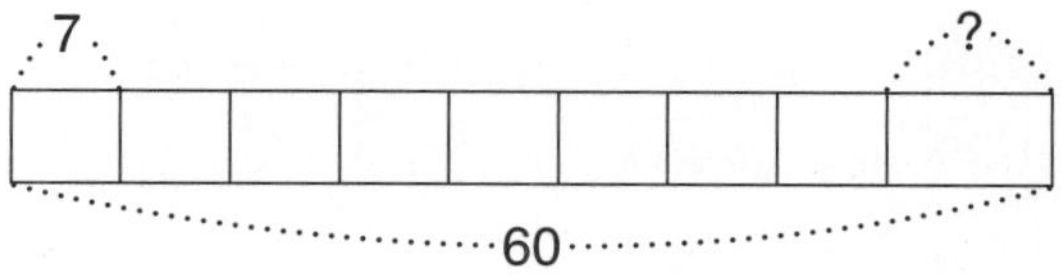

Cost of plants:
$8 \times 7 = 56$
Change:
$60 - 56 = 4$

❹ **1,560 m**
$120 \times 7 = 840$
$120 \times 6 = 720$
$840 + 720 = 1,560$

❺ **15 weeks**
Number of weeks that have passed:
$259 \div 7 = 37$
Weeks left:
$52 - 37 = 15$

Lesson 6 The Multiplication Table of 8 (pp. 18–22)

Think (p. 18)

Follow a procedure similar to the previous lesson. You can use the **Multiplication Chart 8** printout.

Learn (p. 19)

Sofia says there are only 2 new facts, since students have already learned 7 × 8 in the previous lesson. Since they will also learn 8 × 9, they will actually learn 3 new multiplication facts in this lesson, and will then know 99 out of the 100 multiplication facts. Alex points out that all the answers are even (one of the factors, 8, is even).

Do (pp. 20–22)

❹ Students already know that when they multiply a number by 4, they can find the answer by doubling twice. To multiply a number by 8, they can double three times (the first doubling is shown by the equations in the first column in the table on page 21. You can add a column with just the number being multiplied by 8 to the left, and another arrow with × 2 going from it to the next column to show the three doublings). For example, to find 8 × 7, double 7 is 14, double 14 is 28, double 28 is 56.

❽ Rather than division problems with a remainder, as in ❼, this is showing the reverse, or the equation used to verify the answer. To find the number in the blue boxes, we need to divide 74 or 54 by 8.

Answers

8
8
8

❶ 8
48

❷ 16
56

❸ 80
8
72

❹

	20	40
	24	48
	28	56
	32	64
	36	72
20	40	80

❺

56	56
56	56

❻

(a)	8	8
(b)	9	9

❼

(a)	6	6 R 3
(b)	4	4 R 4
(c)	8	8 R 6
(d)	7	7 R 7

❽ (a) 9
(b) 6

Lesson 7 The Multiplication Table of 9 (pp. 23–26)

Think (p. 23)

Follow a procedure similar to the previous lesson. You can use the **Multiplication Chart 9** printout.

Learn (p. 24)

The friends at the bottom of the page are pointing out some patterns they notice. This pattern can be used to easily find the product when multiplying a one-digit number by 9. The tens digit is one less than the number being multiplied by 9, and the ones digit is the difference between 9 and the tens digit. There will be more about this in ❷.

Do (pp. 25–26)

❶ Students should have no trouble understanding this strategy, since they have seen it with every lesson covering strategies for multiplication by 2 through 8. The image at the right is meant to apply to all four of these if you imagine the card being pulled down to expose each row.

❷ Each multiple of 9 is 9 more than the one before, or 10 – 1 more. The tens digit will therefore increase by 1 and the ones digit will decrease by 1, so the sum of the digits will always be 9. This gives the pattern observed in Learn.

❺ Students should realize an extra van, and therefore driver, is needed, even though it will not be full, and not simply write the quotient 6 as the answer.

Answers

9
9

❶ (a) 54
(b) 7
63
(c) 8
72
(d) 9
81

❷ (a) 54
(b) 72
(c) 81

❸ (a) 9 9
(b) 7 7

❹ (a) 4 4 R 8
(b) 7 7 R 7
(c) 5 5 R 3

❺ **7 drivers**
60 ÷ 9 is 6 R 6

❻ **81 tokens shared, 4 tokens left over**
85 ÷ 9 is 9 R 4

❻ Students need to read the problem carefully, and not simply write the quotient 9 for one of the answers. The problem is not asking for how many tokens each child gets, but rather how many tokens in all are shared.

Lesson 8 Multiplying by 8 and 9 (pp. 27–28)

Think (p. 27)

Have your student write an expression and solve it. You may want to cover up Learn or write the problem on a whiteboard.

Learn (p. 27)

This reviews the steps for the multiplication algorithm. Your student should already have a thorough understanding of this algorithm from Dimensions Math® 3A.

Do (p. 28)

5 You may want to show your student a bar model and discuss the two solutions shown for this problem at the right if you did not do so for similar problems in the workbook. Do so particularly if they solved it using the second method at the right. The difference between the two methods is simply that subtraction (9 – 1) is essentially done first in the first method, which often results in simpler calculations. Drawing a bar model in this case (or imagining one, if students have throughly mastered similar problems from Dimensions Math® 3A) allows for an intuitive use of the reverse of the distributive property (factorization), which students will learn formally in Grades 6 or 7:

$(9 \times 99) - (1 \times 99) = (9 - 1) \times 99 = 8 \times 99$

Answers

7,808

1 684

2 3,984

3 (a) 639 (b) 136 (c) 765
(d) 2,472 (e) 6,120 (f) 6,678

4 **1,350 yo-yos**
$150 \times 9 = 1,350$

5 **$792 more**

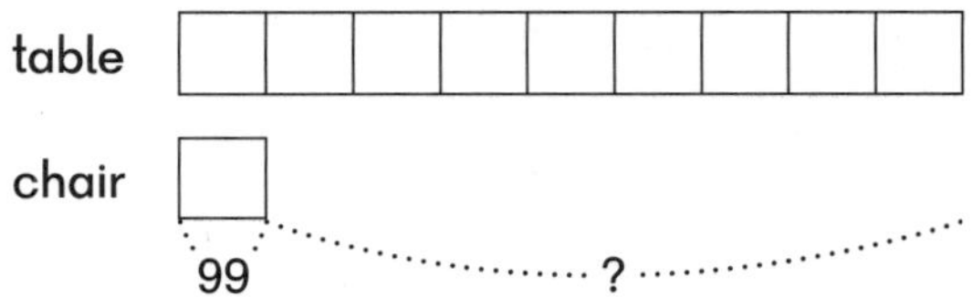

$8 \times 99 = 792$

Or:

$9 \times 99 = 891$

$891 - 99 = 792$

Lesson 9 Dividing by 8 and 9 (pp. 29–30)

Think (p. 29)

Have your student write an expression and solve it. You may want to cover up Learn or write the problem on a whiteboard.

Learn (p. 29)

This reviews the steps for the division algorithm. Your student should already have a thorough understanding of this algorithm from Dimensions Math® 3A.

Do (p. 30)

Assign as many problems from here as you feel would be helpful for your student before proceeding to the workbook.

❸ Students need to read the problem carefully and not simply write the quotient 30 for the answer. The problems is not asking for how many teams there will be, but rather how many students are left over (who will become the referees).

Answers

106 cartons, 0 donuts left over

❶ (a)

$$\begin{array}{r} 12 \\ 8\overline{)97} \\ 8 \\ \hline 17 \\ 16 \\ \hline 1 \end{array}$$

(b)

$$\begin{array}{r} 124 \\ 8\overline{)996} \\ 8 \\ \hline 19 \\ 16 \\ \hline 36 \\ 32 \\ \hline 4 \end{array}$$

(c)

$$\begin{array}{r} 43 \\ 9\overline{)388} \\ 36 \\ \hline 28 \\ 27 \\ \hline 1 \end{array}$$

❷ (a) 11 (b) 122 R 3 (c) 101 R 1
(d) 83 R 6 (e) 62 R 4 (f) 88 R 8

❸ **4 referees**
244 ÷ 8 is 30 R 4

Enrichment

You can, if you want, show your student a "trick" using their hands for finding the multiplication facts for 9. They hold their hands in front of them, and number the fingers 1 to 10 from left to right. They fold down the single finger for the number they are multiplying by 9. The number of fingers to the left of the folded finger is the tens of the answer, and the number of fingers to the right is the ones of the answer. For example, they fold down the 8th finger for 8 × 9. There are 7 fingers to the left, and 2 to the right of the folded finger, so the answer is 72.

Lesson 10 Practice B (pp. 31–32)

You may want to save some of the problems from ❷ and ❸ for ongoing practice later.

If bar models are new for your student, discuss the one shown for ❹ and draw models for ❺ and ❼, particularly if you did not discuss the workbook problems.

Answers

❶ (a) 9 (b) 8
(c) 8 (d) 56
(e) 67 (f) 6

❷ (a) 5,600 (b) 540
(c) 528 (d) 747
(e) 6,273 (f) 5,960

❸ (a) 7 R 6 (b) 3 R 3
(c) 12 R 4 (d) 115 R 4
(e) 42 R 1 (f) 55 R 5

❹ **$72 less**

2 units ⟶ 18
1 unit ⟶ 18 ÷ 2 = 9
8 units ⟶ 8 × 9 = 72

❺ **$3,078**

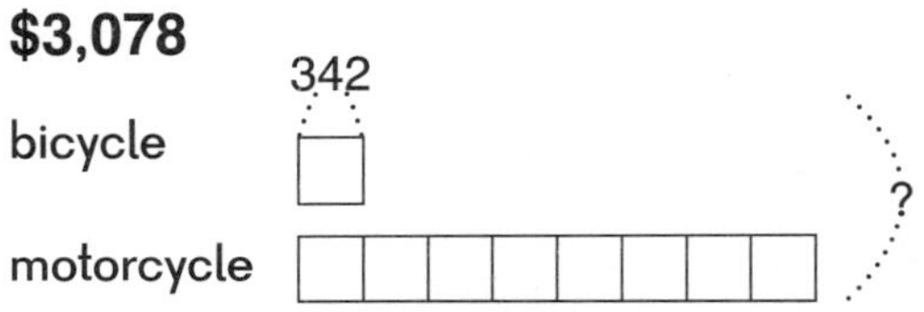

9 × 342 = 3,078
Or
8 × 342 = 2,736
2,736 + 342 = 3,078

❻ **$504**

448 ÷ 8 = 56
56 × 9 = 504

❼ **352 more children**

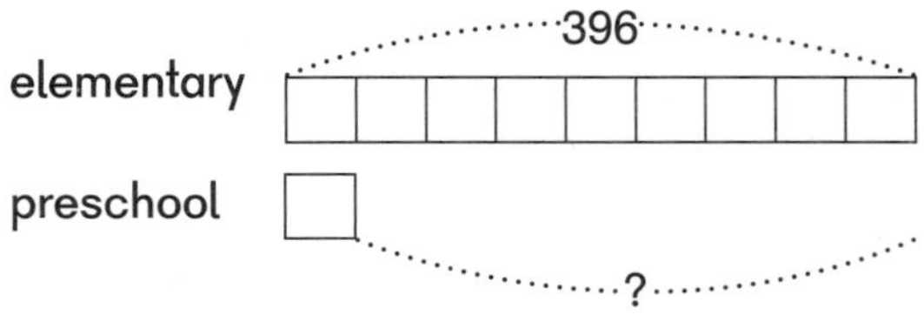

1 unit ⟶ 396 ÷ 9 = 44
8 units ⟶ 8 × 44 = 352
Or 396 − 44 = 352

Chapter 8 Workbook Answers

Exercise 1 pp. 1–3

1. (a) 5
   36
   (b) 10
   54

2. (a) 8 × 6 = **24** + 24 = **48**
   [4] 4

   (b) 7 × 6 = 30 + **12** = **42**
   5 [2]

3. 6 × 9 = 9 × **6** = **54**

4. (a) 9 9
   (b) 6 6

5. 7 3
   45 ÷ 6 is **7** with a remainder of **3**.

6.

P	24	C	3	T	60
X	9	E	0	O	42
I	12	G	7	H	30
D	48	S	2	K	8
E	18	C	36	N	54
S	5	A	6	,	4

GOATS, SHEEP, AND CHICKENS

7. (a) 30
   (b) 6

8. (a) 23 ÷ 6 is **3** with a remainder of **5**.
   (b) 59 ÷ 6 is **9** with a remainder of **5**.
   (c) 50 ÷ 6 is **8** with a remainder of **2**.

9. **11 party favors**
   6 × 8 = 48 (total party favors)
   48 – 37 = 11 (left over favors)

10. **7 shirts**

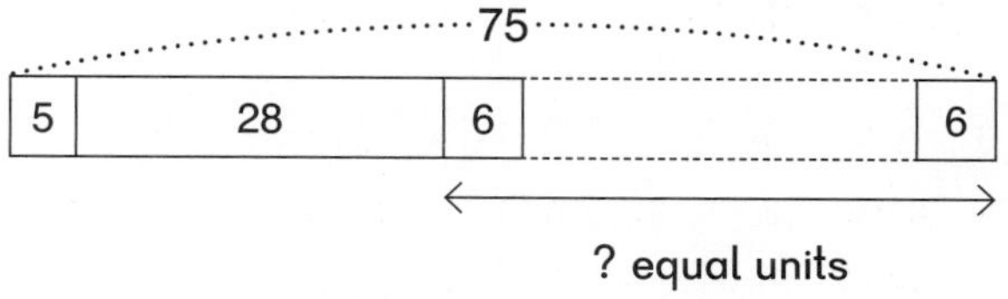

75 – 5 – 28 = 42
42 ÷ 6 = 7

Exercise 2 pp. 4–6

1. 7
   63

2. (a) 7 × 7 = **35** + 14 = **49**
   [5] 2

   (b) 6 × 7 = **21** + 21 = **42**
   [3] 3

   (c) 8 × 7 = 40 + **16** = **56**
   5 [2]

3. 7 × 8 = 8 × **7** = **56**

4. (a) 9 9
   (b) 4 4

5. 8 6
   62 ÷ 7 is **8** with a remainder of **6**.

6.

T	21	A	10	Y	42
C	7	D	9	N	3
W	54	I	5	E	35
A	4	R	6	N	1
O	56	K	8	L	49
S	63	B	28	F	2
_	70	W	48	O	0

IT ALWAY WENT BACK FOR SECONDS

Chapter 8 Workbook Answers

7. (a) 42
   (b) 4

8. (a) 65 ÷ 7 is **9** with a remainder of **2**.
   (b) 50 ÷ 7 is **7** with a remainder of **1**.
   (c) 62 ÷ 7 is **8** with a remainder of **6**.
   (d) 30 ÷ 7 is **4** with a remainder of **2**.
   (e) 48 ÷ 7 is **6** with a remainder of **6**.

9. **5**
   35 ÷ 7 = 5

10. **63**
    9 × 7 = 63

11. **6 friends**
    56 ÷ 7 = 8 (number of boxes of pens)
    8 × 10 = 80 (total number of pens)
    80 − 38 = 42 (number of pens given away)
    42 ÷ 7 = 6 (number of friends)
    This problem should be solvable without a bar model. We need to find the number of pens she gave away, so we need to find the number of pens, which requires us to find the number of boxes of pens. Trying to draw a model would be complex, since the meaning of the units changes. However, if your student is struggling with determining the first step, you could draw a model, working backwards from what the problem asks:

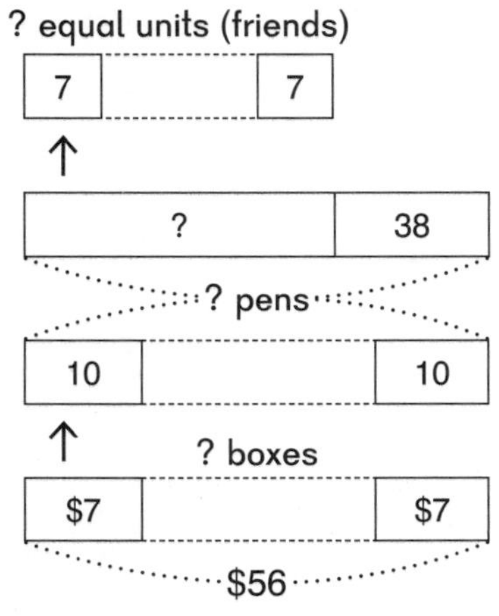

Exercise 3 pp. 7–9

The first two problems serve to remind students that the standard algorithm is a short-cut method to record multiplying the digit in each place and adding in any regrouped digits right away, instead of recording each partial product first and then adding.

1. 63
   420
   5,600
   6,083

		8	6	9
×				7
			6	3
		4	2	0
	5,	6	0	0
	6,	0	8	3

		4	6	
		8	6	9
×				7
	6,	0	8	3

2. 48
   5,400
   5,448

			4	
		9	0	6
×				7
	5,	4	4	8

3. **2,442**
   The previous problem should give students a clue on how to solve this problem mentally. Because there are no tens, there will be no regrouping and the answer is easily found multiplying left to right: 407 × 6 = 2,400 + 42.
   407 → 400 and 7

Chapter 8 Workbook Answers

4

					$^{A}5$	0	$^{B}4$	0	
	$^{C}7$		$^{D}2$	1	6		4		
	$^{E}9$	$^{F}1$			7		$^{G}4$	$^{H}8$	0
$^{I}6$	2	3						0	
2		9			$^{J}3$	0	4	5	
0		$^{K}3$	1	2	6				
2					$^{L}9$	6	$^{M}6$		
		$^{N}1$	8	3	6		4		
$^{O}5$	3	2					$^{P}2$	8	2
		$^{Q}6$	3	7	7				

G 480 N 126
N 1,836 M 642
Q 6,377 A 567
(Students can solve these mentally.)

A 5,040 D 216 E 91
I 623 J 3,045 K 3,126
L 966 O 532 P 282

B 444 C 792 F 1,393
H 805 I 6,202 J 3,696

Exercise 4 pp. 10–12

1

```
     159
 6 ) 958      1
     6
     35       5
     30
      58      9
      54
       4
```

958 ÷ 6 is **159** with a remainder of **4**.
159 × 6 + **4** = 958

2

```
      96
 7 ) 672      9
     63
      42      6
      42
       0
```

672 ÷ 7 = **96**
96 × 7 = 672

3 U 13 R 5 R 14 L 93
A 108 M 32 R 2 L 72 R 4
B 54 E 34 R 4 N 126
AN UMBRELLA

4 **78 beads**
123 + 345 = 468 (total beads)
468 ÷ 6 = 78 (beads in each bag)

5 **$144**

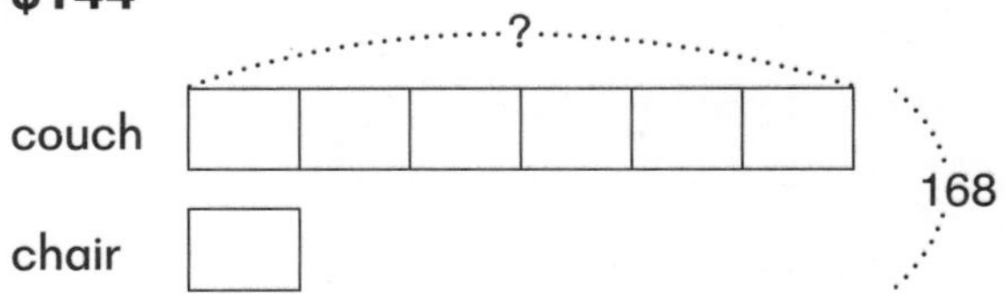

7 units ⟶ 168
1 unit ⟶ 168 ÷ 7 = 24
6 units ⟶ 6 × 24 = 144
Or: 168 − 24 = 144

This problem will generally require a bar model at this level to determine a method of solution. If your student is not comfortable with bar models yet because you started this curriculum at this level, spend some time discussing the solution to this problem. In many of these multi-step problems, students first need to determine the value of one equal unit (if it is not already given).

Chapter 8 Workbook Answers

6 **98 roses**

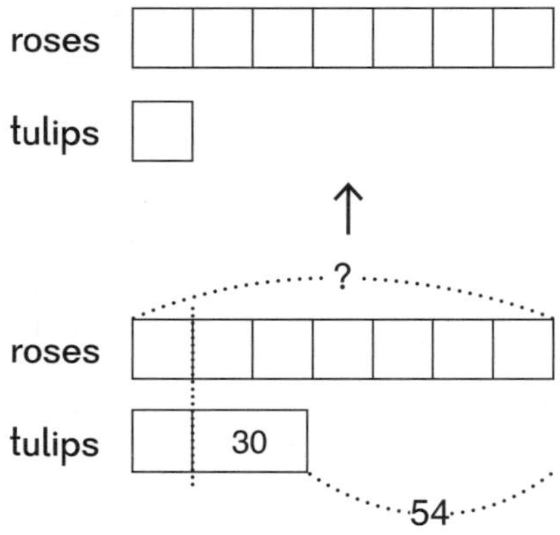

6 units ⟶ 30 + 54 = 84
1 units ⟶ 84 ÷ 6 = 14
7 units ⟶ 7 × 14 = 98

For challenging problems such as this, it is best to look first for something that tells you how many units to draw for each item. In this case, it is the fact that after she sells the tulips, she has 7 times as many roses as tulips. So draw 7 units for roses and 1 for tulips. Then, work backwards and add on a bar for the 30 tulips she sold. The difference between the total bars for each type of flower is 54. It is not necessary to know exactly how long to draw the bar representing the 30 tulips in relation to the parts representing the equal units to be able to see a method of solution from the model. In this situation, one quantity changes, but the other stays the same.

Exercise 5 pp. 13–16

1 (a)

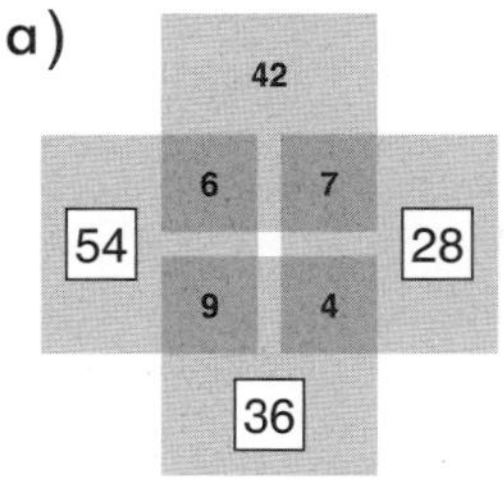

(b)

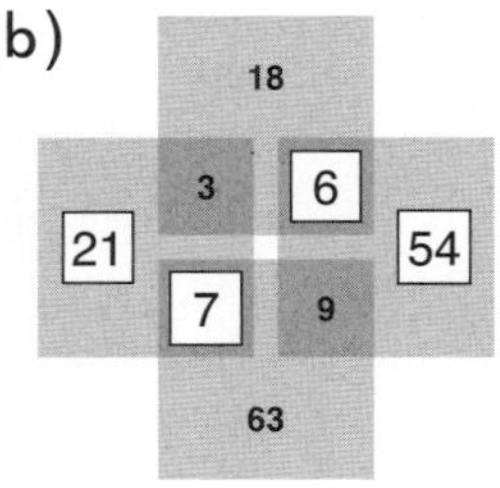

(c)

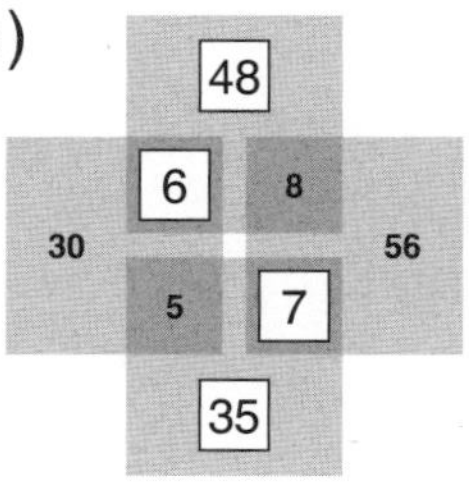

(d)

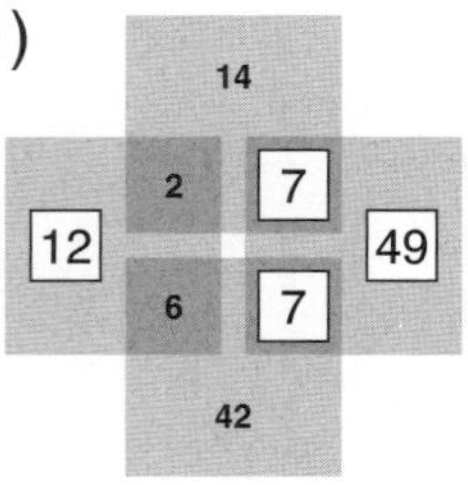

2

A 126	T 78 R 4	L 1,902
U 37 R 3	A 138	N 1,374
R 2,926	A 87	T 53

A TARANTULA

3 (a)

```
    6 3 9
×       7
---------
  4,4 7 3
```

(b)

```
    7 3 5
×       6
---------
  4,4 1 0
```

(c)

```
    1 3 4
6 ) 8 0 9
    6
    -----
    2 0
    1 8
    -----
      2 9
      2 4
    -----
        5
```

(d)

```
      8 9
7 ) 6 2 5
    5 6
    -----
      6 5
      6 3
    -----
        2
```

Students saw these types of problems in Dimensions Math® 3A, as well as earlier levels. They are a good way to determine if your student has a deep understanding of the algorithm, or is simply following a set of steps. If this is the first time your student has seen this type of problem, you may have to help them initially by giving them some hints.

(a) Start by finding a number times 7 that has a product with 3 in the ones place (9 × 7 = 63). It is then easy to then find the digit 7. Then find the number ? such that ? × 7 + 2 = 44.

(b) To find the tens digit (3) in the top factor, find a number ? such that ? × 6 + 3 = _1 (3 × 6 + 3 = 21).

(c) Find the divisor using either the information that 3 × 6 = 18 or 4 × ? = 24. Then find the ones digit of the dividend by adding the remainder to the number above it to get 29: the ones digit must be 9.

(d) All of the missing numbers can be found using addition or subtraction, once we fill in the 5 of 65.

4 **$1,386**

396 ÷ 2 = 198 (cost of 1 bike)

7 × 198 = 1,386

5 **2 candles left over**

320 ÷ 6 is 53 R 2

6 **$340**

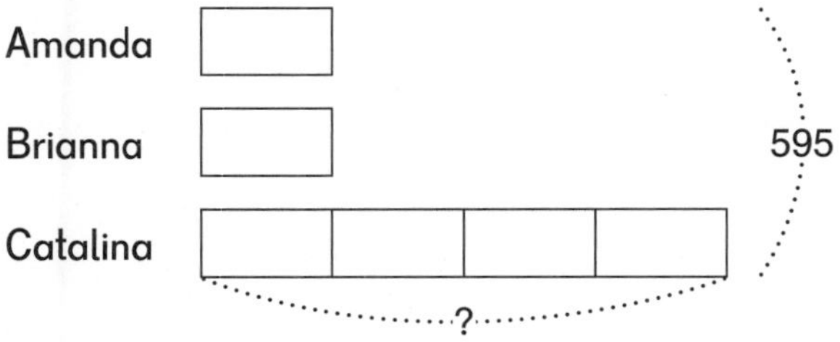

7 units ⟶ 595

1 unit ⟶ 595 ÷ 7 = 85

4 units ⟶ 4 × 85 = 340

7 (a)

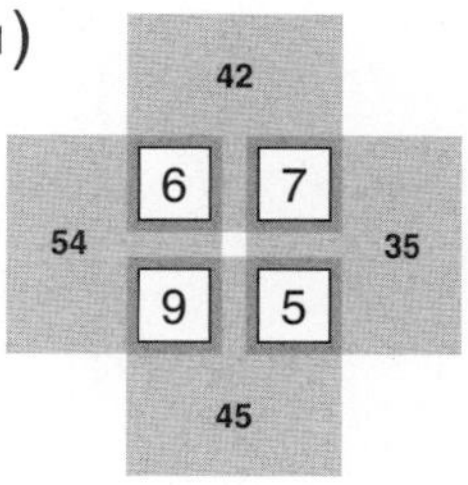

(b)

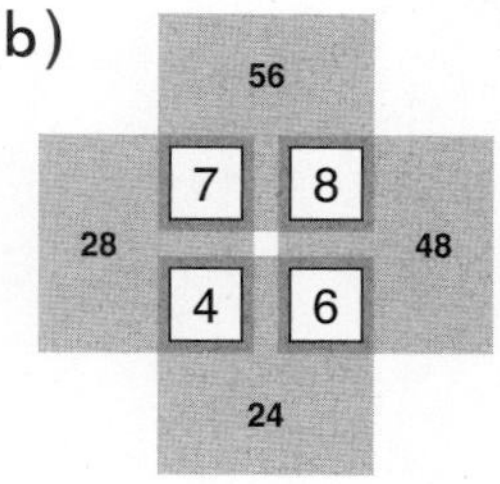

If your student struggles, you can make the problem simpler by letting them use a multiplication table. If both numbers are in the same row or same column, the number in the "intersection" is the number in the header column or row, respectively.

Exercise 6 pp. 17–19

1 48

2 9 × 8 = 10 × 8 − **8** = **72**

3 7 × 8 = **40** + 16 = **56**

(7 split into 5 and 2)

4 (a) 8 ⟶ 16 ⟶ 32 ⟶ 64

64

(b) 4 ⟶ 8 ⟶ 16 ⟶ 32

32

5 (a) 9 9

(b) 3 3

6 8 6

70 ÷ 8 is **8** with a remainder of **6**.

Chapter 8 Workbook Answers

7

80	16	9
2	8	5
24	4	10
7	56	0
32	1	48
40	3	64
160	6	72

38	3	80	18	0	17	65
24	17	6	44	4	95	29
11	14	10	34	16	12	35
28	32	150	84	72	5	64
8	51	22	33	160	99	7
40	1	2	580	9	56	48
19	38	13	95	27	50	85

8 (a) 65 ÷ 8 is **8** with a remainder of **1**.
(b) 50 ÷ 8 is **6** with a remainder of **2**.
(c) 60 ÷ 8 is **7** with a remainder of **4**.
(d) 22 ÷ 8 is **2** with a remainder of **6**.

9 **10 shelves**
75 ÷ 8 is 9 R 3

10 **16 toy dinosaurs**

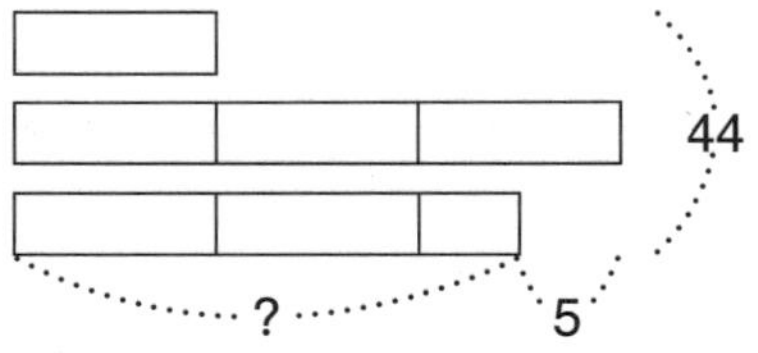

7 units ⟶ 44 + 5 = 49
1 unit ⟶ 49 ÷ 7 = 7
3 units ⟶ 3 × 7 = 21
21 − 5 = 16
The best approach for these types of comparison problems where most of the parts are equal units is to look for a way to make all the parts equal. If Ella had 5 more dinosaurs, she would have 3 units of dinosaurs. So we add 5 to the total, which gives us a value for 7 equal units.

Exercise 7 pp. 20–22

1 (a) 54
(b) 70 − **7** = **63**
(c) **80** − 8 = **72**
(d) 90 − **9** = **81**

2 (a) 5
(b) 45 + 10 − **1** = **54**

3 (a) 9
(b) 37, 62, 56

4 (a) 9 9
(b) 7 7

5 7 6
69 ÷ 8 is **7** with a remainder of **6**.

6

N 2	V 72	P 27
H 36	L 10	T 6
D 81	Y 1	Y 63
E 8	E 18	I 9
U 3	Y 7	N 5
T 45	L 54	S 4

THEY INVENTED SILLY PUTTY

7 (a) 100 ÷ 9 is **11** with a remainder of **1**.
(b) 55 ÷ 9 is **6** with a remainder of **1**.
(c) 89 ÷ 9 is **9** with a remainder of **8**.
(d) 35 ÷ 9 is **3** with a remainder of **8**.

8 **5 cards**
52 ÷ 9 is 5 R 7

Chapter 8 Workbook Answers

9 **$90**

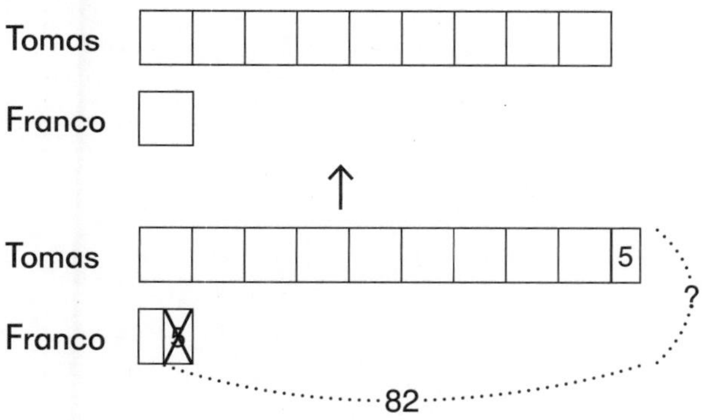

8 units ⟶ 82 – 5 – 5 = 72

1 unit ⟶ 72 ÷ 8 = 9

10 units ⟶ 10 × 9 = 90

We are told that Tomas would have 9 times as much money as Franco if he gave Franco $5, so we can start with a model showing 9 units for Tomas and 1 for Franco. Then we cross off $5 from Franco's and add $5 onto Tomas's bar to show what they actually have. We can see the new difference ($82) is both the amount taken off one bar and the amount added to the other bar. So to find 8 units, we need to subtract 5 twice.

Exercise 8 pp. 23–25

1 81
720
4,500
5,301

```
     5 8 9
  ×      9
  --------
       8 1
     7 2 0
   4,5 0 0
  --------
   5,3 0 1

     8 8
     5 6 9
  ×      9
  --------
   5,3 0 1
```

2 64
400
3,200
3,664

```
     4 6
     4 5 8
  ×      8
  --------
   3,6 6 4
```

3 _ 7,120 H 576 A 568
A 6,354 N 336 O 6,174
C 6,504 R 153 N 456
AN ANCHOR

4 **468 cards**
52 × 9 = 468

5 **625 markers**
9 × 62 = 558
558 + 67 = 625

6 **360 cards**
9 × 5 = 45 (number of students)
45 × 8 = 360

Exercise 9 pp. 26–28

1

```
      1 1 9
  8 ) 9 5 2     1
      8
      ---
      1 5       1
        8
      ---
        7 2     9
        7 2
      -----
          0
```

952 ÷ 8 = **119**
119 × 8 = 952

Chapter 8 Workbook Answers

2

```
     7 4
 9 ) 6 7 2
   6 3
     4 2
     3 6
       6
```

672 ÷ 9 is **74** with a remainder of 6.

74 × 9 + 6 = 672

3 121 R 4 52 R 5 61 R 6 85 R 3

4 + 5 + 6 + 3 = 18 = 9 × 2

4 **57 pieces**

Left over piece: 2 m long

458 ÷ 8 is 57 R 2

5 **24 cookies**

250 – 34 = 216

216 ÷ 9 = 24

6

11	1
22	2
33	3
44	4
55	5
66	6
77	7
88	8
100	0

When hundreds up to 8 hundreds are divided by 9, the digits in the quotient and the remainder are the same as the digit in the hundreds place.

Exercise 8 pp. 29–32

1

×	7	2	8	6	3	10	5	9	1	4
3	21	6	24	18	**9**	30	15	27	3	12
6	42	12	48	**36**	18	60	30	54	6	24
1	7	2	8	6	3	10	5	9	**1**	4
5	35	10	40	30	15	50	**25**	45	5	20
2	14	**4**	16	12	6	20	10	18	2	8
7	**49**	14	56	42	21	70	35	63	7	28
4	28	8	32	24	12	40	20	36	4	**16**
9	63	18	72	54	27	90	45	**81**	9	36
10	70	20	80	60	30	**100**	50	90	10	40
8	56	16	**64**	48	24	80	40	72	8	32

You may have to explain to your student that this is a multiplication table where the numbers that are being multiplied together (the ones in the header column and row) are not in order. If you help them find which number goes where for a few of them, they may see a pattern and be able to do the rest. There is obviously only one possibility for some of them. 1 = 1 × 1, so 1 is the 9th number in the header row and third number in the header column. Similarly, there is only one possibility for 9, 49, and 81. Since 1, 3, 7, and 9 are now filled in, that reduces the possibilities for the others. For example, 4 = 2 × 2 and not 1 × 4 because 1 is already used.

Chapter 8 Workbook Answers

2 L 7,623 E 85 R 24
S 99 K 549 A 6,336
A 304 W 55 H 7,792
WHALE SHARK

3 (a)

```
  757
×   8
-----
6,056
```

(b)

```
  125
×   9
-----
1,125
```

(c)

```
     76
  8)609
    56
    --
     49
     48
     --
      1
```

(d)

```
     86
  9)777
    72
    --
     57
     54
     --
      3
```

4 **763 more apple trees**

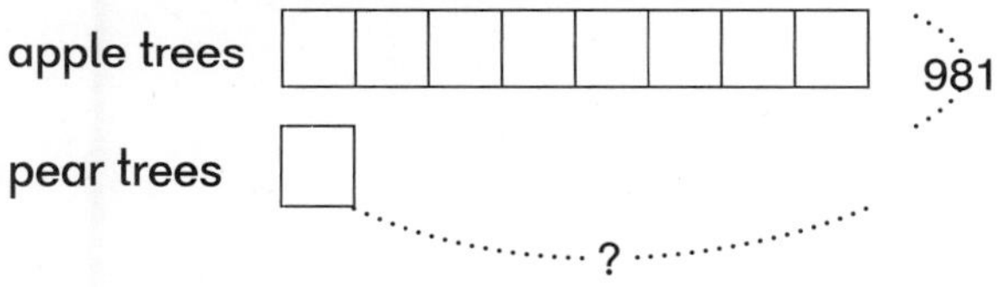

9 units ⟶ 981
1 unit ⟶ 981 ÷ 9 = 109
7 units ⟶ 7 × 109 = 763

5 **192 small bowls**
250 ÷ 8 is 31 R 2
32 boxes
6 × 32 = 192

6 (a) 9
(b) 6

7 **4 more counters**
Number of counters each child gets at first:
126 ÷ 9 = 14
Number of counters each child gets after 2 children leave:
126 ÷ 7 = 18
Difference:
18 − 14 = 4
A bar model would not contribute much to solving this problem, but your student can draw one for each situation if they want. Not all word problems lend themselves to using bar models to solve. Your student will get an idea for which ones a bar model will be useful. At this level, they are usually the ones that involve multiplicative comparison. Later, they will use bar models frequently with word problems involving fractions.

8 **56 bushes**
8 × 7 = 56
If your student multiplied 7 by 9 instead of 8, suggest that they draw a picture. The bushes are in the gaps between the trees, and there are 8 gaps.

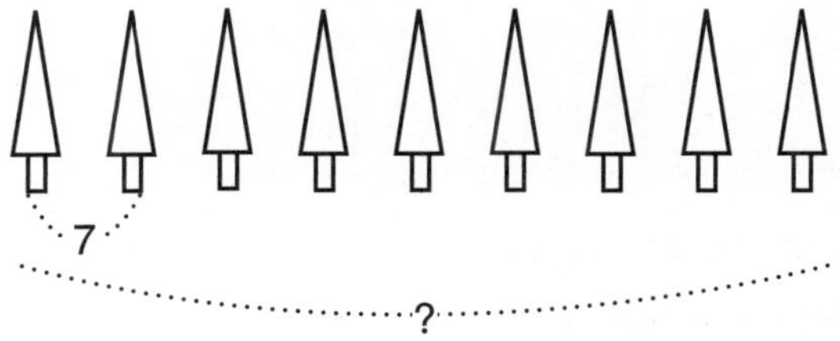

Chapter 8 Workbook Answers

9 **There are 8 spiders**

If they were all beetles, the number of legs would be:

12 × 6 = 72

There are 88 legs, so the number of legs unaccounted for is:

88 − 72 = 16

Spiders need another 2 legs:

16 ÷ 2 = 8

Check:

Number of beetles: 12 − 6 = 4

Number of beetle legs: 4 × 6 = 24

Number of spider legs: 8 × 8 = 64

Total legs: 24 + 64 = 88 ✓

This problem cannot be easily modeled with a bar model. Students encountered similar problems in earlier levels. If your student did not do earlier levels or has forgotten, start out with a simpler problem that they can draw, and then relate the steps in the drawing to equations. For example:

There are 6 cows and chickens. There are 16 legs. How many cows are there?

Each animal has 2 legs, so draw 6 animals and put 2 legs on each.

This uses 12 legs (2 × 6 = 12).

There are 4 legs left (16 − 12 = 4).

Put them on 2 animals (4 ÷ 2 = 2).

There are 2 cows.

Chapter 9 Fractions — Part 1

	Lesson	Page	Objectives
	Chapter Opener	35	
1	Fractions of a Whole	36	Recognize, name, and write common fractions. Find the fraction that makes a whole with another fraction.
2	Fractions on a Number Line	38	Identify and locate fractions on a number line.
3	Comparing Fractions with Like Denominators	39	Compare and order fractions with the same denominator.
4	Comparing Fractions with Like Numerators	40	Compare and order fractions with the same numerator.
5	Practice	41	

Materials

Materials

- Paper strip or ribbon 1 meter long (at least two of them)

Optional

- Fraction tiles

Printouts

(singaporemath.com/higprintouts)

- Fraction Bars
- Fraction Number Lines for Chapter 9

Notes

Fractions

In Dimensions Math® 2B, students learned how to write fractions using fractional notation and to identify fractions that make a whole. If your student did not do Dimensions Math® 2B, and does not understand fractional notation, there is adequate review of the concepts in this chapter.

In this chapter, students will be finding fractions of measurement units. Students learned to measure length, capacity, and mass or weight in the metric system (meters, centimeters, liters, kilograms, grams) and in the U.S. customary system (feet, inches, quarts, cups, pounds, ounces) in Dimensions Math® 2A and 2B. Fractions are used frequently with the U.S. customary system, which is not based on the base-ten system the way the metric system is. Your student needs to be familiar with all of these units of measurement. If they are not, you will have to help your student become familiar with them. Even though Chapter 11 specifically covers measurement, its main objective is converting between units and expressing measurement in compound units, and it also assumes that students are familiar with the measurement units taught earlier in this curriculum.

In Dimensions Math® 2B, students worked with fractions of shapes such as squares or circles. They identified fractions when they could determine that the shape was divided into equal parts. This is reviewed in Lesson 1.

Students will then learn that fractions are numbers; they are also a way to count things, and they can count parts of 1 whole, not simply parts of a shape.

With whole numbers, the object being counted, whether apples, inches, or units on a number line, is the denomination of the number. A fraction, such as three fourths, which is 3 out of 4 equal parts of whole, is written as $\frac{3}{4}$. The denomination is fourths, meaning what is being counted is fourths of a whole. The count, or numeration, is 3 of these fourths. Students will learn that the bottom number is called the "denominator" and the top number is called the "numerator." (If this vocabulary gets in the way of comprehension, students can still use "top number" and "bottom number" instead.)

This curriculum uses the term "fourth," not "quarter," for fractions (except to use common names, such as a quarter circle and a quarter hour).

Number Lines

Number lines are a tool for visualizing the order of numbers; greater numbers are farther to the right on a horizontal number line. Equally spaced tick marks can be drawn between the tick marks for whole numbers, allowing fractions to be located on a number line. So number lines can also be used to visualize the order of fractions.

When students interpret a number line with equally spaced tick marks between 0 and 1, they need to count the intervals, not the tick marks, to determine the value of the first tick mark. (The interval is the part, and the number of equal parts determine the fraction.) Students will learn to interpret the difference between two tick marks as a fraction that counts the parts between the two tick marks. For example, we can add $\frac{2}{7}$ to $\frac{5}{7}$ to get 1. They will not, however, work with addition or subtraction expressions until the next chapter.

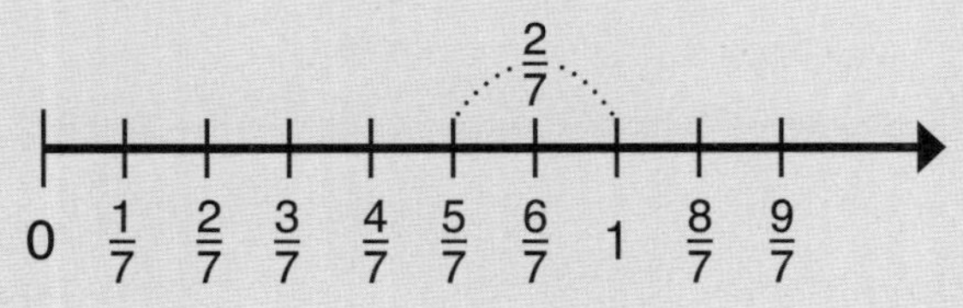

Students will learn about fractions greater than 1, such as $\frac{7}{5}$, as simply a way to express the number of parts past 1. At this level, they will only see improper fractions for fractions greater than 1. They will learn about mixed numbers in Dimensions Math® 4A.

Students will understand that 1 can be written as a fraction with the same numerator and denominator, which can be any number. For the number line above, 1 can be easily interpreted as $\frac{7}{7}$. 1 can also be interpreted as $\frac{2}{2}$ or $\frac{3}{3}$ or $\frac{4}{4}$ and so on. This is the start of an introduction to equivalent fractions, which students will learn about in the next chapter.

Students will now finally be able to interpret the tick marks on a ruler as being fractions of an inch or centimeter.

Comparing Fractions

In Dimensions Math® 2B, students learned to compare unit fractions (fractions with 1 in the numerator) by comparing the size of the parts. For example, $\frac{1}{4}$ is "larger" than $\frac{1}{6}$ because $\frac{1}{4}$ of a shape is larger than $\frac{1}{6}$ of the same shape.

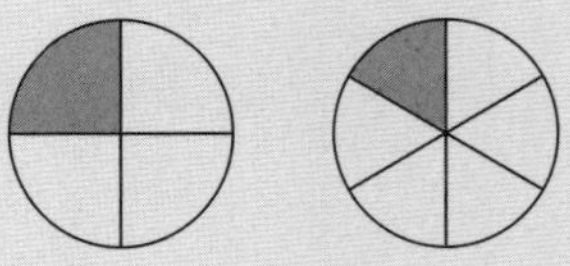

$\frac{1}{4}$ is larger than $\frac{1}{6}$

Students will now learn to compare other fractions besides unit fractions with the same denominator, and to compare fractions with the same numerator. They will now use the terms "greater than" or "less than" to compare fractions, the same terms they use when comparing whole numbers. They will also use inequality symbols with fractions.

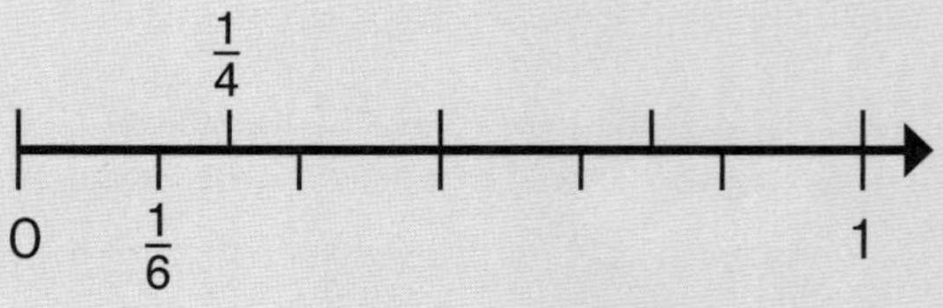

$\frac{1}{4}$ is greater than $\frac{1}{6}$

$\frac{1}{4} > \frac{1}{6}$

Chapter Opener (p. 33)

This Chapter Opener reminds students that fractions count the number of equal parts something (the tape) is divided into. A 1-m tape is used, instead of a two-dimensional shape such as a square or circle, as was used in Dimensions Math® 2B, and the parts are lengths. A measuring tape is similar to a number line. Students will learn about fractions on a number line in this chapter.

Before looking at the Chapter Opener, give your student a meter-long strip of paper or ribbon, tell them that it is 1 meter long, and ask them to measure something that is shorter than a meter. Try to find some length they can measure that is about half of a meter. Ask them to think about how they could and tell you the length more precisely than "shorter than one meter" using only the paper strip or tape they have (they cannot use centimeters). If they do not think of saying that the length is half of a meter, suggest they fold the strip in half.

Then have your student fold another strip into thirds (you may have to help them do this, showing how they can fold it over and adjust before they crease the paper), mark thirds, and find some length that is about a third of a meter. Have them fold the strip for halves into fourths and find something that is about a fourth of a meter. They can then find something that is about two thirds of a meter, and about three fourths of a meter long. The lengths can be approximate. They are measuring to the closest fractional part.

In preparation for Lesson 2, have your student measure something longer than 1 m but shorter than 2 m and give the approximate lengths as the total number of halves, or thirds, or fourths. The object might, for example, be five fourths of a meter long, or three halves of a meter long.

Then look at and discuss the Chapter Opener.

Lesson 1 Fractions of a Whole (pp. 34–38)

Think (p. 34)

Have your student look at Think. Give them a piece of paper to represent the cornbread. You can cut off some of the width of the paper so that it is proportionately similar to the rectangle here. Tell them that the cornbread will only be cut across the width. Have them fold the paper to determine thirds. Even if your student has not learned how to write fractions yet, they can probably answer (a) in words with an idea of what a third of a shape is from every-day experience, and possibly (b) and (c) as well, particularly if they did the Chapter Opener activity. If they do know how to write fractions, have them write the answers using fractional notation. (Food is often used to introduce fractions, since students usually have experience sharing food "equally," even though the parts are not going to be exactly equal.)

Learn (pp. 34–35)

This reviews the concept of fractions and how to write fractions using fractional notation. Make sure your student understands that all parts are equal, that the bottom number of the fraction is the number of parts the whole is divided into, and that the top number is how many parts are counted. If all parts are counted, as in $\frac{3}{3}$, that is the same as 1 whole.

Discuss the definitions for numerator and denominator given at the bottom of page 35.

Answers

(b) 2
(c) 3

1 (a) numerator: 1
denominator: 4
(b) numerator: 7
denominator: 12
(c) numerator: 5
denominator: 6
(d) numerator: 5
denominator: 9

2 (a) $\frac{3}{4}$
(b) $\frac{1}{4}$
(c) $\frac{4}{4}$
(d) $\frac{3}{4}$

3 (a) $\frac{5}{7}$
(b) $\frac{2}{7}$
(c) 7
(d) $\frac{7}{7}$
(e) $\frac{2}{7}$

4 (a) colored: $\frac{5}{8}$
not colored: $\frac{3}{8}$
(b) colored: $\frac{4}{6}$
not colored: $\frac{2}{6}$
(c) colored: $\frac{5}{9}$
not colored: $\frac{4}{9}$
(d) colored: $\frac{3}{5}$
not colored: $\frac{2}{5}$

Do (pp. 36–38)

1 Have your student read each fraction out loud. This problem is likely to be easy and not help much with learning the two words. Instead, ask your student questions such as the following:

- Which fraction has a denominator of 6?
- Which two fractions have the same numerator?
- What do we call the top number in $\frac{7}{12}$?
- Which fraction shows that the whole was divided into 9 equal parts?

2 **3** **4** **5** These problems review the concept of finding the fraction that makes a whole with another fraction (the denominators are the same). Students should easily see that the sum of the numerators of the two fractions is the denominator of each fraction (together, all the parts are counted).

3 This problem reminds students that when counting the shaded parts in a figure such as this (a flat shape divided into equal parts, some of which are shaded), the fraction that is shaded counts all the shaded parts. They do not have to be next to each other.

6 **7** **8** These last three problems introduce a concept that was not covered in Dimensions Math® 2B but was introduced in the Chapter Opener: using fractions in measurement to indicate quantities that are not a whole unit.

6 The beaker shows a liquid volume that measures $\frac{3}{5}$ L. (That the fifths are equal parts can only be seen visually if the sides of the container are vertical. Most measuring cups do not have vertical sides, and marked fractions won't appear to be equally spaced for the same denominators.)

7 Students should know from their study of units of measurement that the lengths are scaled down. Point out the definition of a unit fraction.

8 You can use an actual meter stick and 12-inch ruler to show that a foot is about a third of a meter. This problem reviews the fact that you cannot compare fractions if the whole is not the same. Since 1 m is longer than 1 ft, $\frac{2}{3}$ of 1 m is longer than $\frac{2}{3}$ of 1 ft.

Answers (continued)

5 (a) $\frac{1}{8}$

(b) $\frac{7}{12}$

6 (a) $\frac{3}{5}$ L

(b) 3

(c) $\frac{2}{5}$ L

(d) $\frac{2}{5}$

7 (a) 10 (ten)

(b) $\frac{10}{10}$

(c) $\frac{9}{10}$

(d) $\frac{9}{10}$

8 **No**

The whole is not the same.

Lesson 2 Fractions on a Number Line (pp. 39–42)

Think (p. 39)

Make sure your student understands that the pink strip is a picture of a strip of paper that is longer than 1 meter, similar to a tape measure. The length that is equivalent to 1 meter is between the two dotted lines marked with 0 m and 1 m. Have your student answer the questions. They can answer out loud, or write their answers and compare them to the answers in Learn.

Learn (p. 40)

Discuss the answers and the explanations given by Alex and Sofia. The point to make here is that fractions are numbers, as are whole numbers; they count parts of a whole. Like whole numbers, they can be located on a number line where 1 is the "whole." Students are familiar with both measuring lengths to the nearest whole number of units and with number lines and so should be able to make the connection between a ruler and a number line.

Do (pp. 41–42)

3 The answer to Alex's question is that if the numerator is greater then the denominator, the fraction is greater than 1.

Answers

(a) A: $\frac{1}{5}$ B: $\frac{2}{5}$ C: $\frac{3}{5}$ D: $\frac{4}{5}$

(b) $\frac{4}{5}$

(d) 5

(e) E is 6 fifths, F is 7 fifths

(f) E is $\frac{6}{5}$, F is $\frac{7}{5}$

(g) $\frac{7}{5}$

1 (a) P: $\frac{2}{7}$ Q: $\frac{4}{7}$ R: $\frac{6}{7}$

(b) $\frac{7}{7}$

(c) $\frac{2}{7}$

(d) $\frac{5}{7}$

(e) $\frac{4}{7}$

2 (a) 5

(b) V: $\frac{6}{4}$ W: $\frac{7}{4}$ X: $\frac{8}{4}$

(c) $\frac{5}{4}$, $\frac{6}{4}$, $\frac{7}{4}$

(d) 8

3 (a) $\frac{1}{3}$

(b) A: $\frac{1}{3}$ B: $\frac{2}{3}$ C: $\frac{3}{3}$ D: $\frac{4}{3}$

E: $\frac{5}{3}$ F: $\frac{6}{3}$ G: $\frac{7}{3}$

4 (a) J: $\frac{1}{4}$ K: $\frac{3}{4}$ L: $\frac{7}{4}$

(b) $\frac{5}{4}$ in

5 (a) The second longest ones

(b) In order from third longest to shortest: fourths, eighths, sixteenths.

Lesson 3 Comparing Fractions with Like Denominators (pp. 43–46)

Think (p. 43)

The fractions for the liquid measurements are depicted by rectangles divided into equal parts. Students should be able to interpret the pictures easily enough. The advantage to liquid measurement as a visual tool is that the parts being counted must all be next to each other, at the "bottom," and the fractions can be put in order by height.

Emma is asking how we can compare the fractions using just the numerators and denominators of the written fraction. Students should look at the written fractions and see that the denominators are the same, so the size of the parts are all the same. They just they need to compare the numerator since that is the number of parts.

Learn (p. 44)

Make sure your student understands Mei's explanation of why you can compare the written fractions when the denominator is the same by simply comparing the numerators. Your student should realize that on a horizontal number line, the greater fraction is farther to the right.

Answers

Dion has the most paint left.
Sofia has the least paint left.

1. $\frac{5}{8}$
2. $\frac{2}{5}$
3. $\frac{3}{9}, \frac{5}{9}, \frac{7}{9}$
4. (a)
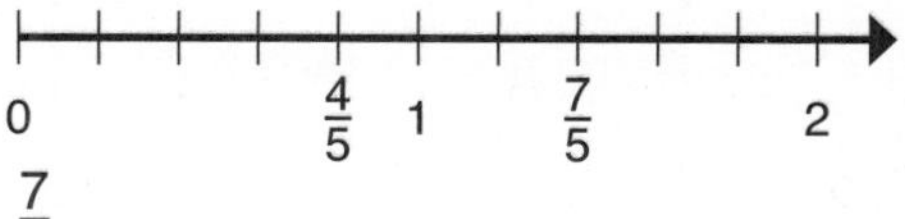

   (b) $\frac{7}{5}$
   (c) 1
5. $\frac{5}{7}$
6. $\frac{11}{12}$
7. (a) < (b) =
   (c) < (d) >
   (e) > (f) >
8. (a) $0, \frac{1}{2}, 1$ (b) $\frac{3}{8}, \frac{5}{8}, \frac{6}{8}$
   (c) $\frac{2}{6}, \frac{3}{6}, \frac{5}{6}, \frac{8}{6}$ (d) $\frac{5}{8}, \frac{7}{8}, 1, \frac{9}{8}, 2$
9. (a) Olivia
   (b) $\frac{3}{10}$ L more

Do (pp. 45–46)

4. This problem uses a number line in order to help students compare fractions, including ones that are greater than 1. If you are not letting your student write in the textbook, you can use the **Fraction Number Lines for Chapter 9** printout.

5. By now, students should not need a visual aid to compare these fractions.

9. Students just need to determine what makes a whole with $\frac{7}{10}$, not write an equation yet.

Lesson 4 Comparing Fractions with Like Numerators (pp. 47–50)

Use the **Fraction Bars** printout. Cut apart each of the labeled bars. Have your student color one part on the left for each, put the bars in order according to the size of the shaded part, and then write the fraction for the shaded part on the bar. Write the fractions in order from least to greatest.

$$\frac{1}{10} < \frac{1}{9} < \frac{1}{8} < \frac{1}{7} < \frac{1}{6} < \frac{1}{5} < \frac{1}{4} < \frac{1}{3} < \frac{1}{2}$$

Discuss this order with respect to the numerators and denominators. The numerators are all 1, so the fractions are all 1 part. The denominators decrease as the size of the parts increases. With the fraction bars, your student should see that a greater denominator means a smaller part.

Think and Learn (pp. 47–48)

Students should be able to see from the pictures how to put the fractions in order, using the height of the colored bars. Discuss Sofia's question. Each picture shows three shaded parts (the numerators), but the size of the parts are different (the denominators). The number lines at the bottom of page 48 reinforce the idea that if the denominator is greater, the part is smaller.

Answers

Emma has the most water.

Mei has the least water.

1. $\frac{2}{3}$

2. $\frac{5}{9}$

3. 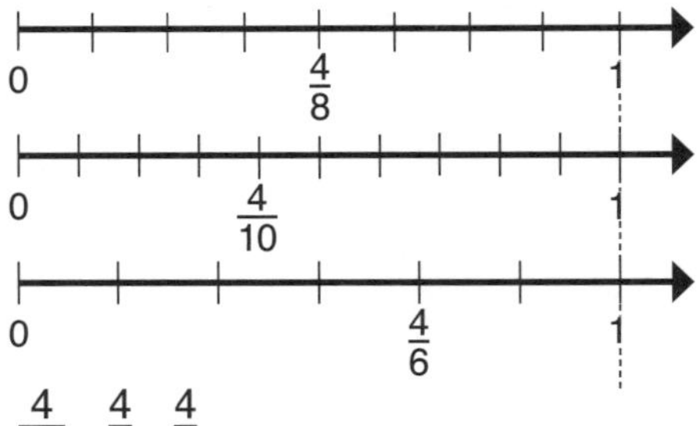

   $\frac{4}{10}$, $\frac{4}{8}$, $\frac{4}{6}$

4. $\frac{3}{4}$

5. $\frac{11}{16}$

6. (a) $<$ (b) $>$
   (c) $<$ (d) $>$
   (e) $<$ (f) $<$

7. (a) $\frac{1}{8}$, $\frac{1}{6}$, $\frac{1}{3}$ (b) $\frac{7}{8}$, $\frac{7}{6}$, $\frac{7}{5}$
   (c) $\frac{3}{8}$, $\frac{3}{7}$, $\frac{3}{5}$, $\frac{3}{4}$ (d) 0, $\frac{2}{8}$, $\frac{2}{5}$, 1

8. The birch seedling

Do (pp. 49–50)

3 You can use the **Fraction Number Lines for Chapter 9** printout. Make sure your student counts the parts (intervals) and not the tick marks.

4 By now, students should not need a visual aid to compare the fractions.

7 For (d), students should simply realize that the two fractions are both less than 1, and not need to think of 1 as a fraction with the same numerator as the other fractions ($\frac{2}{2}$).

Lesson 5 Practice (pp. 51–52)

The workbook exercise for this lesson includes some multiplication and division practice.

6 This problem is different from those students have seen before, since all the numerators or all the denominators are not the same. If your student has trouble, ask them to first compare the fractions to 1.

(a) Only $\frac{7}{3}$ is greater than 1, so the other two fractions are less than 1 and only need to be compared to each other; they have the same denominator.

(d) Only $\frac{7}{5}$ is greater than 1. We can compare $\frac{4}{9}$ to $\frac{4}{8}$ (same numerator) and then compare $\frac{4}{8}$ to $\frac{7}{8}$ (same denominator).

7 There is only one option here. Students should realize that the denominator must be less than 5 for the fraction to be greater than $\frac{3}{5}$ and have the same numerator.

Enrichment

- Have your student estimate fractions. Use the **Fraction Bars** printout. Cut apart the bars on the last page, which are not divided into parts. Color a portion of a bar and ask your student about how much is shaded. Then let them check with the fraction bars on the first page. Alternately, give them three choices and have them select which they think is the best choice. You could also ask your student to color a specific fraction of the bar. They then check with the fractions on the first page to see how close they colored the correct amount.

Answers

1 (a) colored: $\frac{4}{8}$
not colored: $\frac{4}{8}$
(b) colored: $\frac{7}{12}$
not colored: $\frac{5}{12}$

2 (a) $\frac{2}{7}$
(b) $\frac{2}{8}$
(c) $\frac{5}{10}$
(d) $\frac{6}{6}$

3 (a) K: $\frac{1}{7}$ L: $\frac{3}{7}$ M: $\frac{6}{7}$
(b) P: $\frac{1}{5}$ Q: $\frac{3}{5}$ R: $\frac{7}{5}$

4 $\frac{5}{3}$ and $\frac{9}{7}$

5 (a) $<$ (b) $>$
(c) $>$ (d) $>$
(e) $=$ (f) $>$

6 (a) $\frac{2}{7}, \frac{5}{7}, \frac{7}{3}$ (b) $\frac{5}{12}, \frac{5}{9}, \frac{5}{7}$
(c) $0, \frac{1}{3}, 1, \frac{5}{3}$ (d) $\frac{4}{9}, \frac{4}{8}, \frac{7}{8}, \frac{7}{5}$

7 $\frac{3}{4}$

8 $\frac{1}{3}$

About $\frac{4}{5}$ of the bar is shaded.

Chapter 9 Workbook Answers

Exercise 1 pp. 33–36

1 (a) **3** out of **5**

(b) numerator: 3 denominator: 5

(c) $\frac{1}{5}$

(d) 3

(e) 5

(f) $\frac{\mathbf{2}}{5}$

2 (a) **7** out of **10**

(b) $\frac{7}{\mathbf{10}}$

(c) 10

(d) $\frac{7}{\mathbf{10}}$ and $\frac{\mathbf{3}}{10}$ make $\frac{\mathbf{10}}{10}$

3 R $\frac{2}{5}$ I $\frac{5}{9}$ C $\frac{3}{9}$

L $\frac{5}{6}$ A $\frac{3}{7}$ C $\frac{3}{10}$

D $\frac{5}{12}$ E $\frac{1}{7}$ O $\frac{3}{4}$

A CROCODILE

4 Which parts are shaded can vary.

(a)

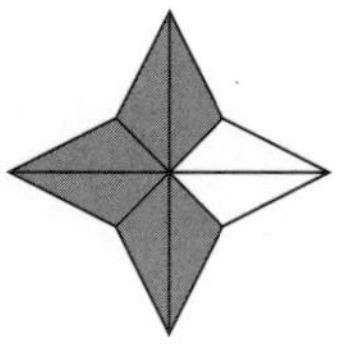

(b)

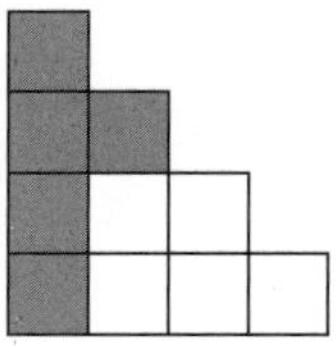

(c)

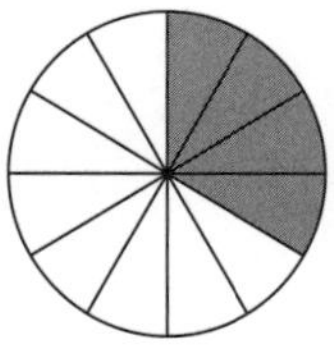

(d)

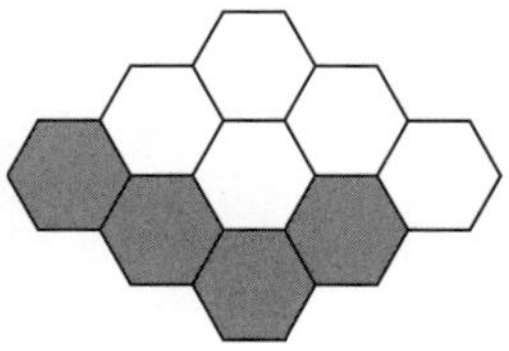

(e)

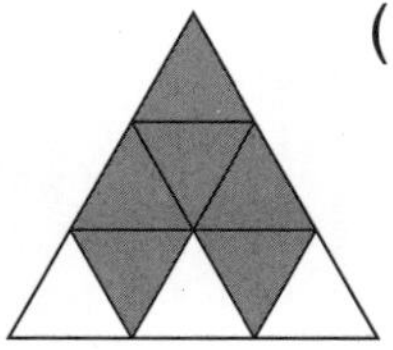

(f)

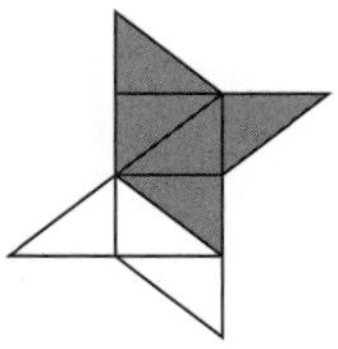

5

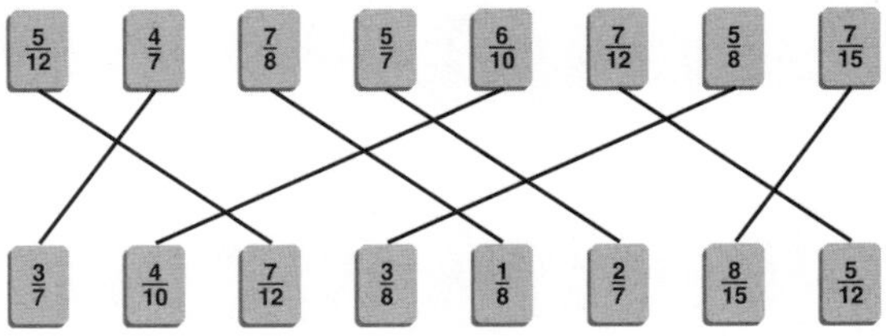

6 Which parts are shaded can vary.

(a)

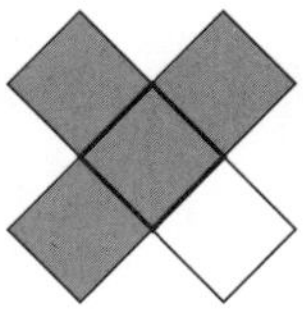

(b)

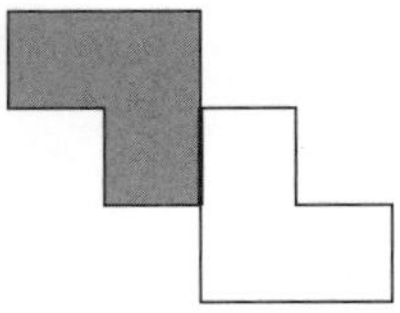

(c)

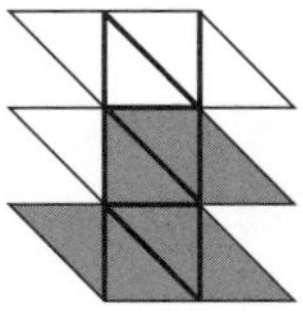

(d)

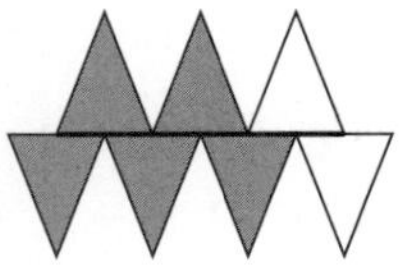

(e)

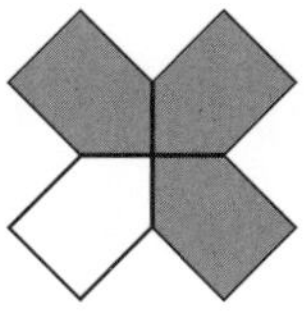

(f)

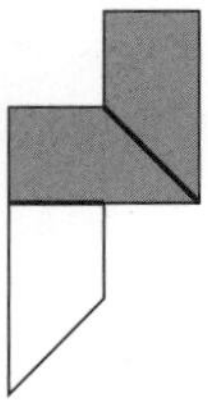

Exercise 2 pp. 37–39

1 (a) $\frac{3}{\mathbf{5}}$

(b) $\frac{3}{5}$

(c) $\frac{3}{5}$

2 (a) 5

(b) 5

(c) 1

(d) 3

(e) $\frac{\mathbf{3}}{5}$

(f) $\frac{4}{5}$

Chapter 9 Workbook Answers

3 (a) 3
(b) 5
(c) 6
(d) 3

4 (a) $\frac{1}{4}$
(b) R: $\frac{3}{4}$ Q: $\frac{5}{4}$ P: $\frac{8}{4}$
(c) ... **Q** is ... longer than ... **R**
(d) $\frac{\mathbf{5}}{\mathbf{4}}$

5 (a)
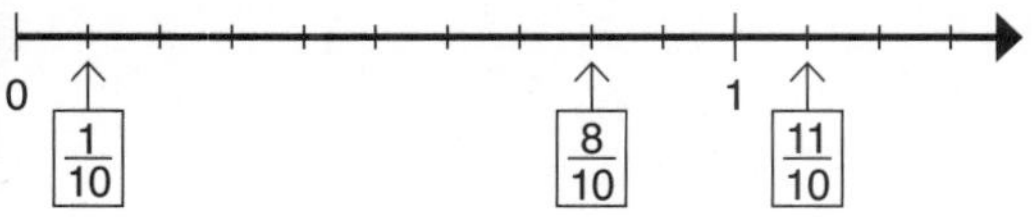

(b)
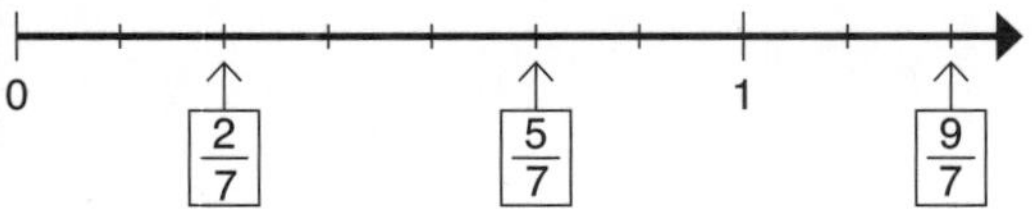

(c)

(d)
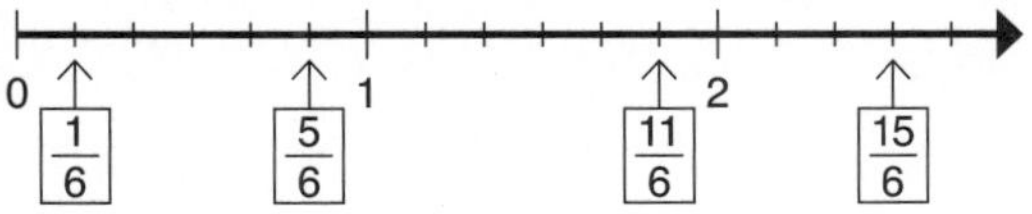

(e) $\frac{1}{10}$, $\frac{8}{10}$, $\frac{2}{7}$, $\frac{5}{7}$, $\frac{5}{12}$, $\frac{11}{12}$, $\frac{1}{6}$, $\frac{5}{6}$
(f) $\frac{11}{10}$, $\frac{9}{7}$, $\frac{15}{12}$, $\frac{11}{6}$

6 (a) 25 (b) 1,000
(c) $\frac{\mathbf{27}}{3}$ (d) $\frac{12}{\mathbf{4}}$

This problem is asking students to informally extrapolate from knowing which fractions can represent a whole to a connection between fractions greater than 1 and division. If your student struggles with this, it is not necessary to explain the concept; they will learn it formally in Dimensions Math® 4.

Exercise 3 pp. 40–42

1 $\frac{3}{5}$ (circled) $\frac{2}{5}$ $\frac{7}{10}$ (circled) $\frac{4}{10}$
$\frac{2}{7}$ (circled) $\frac{3}{7}$ $\frac{3}{6}$ (circled) $\frac{4}{6}$

2 (a) $\frac{7}{8}$ (circled) $\frac{3}{8}$ $\frac{5}{8}$
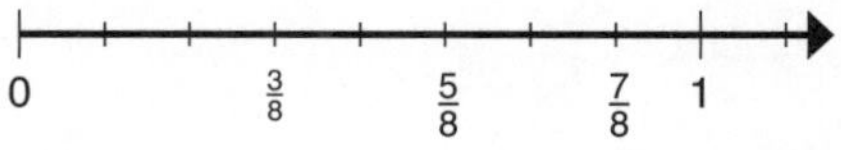

(b) $\frac{1}{3}$ $\frac{4}{3}$ (circled) $\frac{3}{3}$
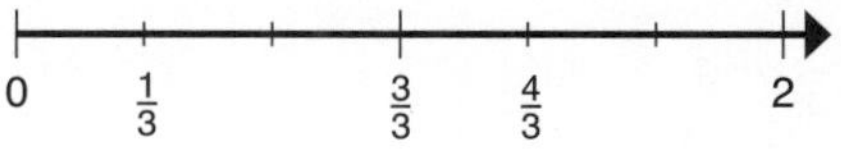

4 $\frac{4}{9}$
$\frac{5}{9}$ (circled)
$\frac{3}{9}$

5 $\frac{7}{12}$
$\frac{9}{12}$
$\frac{5}{12}$ (circled)

6 (a) $\frac{9}{10}$ $\frac{5}{10}$ $\frac{7}{10}$ $\frac{2}{10}$ (circled)
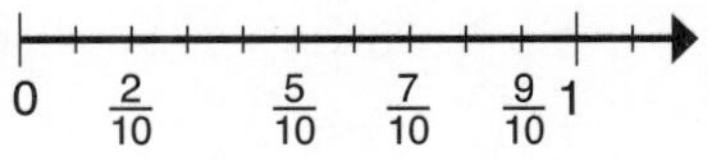

(b) $\frac{7}{4}$ $\frac{3}{4}$ (circled) $\frac{8}{4}$ $\frac{5}{4}$
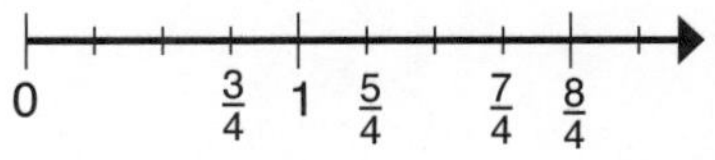

7 $\frac{8}{10}$ m, $\frac{10}{10}$ m, $\frac{14}{10}$ m

8 (a) $\frac{5}{4}$ (b) $\frac{10}{10}$

9 (a) $\frac{2}{12}$ (b) $\frac{2}{7}$

Chapter 9 Workbook Answers

10 (a) $\frac{3}{6}, \frac{5}{6}, \frac{7}{6}, \frac{9}{6}$

(b) $\frac{3}{8}, \frac{5}{8}, \frac{7}{8}, 1, \frac{9}{8}$

11 (a) $1, \frac{9}{12}, \frac{7}{12}, \frac{5}{12}, 0$

(b) $2, \frac{5}{4}, 1, \frac{3}{4}, \frac{1}{4}$

Exercise 4 pp. 43–46

1 $\frac{1}{6}$ $\frac{3}{4}$ (circled)

$\frac{1}{4}$ (circled) $\frac{3}{5}$

2 $\frac{3}{8}$ (circled) $\frac{5}{7}$

$\frac{3}{4}$ $\frac{5}{9}$ (circled)

3 (a)

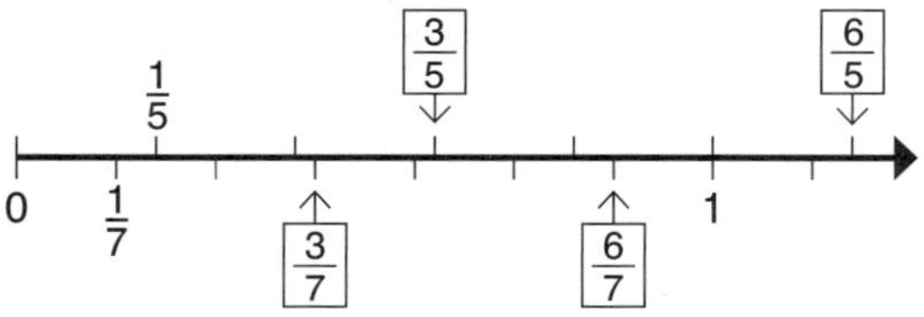

(b) $\frac{3}{5}$ (c) $\frac{6}{7}$

If necessary, help your student interpret this "double" number line that has two sets of tick marks. They will see more of them in the workbook. You can draw bars at the tick marks, if needed, to show that the tick marks on the top are for fifths and those on the bottom are for sevenths.

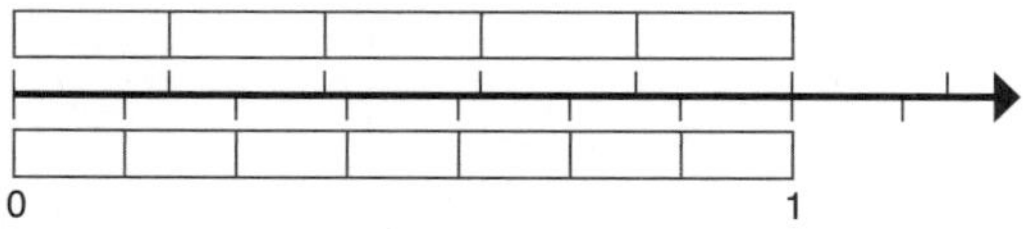

4

Least								Greatest
$\frac{3}{12}$	$\frac{3}{11}$	$\frac{3}{10}$	$\frac{3}{9}$	$\frac{3}{8}$	$\frac{3}{7}$	$\frac{3}{6}$	$\frac{3}{5}$	$\frac{3}{4}$
Blue	Red	Yellow	White	Black	Blue	Black	Red	White

Check that your student has colored in the flags correctly. There is a maritime signal flag for each letter of the alphabet. Your student might be interested in researching what the other maritime flags look like.

5

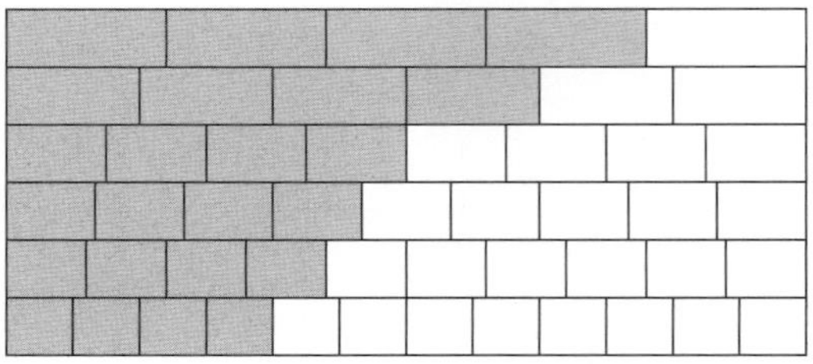

(a) $\frac{4}{8} < \frac{4}{5}$ (b) $\frac{4}{10} < \frac{4}{6}$ (c) $\frac{4}{9} > \frac{4}{12}$

6

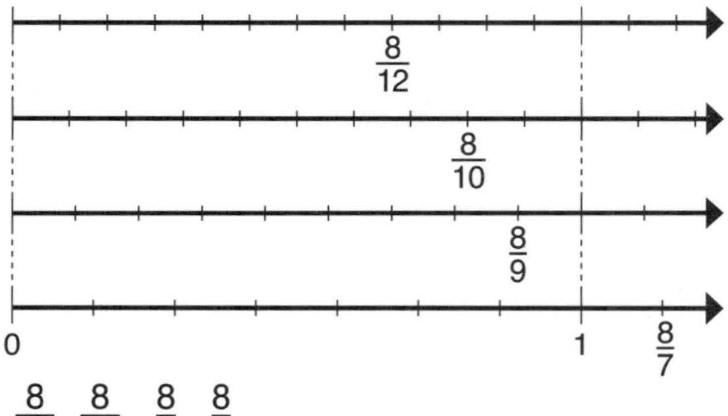

$\frac{8}{12}, \frac{8}{10}, \frac{8}{9}, \frac{8}{7}$

7 (a) $\frac{1}{4}$

(b) $\frac{7}{4}$

8 (a) $\frac{2}{8}$

(b) $\frac{9}{13}$

9 (a) $\frac{1}{5}, \frac{1}{3}, \frac{1}{2}$

(b) $\frac{5}{10}, \frac{5}{9}, \frac{5}{7}, \frac{5}{5}$

Chapter 9 Workbook Answers

10 (a) $\frac{5}{5}, \frac{5}{9}, \frac{5}{12}, 0$

(b) $\frac{2}{5}, \frac{2}{7}, \frac{2}{9}, \frac{2}{10}, \frac{2}{15}$

11 Answers can vary. Possible solutions:

(a) $\frac{5}{\mathbf{8}} < \frac{5}{7}$ (b) $\frac{3}{10} > \frac{\mathbf{3}}{12}$

Exercise 5 pp. 47–50

1

544	1,460	4,123
32 R 1	157 R 1	70 R 4

2 C

A: parts are not equal

B: parts are not equal

D: divided into sixths, not fourths

3 (a) $\frac{4}{9}$

(b) $\frac{4}{9}$

4 Which parts are shaded can vary.

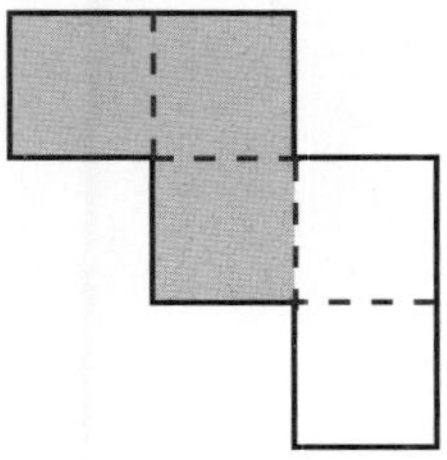

5

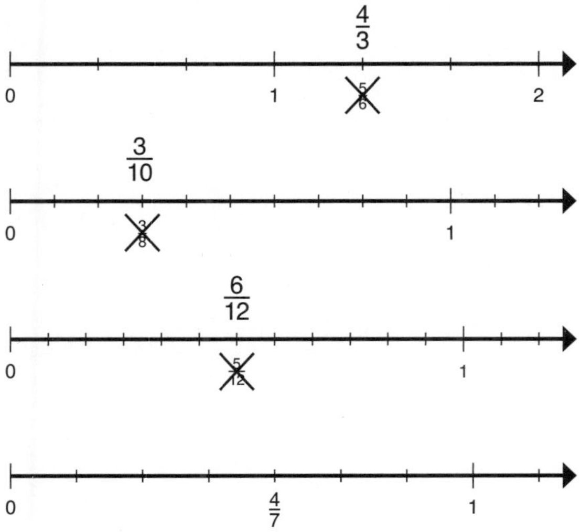

6 (a)

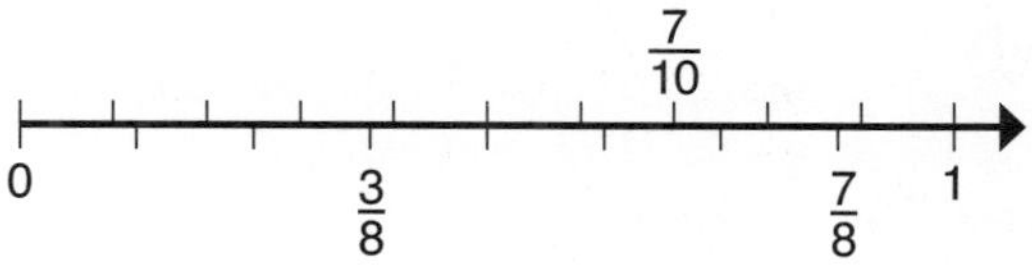

$\frac{3}{8}, \frac{7}{10}, \frac{7}{8}$

(b)

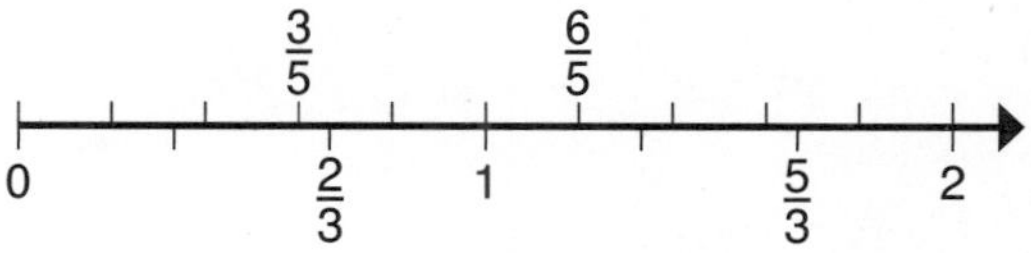

$\frac{3}{5}, \frac{2}{3}, \frac{6}{5}, \frac{5}{3}$

7 (a) < (b) > (c) >
(d) > (e) > (f) <

8 $\frac{4}{8}$

9 $\frac{3}{8}$ of the pizza

Students can draw a picture of either a round or rectangular pizza, if needed, to see that Gavin ate $\frac{2}{8}$ of the pizza.

10 (a) $\frac{2}{7}, \frac{3}{7}, \frac{3}{6}, \frac{5}{6}, \frac{7}{6}$

Put the fractions with the same denominators in order. Then compare the two fractions with the same numerator.

(b) $\frac{5}{12}, \frac{9}{12}, 1, \frac{9}{8}, \frac{12}{8}$

Put the fractions with the same denominators in order. One group is less than 1, and the other is greater than 1.

(c) $\frac{1}{5}, \frac{1}{2}, \frac{3}{3}, \frac{8}{4}, 3$

Students will have to realize that $\frac{8}{4}$ is 2.

Chapter 9 Workbook Answers

11 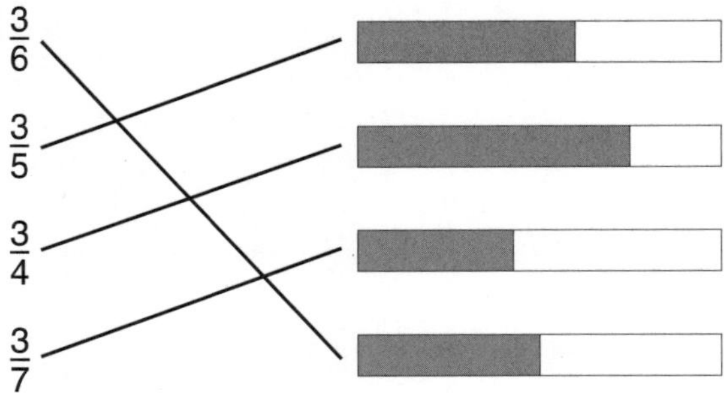

12 One of the cuts divides the cake into two layers.

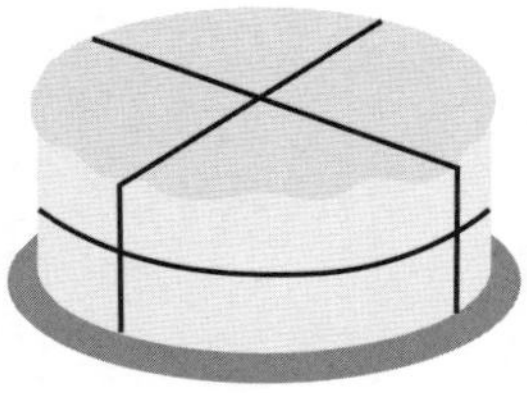

Chapter 10 Fractions — Part 2

	Lesson	Page	Objectives
	Chapter Opener	53	
1	Equivalent Fractions	54	Identify equivalent fractions using bar models or number lines.
2	Finding Equivalent Fractions	55	Find equivalent fractions by multiplying the numerator and denominator by the same number.
3	Simplifying Fractions	56	Find equivalent fractions by dividing the numerator and denominator by the same number. Find the simplest form of a fraction.
4	Comparing Fractions — Part 1	58	Compare and order fractions by using equivalent fractions.
5	Comparing Fractions — Part 2	60	Compare and order fractions by comparing them to $\frac{1}{2}$ and 1.
6	Practice A	62	
7	Adding and Subtracting Fractions — Part 1	63	Add and subtract fractions with the same denominator.
8	Adding and Subtracting Fractions — Part 2	64	Add and subtract fractions with the same denominator and simplify the answer.
9	Practice B	65	

Materials

Materials

Optional

- Fraction circles
- Fraction tiles
- Playing cards

Printouts

(singaporemath.com/higprintouts)

- Chapter 10 Opener
- Equivalent Fractions Puzzle
- Fraction Bars
- Fraction Bars to Twentieths
- Lesson 10-2
- Lesson 10-3
- Multiplication Chart
- Number Cards 0–100

Notes

Equivalent Fractions

In this chapter, students will understand and find equivalent fractions, find the simplest form of a fraction, and use equivalent fractions as another strategy for comparing and ordering fractions.

Fractions are equal, or "equivalent," if they have the same value; that is, they represent the same number. Students already know that fractions with the same numerator and denominator are equal; they all have a value of 1. They also may already have an intuitive understanding of some equivalent fractions, from seeing fractions on a shape or number line, such as $\frac{1}{2} = \frac{2}{4}$.

Number lines are used to visualize equivalent fractions. On a number line, equivalent fractions are located at the same point. If the number lines are shown separately for each fraction, the distance to 1 is the same on each number line.

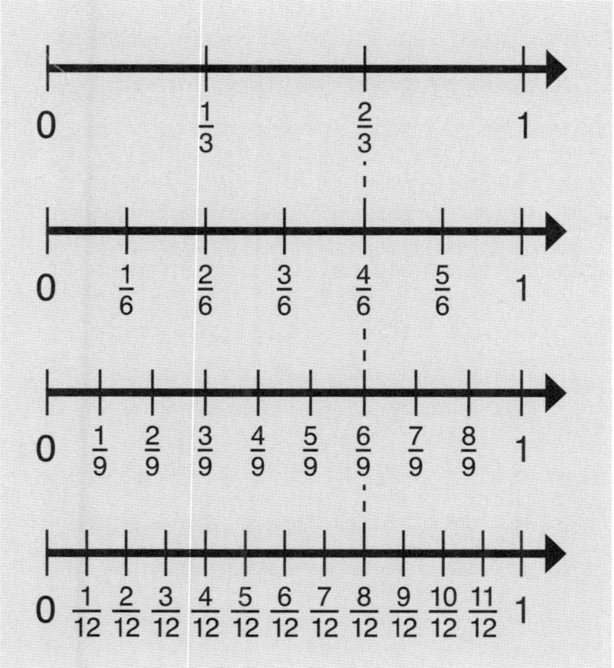

Bar models are also used to visualize equivalent fractions. Since students will be using bar models to interpret and solve fraction word problems involving fractions later, it is important that they are familiar with representing equivalent fractions with bar models.

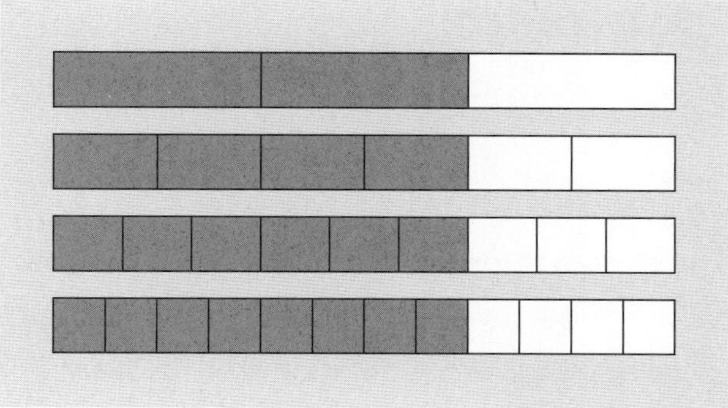

To find an equivalent fraction, we can multiply or divide the numerator or denominator by the same number.

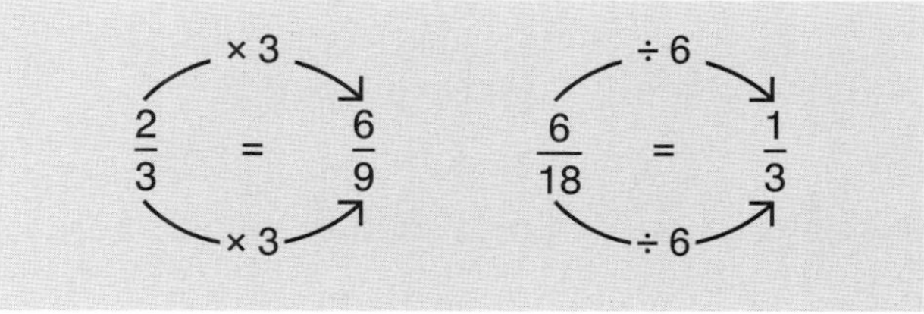

Students will see problems where they need to fill in a missing numerator or denominator. They can solve a problem such as $\frac{1}{4} = \frac{?}{12}$ by reasoning that since $4 \times 3 = 12$, 1 should be multiplied by 3, so $\frac{1}{4} = \frac{3}{12}$. Since the denominators will generally be 24 or less, if students know their multiplication facts well, this should be easy. This strategy cannot be used to solve a problem such as $\frac{6}{9} = \frac{?}{12}$ since students have only learned to multiply by a whole number. Students will only see how to solve this type of problem at this level in an optional Challenge problem in the workbook.

Simplifying Fractions

When we divide the numerator or denominator by the same number to get an equivalent fraction, we are "simplifying" the fraction. This can be done in steps.

$$\frac{6}{18} \overset{\div 2}{=} \frac{3}{9} \overset{\div 3}{=} \frac{1}{3}$$

The simplest form of a fraction is one where there is no whole number that both the numerator and denominator can be divided by (other than 1) in order to further simplify the fraction. The simplest form of $\frac{6}{18}$ is $\frac{1}{3}$.

In order to simplify a fraction and find its simplest form, students will have to determine a number that both the numerator and denominator can be divided by. At this level the numbers are less than 24, except for rare occasions in the workbook. If students cannot immediately see what number to divide by to get the simplest form, they can easily try dividing first by 2, then by 3, then by 4, etc. They should realize that the easiest way to simplify a fraction is in steps, in which case they will only have to recognize even numbers; that 3, 6, 9, 12, 18, 21 and 24 can be divided by 3; that 10 and 15 can be divided by 5; and that 7, 14, and 21 can be divided by 7. Students will formally learn about common factors and how to find the greatest common factor in Dimensions Math® 4A.

The easiest first step in simplifying a fraction is to recognize whether both the numerator and denominator are even and, if so, to divide the numerator and denominator by 2 as the first step, and for any subsequent steps until they are no longer both even. When they are not both even, they can check if both can be divided by 3 (the sum of the digits for both is a multiple of 3) or 5 (the ones digit is 0 or 5). After simplifying as much as possible this way, they can check whether both numbers can be divided by 7.

Students will learn to identify two fractions as equivalent fractions even when the numerator or denominator of one is not a simple multiple of the numerator or denominator of the other by finding the simplest form of both. For example, $\frac{6}{9}$ and $\frac{8}{12}$ are equivalent fractions; the simplest fraction for both is the same, $\frac{2}{3}$.

Comparing Fractions

In the previous chapter, students learned to compare fractions with the same denominator or the same numerator. In this chapter, students will use equivalent fractions to compare fractions that do not have the same numerator or denominator.

We can find equivalent fractions of one or both of the fractions being compared where the equivalent fractions have the same denominator or the same numerator. This may be challenging for some students because they need to recognize when one number is a multiple of the other, but at this level the numerators or denominators will generally be 16 or less.

For example, to compare $\frac{5}{8}$ and $\frac{3}{4}$, students need to recognize that 8 and 4 are "related" in that they can multiply 4 by 2 to get 8. They then find an equivalent fraction for $\frac{3}{4}$ with the same denominator as $\frac{5}{8}$. To compare $\frac{6}{7}$ and $\frac{3}{4}$, they need to recognize that 6 and 3 are "related" so they can find an equivalent fraction for $\frac{3}{4}$ with the same numerator as $\frac{6}{7}$.

(The guide will use the non-mathematical term "related" rather than the mathematical term "multiple" since students do not formally learn the term multiple until Dimensions Math® 4A. If your student has no trouble understanding what you mean if you say 8 is a multiple of 4, you can use that term instead, since its meaning is fairly obvious.)

When neither the numerators nor the denominators are related, students will systematically list fractions for each until they find ones with either the same numerator or the same denominator. If students do need to list equivalent fractions for both fractions they are comparing, they will only have to list at most five of each.

Students will also compare fractions by comparing them to 1 or to $\frac{1}{2}$.

These strategies will allow students to compare a set of fractions without having to first find common multiples, and without using some procedure without understanding it (such as "cross multiply"). They will formally learn to find common multiples in Dimensions Math® 4A, and the lowest common multiple of the denominator in Dimensions Math® 5A.

Adding and Subtracting Fractions

In Lessons 7 and 8, students will add and subtract fractions with the same denominator. The lessons may look like they will be long, but they should be easy; all students are doing are adding and subtracting numerators, and the sums and differences are all within 20.

Activities

- After Lesson 2
  Materials: Number cards 1–24
  Purpose: Create equivalent fractions.
  Procedure: Select a set of numbers that form equivalent fractions and have your student use all of them to make equivalent fractions. Use problems in the textbook or workbook for ideas of which numbers to use.
  Examples:

  4, 10, 8, 5 $\frac{8}{10} = \frac{4}{5}$

  12, 4, 6, 3, 8, 9 $\frac{3}{4} = \frac{6}{8} = \frac{9}{12}$

- After Lesson 3
  Materials: **Equivalent Fractions Puzzle** printout
  Purpose: Match equivalent fractions.
  Procedure: Have your student cut apart the triangles for the puzzle. They then match the sides with equivalent fractions. The puzzle will form a hexagon, as shown on the answer page.

- After Lesson 3
  Purpose: Create fractions in simplest form.
  Procedure: Write 5 or so numbers between 1 and 12 and have your student use them to make as many fractions (less than 1) in simplest form they can. (This can be done as a game. See the example under Games.)

Games

- After Lesson 3
  Materials: Number cards 1–12, as many sets as players (or playing cards with Kings removed; Jack is 11 and Queen is 12)
  Purpose: Create fractions in simplest form.
  Goal: Get the most points.
  Procedure: Shuffle the cards and turn them face down in the middle. Each player draws 6 cards and uses the numbers to write as many fractions less than 1 in simplest form as possible. For example, a player draws the cards 3, 4, 5, 8, 9, and 12. They can write the fractions $\frac{3}{4}$, $\frac{3}{5}$, $\frac{3}{8}$, $\frac{4}{5}$, $\frac{5}{8}$, $\frac{5}{9}$, $\frac{5}{12}$, and $\frac{8}{9}$. Players get as many points as fractions they formed for that round. Game can continue as many rounds as agreed upon in advance and players can keep a running total. The player with the most points at the end wins.
  Variation: Students draw fewer than six cards.
  Variation: Use number cards 1–24.

Chapter Opener (p. 53)

This Chapter Opener serves to get students to start thinking about ways to compare fractions when the denominators or numerators are not the same.

Use the **Chapter 10 Opener** printout. Each fraction circle is the same size. Have your student use them to compare the fractions. They could cut out each circle and then cut out the fraction each friend ate from the fraction circles divided into thirds, twelfths, and sixths. They can then compare the sizes. They will see that Dion and Alex ate the same amount of pizza, and Emma ate less pizza than either of them.

Then have them lay the pieces on top of the last fraction circle, which is divided into twelfths. They should see that both $\frac{1}{3}$ and $\frac{2}{6}$ are the same as $\frac{4}{12}$.

Alternately, if you have a set of fraction tiles or circles, you can let your student decide how to use them to compare the fractions.

Lesson 1 Equivalent Fractions (pp. 54–57)

Think (p. 54)

You might want to give your student the directions out loud and not have them look at the textbook yet. You can fold a sheet of paper into fourths, either horizontally or vertically, and cut apart the strips, or cut strips from the last page of the **Fraction Bars** printout. If your student follows the directions, they should end up with something similar to the last set of three strips on page 54. Ask them the questions at the bottom of the page. You can have them place the bars on paper or a whiteboard so they can write the fractions for the colored parts next to the strips. They should look at the written fractions and make any observations they can about the numbers in the fractions. They may simply say that all three of them stand for the same amount colored, or they may observe that the number in the denominator is double the number in the numerator each time.

Learn (p. 55)

Discuss the information on this page. Dion says that equivalent fractions have the same value. The prefix equi- means equal, so the word means "equal value." Because they have equal value, they are located at the same place on a number line, just like a fraction such as $\frac{5}{5}$ was at the same place as 1 on a number line in the previous chapter. (They could imagine the number lines at the bottom of the page superimposed on each other.)

Answers

Other equal fractions: $\frac{1}{4} = \frac{2}{8}$ and $\frac{3}{4} = \frac{6}{8}$

1. $\frac{3}{6}$

2. (a) $\frac{4}{6}$
   (b) $\frac{6}{9}$
   (c) $\frac{8}{12}$

3. (a) $\frac{3}{12}$ $\frac{6}{12}$ $\frac{9}{12}$
   $\frac{1}{4}$ $\frac{2}{4}$ $\frac{3}{4}$
   (b) $\frac{1}{4}$
   (c) $\frac{3}{4}$
   (d) $\frac{6}{12}$

4. (a) $\frac{1}{2}$
   (b) $\frac{2}{5}$

5. $\frac{1}{2} = \frac{2}{4} = \frac{3}{6} = \frac{4}{8} = \frac{5}{10}$
   $\frac{1}{3} = \frac{2}{6} = \frac{3}{9}$ $\quad$ $\frac{2}{3} = \frac{4}{6} = \frac{6}{9}$
   $\frac{1}{4} = \frac{2}{8}$ $\quad$ $\frac{3}{4} = \frac{6}{8}$
   $\frac{1}{5} = \frac{2}{10}$ $\quad$ $\frac{2}{5} = \frac{4}{10}$ $\quad$ $\frac{3}{5} = \frac{6}{10}$

Do (pp. 56–57)

5. Students can use a ruler to see which vertical lines line up. You can extend this problem by using the **Fraction Bars to Twentieths** printout.

Lesson 2 Finding Equivalent Fractions (pp. 58–60)

Think (p. 58)

Instead of going directly to the textbook, you can give your student the **Lesson 10-2** printout. Ask them to shade the same half of each bar for the set of bars on the left, and the same third of each bar for the set of bars on the right. Ask them to write the fraction shaded next to each bar. Discuss any observations they make of both the bars and the written fractions. Try to get them to relate their observations for the bars to the numbers in the written fractions. For example, if they observe that half of the total number of parts are shaded, they could also observe that the denominator is always twice the numerator.

Learn (pp. 58–59)

This gives some observations that could be made. The primary observations are the last two, made by Emma and Alex. Students should conclude that if the numerator and denominator are multiplied by the same number, the resulting fraction is equivalent to the original fraction.

Do (p. 60)

❷ This problem helps prepare students for the next problem. To solve $\frac{2}{3} = \frac{?}{9}$, they need to identify what number 3 must be multiplied by to get 9, and then multiply 2 by the same number to find the unknown numerator.

Answers

Answers can vary, Examples:
$\frac{1}{2} = \frac{5}{10}$, $\frac{1}{3} = \frac{5}{15}$

❶ $\frac{3}{4} = \frac{\mathbf{6}}{8} = \frac{9}{\mathbf{12}}$

❷ $\frac{2}{3} = \frac{\mathbf{6}}{9} = \frac{10}{\mathbf{15}}$

(numerators: × 3, × 5; denominators: × 3, × 5)

❸ (a) $\frac{\mathbf{3}}{12}$ (b) $\frac{\mathbf{6}}{15}$ (c) $\frac{\mathbf{6}}{14}$

(d) $\frac{6}{\mathbf{18}}$ (e) $\frac{3}{\mathbf{24}}$ (f) $\frac{4}{\mathbf{8}}$

❹ Answers can vary. Examples:

(a) $\frac{3}{15}$, $\frac{4}{20}$, $\frac{5}{25}$

(b) $\frac{4}{14}$, $\frac{6}{21}$, $\frac{8}{28}$, $\frac{10}{35}$

❸ Students will need to determine what number the denominator was multiplied by for (a)–(c) and what number the numerator was multiplied by for (d)–(f).

❹ Answers can vary since students have not yet learned to systematically list equivalent fractions by first multiplying the numerator and denominator by 2, then 3, then 4, and so on, and are not required to. So $\frac{100}{500}$ is a valid equivalent fraction for $\frac{1}{5}$, for example.

Lesson 3 Simplifying Fractions (pp. 61–64)

Think (p. 61)

Before looking at the textbook, give your student a copy of the **Lesson 10-3** printout and ask them to color the first 8 parts of the top bar and write the fraction that is shaded. Then have them find bars that show equivalent fractions of this fraction, color those bars the same way, and write the equivalent fractions. They can cut out the strips in order to align them with each other. Discuss any observations they make, asking them how they can "go" from the fraction with the greater denominator to an equivalent fraction with a lesser denominator.

Learn (pp. 61–62)

On page 61, for the orange bars, your student should observe that every 2 units in the twelfths bar becomes 1 unit in the sixths bar, and then every 2 units of the sixths bar becomes 1 unit of the thirds bar. So both the number of shaded parts and the total number of parts are divided by 2 and then by 2 again to get the equivalent fractions. For the green bars, every 4 units in the twelfths bar becomes 1 unit in the thirds bar, so both the numerator and denominator are divided by 4.

Ask your student if the units for the last bar showing thirds could be combined so that there are equal units for shaded and unshaded parts. They cannot. Tell them that $\frac{2}{3}$ is the "simplest" fraction of the three factions here ($\frac{8}{12}$, $\frac{4}{6}$, and $\frac{2}{3}$). It has the fewest possible equal parts, and is the easiest to imagine, or picture, in our minds.

Answers

$\frac{4}{6}$

$\frac{2}{3}$

$\frac{2}{3}$

$\frac{2}{3}$

1. (a) $\frac{9}{12} = \frac{6}{8} = \frac{3}{4}$
   (b) $\frac{3}{4}$
2. $\frac{8}{16}$ in $= \frac{4}{8}$ in $= \frac{2}{4}$ in $= \frac{1}{2}$ in
3. (a) $\frac{4}{5}$ (b) $\frac{1}{3}$
   (c) $\frac{5}{6}$ (d) $\frac{3}{6}$
   (e) $\frac{3}{4}$ (f) $\frac{1}{2}$
4. $\frac{2}{3}$ $\frac{2}{3}$
5. (a) $\frac{2}{3}$ (b) $\frac{1}{2}$
   (c) $\frac{3}{4}$ (d) $\frac{1}{2}$
   (e) $\frac{1}{5}$ (f) $\frac{5}{6}$
6. $\frac{5}{10}$ $\frac{4}{8}$ $\frac{7}{14}$ $\frac{3}{6}$
   A fraction is equal to $\frac{1}{2}$ if the denominator is twice the numerator.

Discuss page 62. Point out that we can simplify a fraction to its simplest form in either one step or more than one step. Discuss Alex's question at the bottom of the page. A fraction is in its simplest form if there is no number greater than 1 that both the numerator and denominator can be divided by so that there is no remainder.

Do (pp. 63–64)

❶ Your student may notice that this problem is the "reverse" of ❶ in the previous lesson.

❹ This problem points out that two fractions may be equivalent even if we cannot think of a number to multiply or divide both the numerator and denominator of one fraction by to get the other fraction. The way to see if they are equivalent is to put both of them in simplest form. If the simplest forms of both fractions are the same, the fractions are equivalent.

❻ Students will be comparing fractions to $\frac{1}{2}$ by comparing the numerator to the denominator in Lesson 5. Your student could answer that the numerator is half of the denominator. Students have not yet formally learned the connection between division and fractions (e.g. $\frac{1}{2}$ of $12 = \frac{12}{2} = 12 \div 2 = 6$) but can certainly intuit it by now.

Reinforcement

Equivalent fractions are important in computations with fractions, so it is worth spending time making sure your student can recognize them. One way to further investigate equivalent fractions with even greater denominators than they will encounter in the textbook or workbook is with a multiplication chart.

You can use the **Multiplication Chart** printout. Point out two rows, such as 3 and 4 or 3 and 8. Ask your student to think of the top number as the numerator and the bottom number as the denominator of a fraction for the numbers in the same column. List them. For example:

×	1	2	3	4	5	6	7	8	9	10
1	1	2	3	4	5	6	7	8	9	10
2	2	4	6	8	10	12	14	16	18	20
3	3	6	9	12	15	18	21	24	27	30
4	4	8	12	16	20	24	28	32	36	40
5	5	10	15	20	25	30	35	40	45	50
6	6	12	18	24	30	36	42	48	54	60
7	7	14	21	28	35	42	49	56	63	70
8	8	16	24	32	40	48	56	64	72	80
9	9	18	27	36	45	54	63	72	81	90
10	10	20	30	40	50	60	70	80	90	100

$\frac{3}{4}, \frac{6}{8}, \frac{9}{12}, \frac{12}{16}, \frac{15}{20}, \frac{18}{24}, \frac{21}{28}, \frac{24}{32}, \frac{27}{36}, \frac{30}{40}$

$\frac{3}{8}, \frac{6}{16}, \frac{9}{24}, \frac{12}{32}, \frac{15}{40}, \frac{18}{48}, \frac{21}{56}, \frac{24}{64}, \frac{27}{72}, \frac{30}{80}$

Your student should notice the fractions in each list are equivalent to the first fraction in. Both the numerator and denominator of the first fraction is multiplied by the same number to get each subsequent fraction.

Point out that we cannot always simply multiply or divide directly to show that two fractions are equal. For example, $\frac{15}{20} = \frac{21}{28}$; both of them are equal to $\frac{3}{4}$, and so are equal to each other.

Lesson 4 Comparing Fractions — Part 1 (pp. 65–68)

Think (p. 65)

Use the **Fraction Bars** printout. Have your student shade the fractions for the three lengths given in this problem to find the answer. They can cut the strips apart. Then ask them if they can think of a way to put the fractions in order without fraction bars. They might think of using equivalent fractions in some way, since that was the previous lesson.

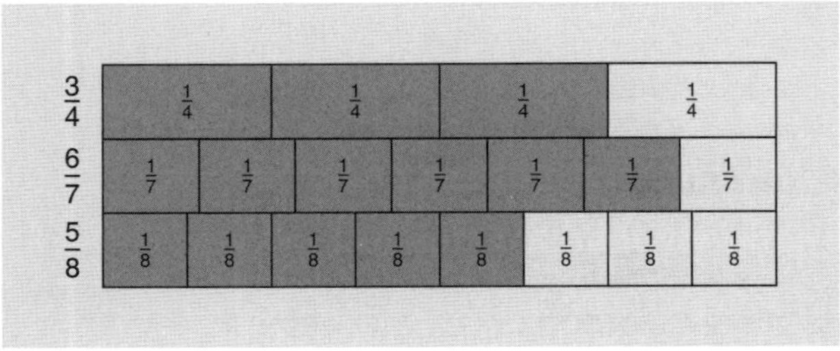

If your student cannot come up with a strategy, you can ask them to compare $\frac{3}{4}$ and $\frac{5}{8}$ by making an equivalent fraction with one of the two fractions, reminding them they can compare fractions with the same denominator. Similarly, you can ask them to compare $\frac{3}{4}$ and $\frac{6}{7}$ by making an equivalent fraction with one of them, reminding them they can compare fractions with the same numerator. Alternately, proceed directly to Learn.

Learn (p. 66)

Dion recognizes that he can find an equivalent fraction for $\frac{3}{4}$ with the same denominator as $\frac{5}{8}$, and use that to compare those two fractions.

Answers

Emma's ribbon is the shortest.
Dion's ribbon is the longest.

1. $\frac{7}{10}$

2. $\frac{5}{9}$

3. (a) $<$ $(\frac{4}{6} < \frac{5}{6})$ (b) $>$ $(\frac{4}{8} > \frac{3}{8})$
   (c) $<$ $(\frac{2}{9} < \frac{3}{9})$ (d) $>$ $(\frac{6}{8} > \frac{5}{8})$
   (e) $>$ $(\frac{4}{10} > \frac{3}{10})$ (f) $>$ $(\frac{5}{12} > \frac{4}{12})$

4. $\frac{2}{5}$

5. (a) $=$ $(\frac{1}{2} = \frac{1}{2})$ (b) $>$ $(\frac{6}{7} > \frac{6}{10})$
   (c) $>$ $(\frac{6}{9} > \frac{6}{21})$ (d) $<$ $(\frac{9}{21} < \frac{9}{8})$
   (e) $>$ $(\frac{10}{11} > \frac{10}{16})$ (f) $=$ $(\frac{2}{3} = \frac{2}{3})$

6. (a) $\frac{2}{3}, \mathbf{\frac{4}{6}}, \mathbf{\frac{6}{9}}, \mathbf{\frac{8}{12}}$
   $\frac{3}{4}, \mathbf{\frac{6}{8}}, \mathbf{\frac{9}{12}}, \mathbf{\frac{12}{16}}$
   (b) $\frac{3}{4}$

7. (a) $>$ $\frac{2}{3}, \frac{4}{6}, \frac{6}{9}, \frac{8}{12}, \frac{10}{15}$ $\frac{10}{15} > \frac{9}{15}$
   $\frac{3}{5}, \frac{6}{10}, \frac{9}{15}$ or $\frac{6}{9} > \frac{6}{10}$
   (b) $<$ $\frac{1}{2}, \frac{2}{4}, \frac{3}{6}$ $\frac{3}{6} < \frac{4}{6}$
   $\frac{2}{3}, \frac{4}{6}$
   (c) $>$ $\frac{5}{6}, \frac{10}{12}, \frac{15}{18}, \frac{20}{24}$ $\frac{20}{24} > \frac{9}{24}$
   $\frac{3}{8}, \frac{6}{16}, \frac{9}{24}$
   (d) $>$ $\frac{3}{4}, \frac{6}{8}, \frac{9}{12}$ $\frac{9}{12} > \frac{8}{12}$
   $\frac{4}{6}, \frac{8}{12}$

Emma recognizes that she can find an equivalent fraction for $\frac{3}{4}$ with the same numerator as $\frac{6}{7}$ and use that to compare those two fractions.

Once it is established that $\frac{5}{8}$ is less than $\frac{3}{4}$ and $\frac{3}{4}$ is less than $\frac{6}{7}$, the three fractions can be put in order.

Do (pp. 67–68)

1 2 Students should notice that they can divide the parts for one of the fraction circles or bars to have parts the same size as the parts in the other fraction circle or bar. There are then twice or three times as many parts, so they can multiply to make an equivalent fraction that has the same denominator as the other fraction.

3 Students are expected to use the strategy of finding an equivalent fraction for one of the fractions with the same denominator as the other fraction, although in some cases they could find an equivalent fraction with the same numerator as the other fraction. Generally students find it easier to compare fractions when the denominators are the same, since the numerators will be in the same order as the fractions themselves.

4 Students should notice that they can find an equivalent fraction for one of the two fractions with the same number of parts as the other fraction; that is, the numerators are the same.

5 Students are expected to find an equivalent fraction so that the numerators are the same, although they could make the denominators the same for (a) or (f).

6 Neither the numerators nor the denominators are "related" for $\frac{2}{3}$ and $\frac{3}{4}$ (and both are in simplest form), so it is not possible to find an equivalent fraction for only one of them in order to compare them. This problem shows students they can systematically list equivalent fractions for both until they see two that they can compare, either because they have the same denominator (as Sofia is doing) or the same numerator (as Alex is doing). If your student is not struggling, you can suggest that they do this for the fraction with the greatest denominator first, until they see a denominator that is "related" to the denominator of the other fraction, and then simply find the corresponding equivalent fraction.

7 Students can use the method of listing equivalent fractions for both fractions. For (a), they could list equivalent fractions for $\frac{3}{5}$ until they get to $\frac{9}{15}$, see that 15 is "related" to 3, and find the equivalent fraction for $\frac{2}{3}$ with a denominator of 15. For (b) and (c), some students may simply know the answer from visualizing the fraction bars.

Lesson 5 Comparing Fractions — Part 2 (pp. 69–72)

Think (p. 69)

Have students read the problem and think of ways to put the fractions in order. Students might notice based on their experience with fraction bars that $\frac{2}{5}$ must be the least. They may compare $\frac{5}{6}$ and $\frac{8}{9}$ by listing equivalent fractions, which is tedious. Point out the hints at the bottom of the page. Students should realize that $\frac{2}{5}$ is less than $\frac{1}{2}$ and the other two fractions are greater than $\frac{1}{2}$, but may not be able to use Emma's hint yet.

Learn (p. 70)

Students learned earlier that a fraction is equal to $\frac{1}{2}$ if the denominator is twice the numerator. Fractions equivalent to $\frac{1}{2}$ will always have an even number in the denominator.

To compare $\frac{2}{5}$ to $\frac{1}{2}$, Dion compares $\frac{2}{5}$ to $\frac{2}{4}$, an equivalent fraction of $\frac{1}{2}$ with the same numerator as $\frac{2}{5}$. Other strategies are possible. From experience with fraction bars, your student may be able to easily visualize $\frac{2}{5}$ and "see" that it is less than $\frac{1}{2}$. Or, they may intuitively know that 2 is less than half of 5, so $\frac{2}{5}$ must be less than $\frac{1}{2}$. Or, they could find an equivalent fraction of $\frac{2}{5}$ that has an even number in the denominator, $\frac{4}{10}$, which they know is less than $\frac{1}{2}$, since 10 is more than double 4.

To compare $\frac{5}{6}$ to $\frac{1}{2}$, Dion finds an equivalent fraction of $\frac{1}{2}$ with a denominator of 6, $\frac{3}{6}$. Your students might easily know that half of 6 is 3, which is less than the 5 in $\frac{5}{6}$, so $\frac{5}{6}$ is greater than $\frac{1}{2}$.

Answers

Mei skateboarded the longest distance.
Sofia skateboarded the shortest distance.

1. $\frac{5}{8}$
2. $\frac{1}{2}$
3. $\frac{5}{8}$
4. $\frac{3}{8}, \frac{3}{10}, \frac{5}{11}, \frac{2}{5}, \frac{3}{7}$
5. (a) $\frac{1}{4} < \frac{5}{7}$ $(\frac{1}{4} < \frac{1}{2}, \frac{5}{7} > \frac{5}{10})$
   (b) $\frac{2}{3} > \frac{1}{5}$ $(\frac{2}{3} > \frac{2}{4}, \frac{1}{5} < \frac{1}{2})$
   (c) $\frac{1}{3} < \frac{5}{8}$ $(\frac{1}{3} < \frac{1}{2}, \frac{5}{8} > \frac{5}{10})$
6. $\frac{6}{7}$
7. (a) > (b) >
   (c) < (d) >
8. $\frac{1}{4}, \frac{5}{12}, \frac{2}{3}$
9. (a) $\frac{1}{2}, \frac{5}{8}, \frac{3}{4}$ (b) $\frac{2}{5}, \frac{7}{10}, \frac{7}{8}$
   (c) $\frac{3}{8}, \frac{1}{2}, \frac{3}{4}, \frac{5}{6}$ (d) $\frac{1}{3}, \frac{1}{2}, \frac{5}{6}, \frac{7}{8}$

To compare $\frac{5}{6}$ to $\frac{8}{9}$, Emma compares both fractions to 1. Students can refer to the fraction bars at the bottom of the page. Emma's method is used when the numerators are one less than the denominators. The difference with 1 is then a unit fraction.

$\frac{1}{9}$ is less than $\frac{1}{6}$, so $\frac{8}{9}$ is "closer to" 1 than $\frac{5}{6}$, and $\frac{8}{9}$ is greater than $\frac{5}{6}$.

Do (pp. 71–72)

❶ ❷ ❸ These first three problems are related. The fraction bars verify the friends' thinking. Be sure to discuss the thought bubbles. For ❶, Sofia knows that $\frac{5}{8}$ is greater than $\frac{4}{8}$, so $\frac{5}{8}$ is greater than $\frac{1}{2}$. For ❷, Mei knows that $\frac{4}{9}$ is less than $\frac{4}{8}$, so $\frac{4}{9}$ is less than $\frac{1}{2}$. Therefore, for ❸, we know that $\frac{4}{9}$ is less than $\frac{5}{8}$.

❹ Students may be able to easily determine whether some of these are less than $\frac{1}{2}$ by visualizing the fraction. They can compare the rest to an equivalent fraction of $\frac{1}{2}$ with either the same numerator or the same denominator.

❺ Students are expected to compare these fractions by comparing each to $\frac{1}{2}$. For all three of them, one of the fractions is a unit fraction, and so is easy to compare to $\frac{1}{2}$. Your student does not have to justify a correct answer with equivalent fractions unless you feel you should require it. From experience with fractions, they might easily visualize that each of the other fractions are greater than $\frac{1}{2}$.

❻ Students should notice that the numerator is one less than the denominator for each of these, which is why Alex is using Emma's method from Learn.

❼ Students are expected to compare each of the fractions to 1, as in ❻, by comparing the unit fractions needed to make 1.

❽ Discuss the ideas being used by the friends. Emma recognizes that the denominators are "related" and so finds equivalent fractions for $\frac{2}{3}$ and $\frac{1}{4}$ with denominators of 12. Dion recognizes that since one of them is greater than $\frac{1}{2}$, he only needs to compare the two that are less than $\frac{1}{2}$.

❾ In general, the first step in comparing a set of fractions in this lesson and the rest of this level should be to first group the fractions by whether they are less than $\frac{1}{2}$, between $\frac{1}{2}$ and 1, or greater than 1. The next step is to compare the fractions within each of those groups. They will not always be able to easily use Emma's method. Use your discretion for whether you want to require your student to explain their reasoning. Possible reasoning:

(a) $\frac{5}{8}$ and $\frac{3}{4}$ are both greater than $\frac{1}{2}$.
$\frac{3}{4} = \frac{6}{8}$, $\frac{5}{8} < \frac{6}{8}$

(b) $\frac{2}{5}$ is less than $\frac{1}{2}$, $\frac{7}{8}$ and $\frac{7}{10}$ are greater than $\frac{1}{2}$. $\frac{7}{10} < \frac{7}{8}$

(c) $\frac{3}{8}$ is less than $\frac{1}{2}$, $\frac{3}{4}$ and $\frac{5}{6}$ are greater than $\frac{1}{2}$. Both of the fractions $\frac{3}{4}$ and $\frac{5}{6}$ have numerators one less than the denominator. $\frac{5}{6}$ is closer to 1.

(d) $\frac{1}{3}$ is less than $\frac{1}{2}$, $\frac{5}{6}$ and $\frac{7}{8}$ are greater than $\frac{1}{2}$. Both of the fractions $\frac{5}{6}$ and $\frac{7}{8}$ have numerators one less than the denominator. $\frac{7}{8}$ is closer to 1.

Lesson 6 Practice A (pp. 73–74)

1 For (c) and (f), students will not be able
2 to multiply the numerator and denominator of the second fraction to find the third equivalent fraction; they will need to go back to the first fraction for both.

6 Students can use any strategy they want. They might easily find the answer without even having to specifically find equivalent fractions, for example. It should be easy by now to know from experience that $\frac{1}{3}$ is less than $\frac{5}{6}$. For (a) and (b), they can find equivalent fractions with the same denominator. For (c) and (d), they can find equivalent fractions with the same numerator. For (e), one fraction is greater than 1. For (f), they can compare the fractions to 1.

7 (a) All of the fractions are greater than $\frac{1}{2}$. $\frac{2}{3}=\frac{8}{12}$, $\frac{3}{4}=\frac{9}{12}$, $\frac{7}{12}<\frac{8}{12}<\frac{9}{12}$

(b) $\frac{5}{7}$ and $\frac{5}{9}$ are greater than $\frac{1}{2}$. $\frac{5}{9}<\frac{5}{7}$

(c) $\frac{4}{8}=\frac{1}{2}$, and the rest are greater than $\frac{1}{2}$.

(d) $\frac{6}{5}>\frac{1}{2}$, $\frac{3}{10}$ and $\frac{3}{8}$ are both less than $\frac{1}{2}$. The two greater than $\frac{1}{2}$ both have the same numerators.

Answers

1 (a) $\frac{2}{10}$ (b) $\frac{2}{3}$ (c) $\frac{2}{4}=\frac{3}{6}$
(d) $\frac{3}{5}$ (e) $\frac{3}{4}$ (f) $\frac{2}{6}=\frac{3}{9}$

2 (a) $\frac{6}{10}$ (b) $\frac{10}{15}$ (c) $\frac{4}{8}=\frac{6}{12}$
(d) $\frac{3}{4}$ (e) $\frac{2}{14}$ (f) $\frac{4}{6}=\frac{6}{9}$

3 Answers can vary. Examples:
(a) $\frac{2}{3}$, $\frac{8}{12}$
(b) $\frac{2}{4}$, $\frac{5}{10}$
(c) $\frac{6}{6}$, $\frac{11}{11}$

4

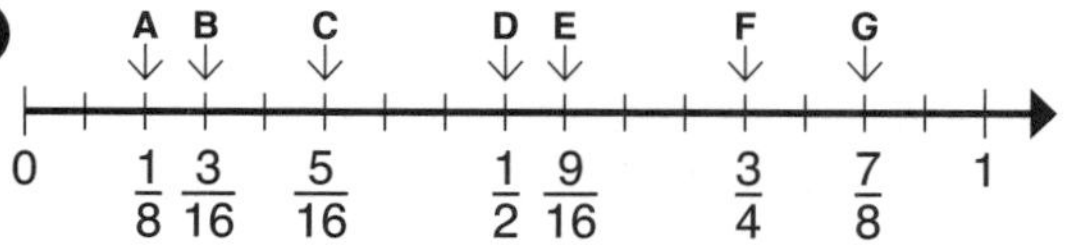

5 (a) $\frac{3}{5}$ (b) $\frac{1}{2}$ (c) $\frac{1}{2}$
(d) $\frac{2}{3}$ (e) $\frac{5}{6}$ (f) $\frac{7}{8}$
(g) $\frac{9}{10}$ (h) $\frac{3}{4}$ (i) $\frac{2}{3}$
(j) $\frac{7}{9}$ (k) $\frac{1}{2}$ (l) $\frac{1}{2}$

6 (a) < (b) <
(c) < (d) >
(e) < (f) >

7 (a) $\frac{7}{12}$, $\frac{2}{3}$, $\frac{3}{4}$ (b) $\frac{1}{2}$, $\frac{5}{9}$, $\frac{5}{7}$
(c) $\frac{4}{8}$, $\frac{7}{9}$, $\frac{7}{8}$, $\frac{7}{5}$ (d) $\frac{3}{10}$, $\frac{3}{8}$, $\frac{1}{2}$, $\frac{6}{5}$

8 **Fang**
$\frac{1}{4}=\frac{2}{8}$, $\frac{3}{8}>\frac{2}{8}$

Lesson 7 Adding and Subtracting Fractions — Part 1 (pp. 75–79)

Think (p. 75)

Have your student read the problem and find the answers. They probably won't find it difficult, and will simply add or subtract the number of eighths. You can ask them to write an equation or wait until Learn to see the addition and subtraction equations with fractions.

Learn (pp. 75–76)

Two ways to visualize adding fractions or subtracting fractions with the same denominator are shown: a vertical "bar model" with the lowest units colored, and a number line model. The numerators all count the parts—eighths—so we can simply add or subtract the numerators to get the total or the difference in number of parts.

Do (pp. 77–79)

In the first four problems, both a bar model and a number line are provided to help students visualize the process.

3 Students should think of 1 as $\frac{4}{4}$ and find the numerator of the difference by subtracting 3 from 4.

4 If the sum is an equivalent fraction of 1, students should write a final answer of 1. If the numerator is 0, there are no parts, and they should write the final answer as 0.

Answers

(a) $\frac{7}{8}$

$\frac{7}{8}$

(b) $\frac{3}{8}$

$\frac{3}{8}$

1 $\frac{5}{7}$

2 $\frac{4}{9}$

3 $\frac{1}{4}$

4 (a) $\frac{3}{5}$

(b) $\frac{5}{5} = 1$

(c) $\frac{3}{5}$

(d) $\frac{4}{5}$

(e) $\frac{0}{5} = 0$

(f) $\frac{3}{5}$

5 (a) $\frac{3}{4}$ (b) $\frac{7}{8}$

(c) $\frac{1}{6}$ (d) $\frac{3}{10}$

(e) $\frac{7}{10}$ (f) $\frac{11}{12}$

6 (a) $\frac{2}{9}$ (b) $\frac{3}{7}$

(c) $\frac{2}{4}$ (d) $\frac{11}{12}$

7 $\frac{2}{3}$ more

8 $\frac{9}{10}$ kg

$\frac{3}{10} + \frac{4}{10} + \frac{2}{10} = \frac{9}{10}$

Lesson 8 Adding and Subtracting Fractions — Part 2 (pp. 80–82)

Think (p. 80)

Have your student read the problem and find the answer. The difference here from the previous lesson is that the answer can be simplified.

Learn (p. 80)

This shows a vertical model for the paint in the cans. Students should not have any difficulty simplifying the fraction if they mastered Lesson 2.

Do (pp. 81–82)

4 In order to subtract from 1, we need to think of the equivalent fraction for 1 with a denominator the same as the fraction being subtracted. In this case they need to simplify the answer since it is not in simplest form.

Tell your student that from now on they should always express their final answers for fraction problems in simplest form, even when the problem does not specifically say to do so.

Answers

$\frac{2}{3}$

1 $\mathbf{\frac{4}{6}} = \frac{2}{3}$

2 $\mathbf{\frac{2}{4}} = \frac{1}{2}$

3 (a) $\mathbf{\frac{4}{8}} = \frac{1}{2}$ (b) $\mathbf{\frac{8}{10}} = \frac{4}{5}$

(c) $\mathbf{\frac{4}{6}} = \frac{2}{3}$ (d) $\mathbf{\frac{4}{12}} = \frac{1}{3}$

4 $\mathbf{\frac{4}{6}} = \frac{2}{3}$

5 (a) $\mathbf{\frac{6}{9}} = \frac{2}{3}$ (b) $\mathbf{\frac{10}{12}} = \frac{5}{6}$

6 (a) $\frac{6}{8} = \frac{3}{4}$ (b) $\frac{8}{10} = \frac{4}{5}$

(c) $\frac{3}{9} = \frac{1}{3}$ (d) $\frac{5}{15} = \frac{1}{3}$

7 (a) $\mathbf{\frac{5}{8}}$ **lb**

$\frac{7}{16} + \frac{3}{16} = \frac{10}{16} = \frac{5}{8}$

(b) $\mathbf{\frac{1}{4}}$ **lb more**

$\frac{7}{16} - \frac{3}{16} = \frac{4}{16} = \frac{1}{4}$

Lesson 9 Practice B (pp. 83–84)

2 Students should simplify after adding or subtracting in order to compare the values.

The workbook exercise includes some problems that review addition, subtraction, multiplication, and division. The next chapter does include problems that involve these operations on whole numbers.

Answers

1
(a) $\frac{5}{8}$
(b) $\frac{7}{7} = 1$
(c) $\frac{9}{9} = 1$
(d) $\frac{5}{6}$
(e) $\frac{6}{10} = \frac{3}{5}$
(f) $\frac{10}{15} = \frac{2}{3}$
(g) $\frac{3}{6} = \frac{1}{2}$
(h) $\frac{10}{10} = 1$
(i) $\frac{10}{16} = \frac{5}{8}$
(j) $\frac{4}{9}$
(k) $\frac{3}{6} = \frac{1}{2}$
(l) $\frac{3}{5}$
(m) $\frac{6}{10} = \frac{3}{5}$
(n) $\frac{3}{12} = \frac{1}{4}$
(o) $\frac{5}{15} = \frac{1}{3}$
(p) $\frac{4}{6} = \frac{2}{3}$
(q) $\frac{3}{8}$
(r) $\frac{8}{16} = \frac{1}{2}$

2
(a) =
$1 = 1$
(b) <
$\frac{3}{10} < \frac{2}{3}$
(c) >
$\frac{5}{7} > \frac{5}{8}$
(d) <
$\frac{3}{4} < \frac{3}{2}$
(e) =
$\frac{1}{4} = \frac{1}{4}$
(f) >
$\frac{2}{3} > \frac{1}{3}$

3 **Kalama, $\frac{1}{4}$ mile**
$\frac{7}{8} - \frac{5}{8} = \frac{2}{8} = \frac{1}{4}$

4 **$\frac{5}{6}$ ft**
$\frac{5}{12} + \frac{3}{12} + \frac{2}{12} = \frac{10}{12} = \frac{5}{6}$

5 **$\frac{1}{2}$ m**
$\frac{8}{8} - \frac{3}{8} - \frac{1}{8} = \frac{4}{8} = \frac{1}{2}$

6 **$\frac{1}{3}$ km**
$\frac{8}{9} - \frac{5}{9} = \frac{3}{9} = \frac{1}{3}$

Chapter 10 Workbook Answers

Exercise 1 pp. 51–54

1 $\frac{2}{4}$ $\frac{3}{6}$ $\frac{4}{8}$ $\frac{5}{10}$ $\frac{6}{12}$

2 $\frac{6}{8}$ $\frac{9}{12}$

3 $\frac{4}{6}$ $\frac{6}{9}$

4 Which parts are shaded can vary.

(a)

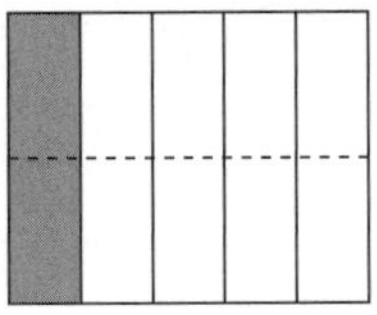

$\frac{2}{10}$

(b)

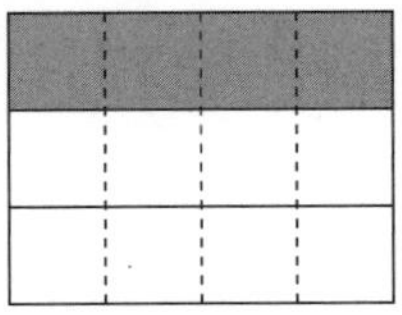

$\frac{4}{12}$

(c)

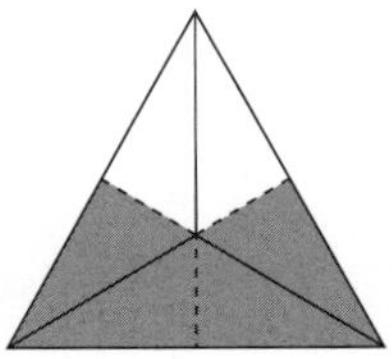

$\frac{4}{6}$

(d)

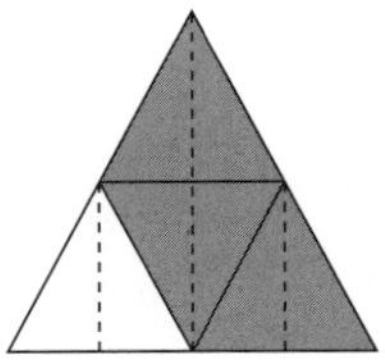

$\frac{6}{8}$

(e)

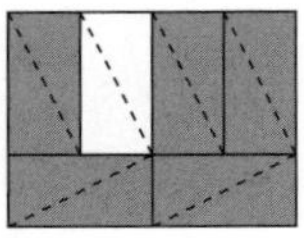

$\frac{10}{12}$

(f)

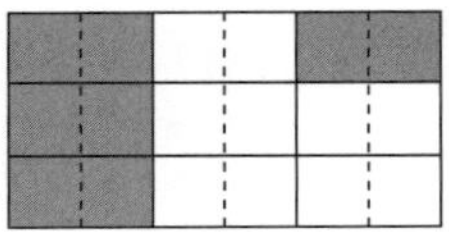

$\frac{8}{18}$

5 (a)

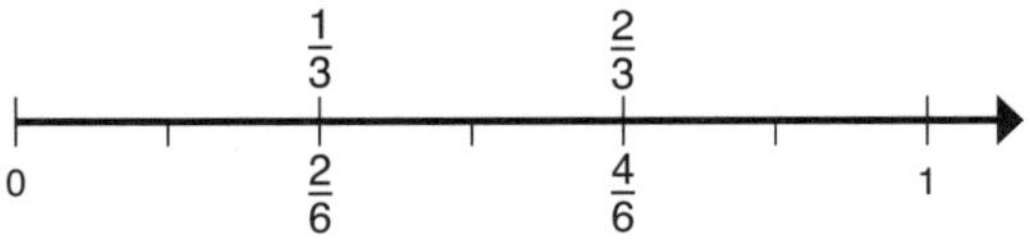

(b)

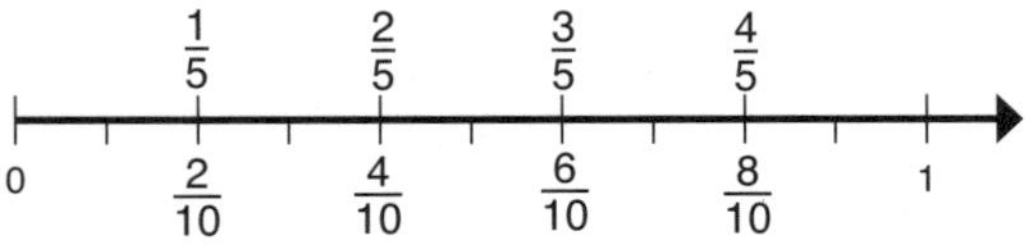

(c)

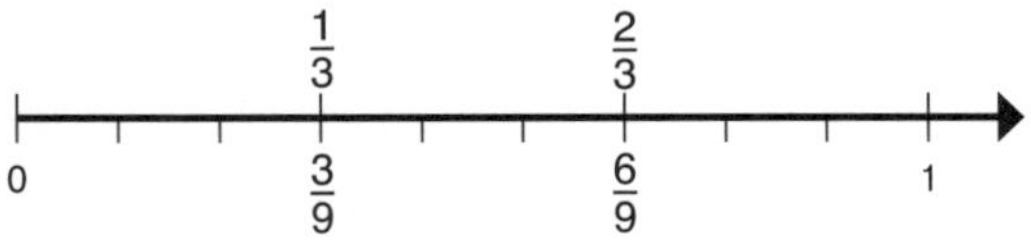

(d)

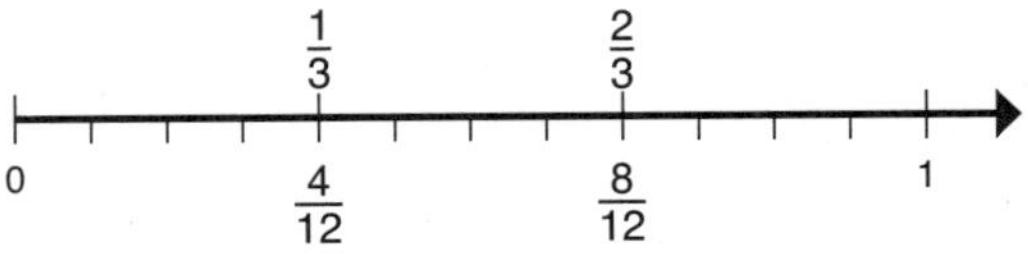

(e)

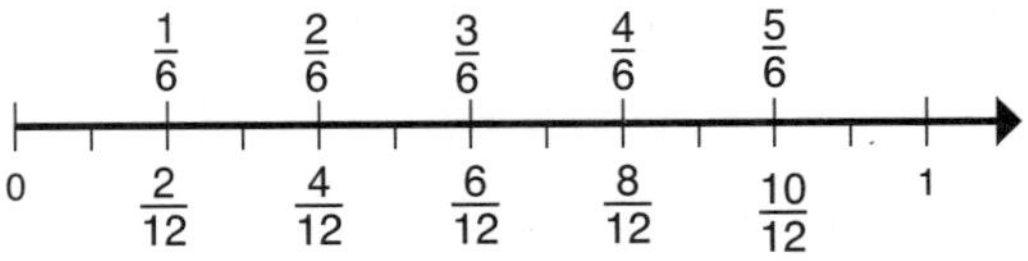

(f)

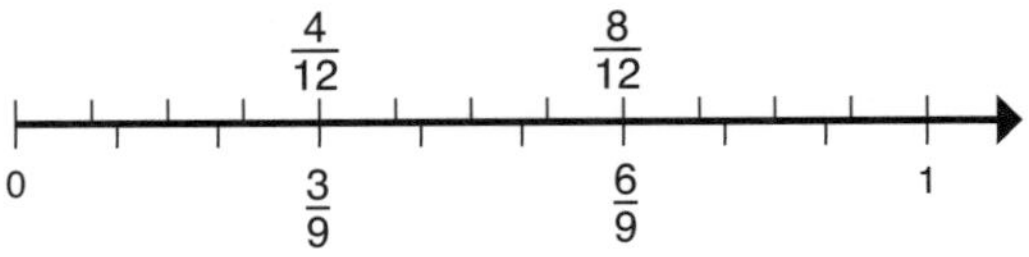

6 Which parts are shaded can vary.

(a)

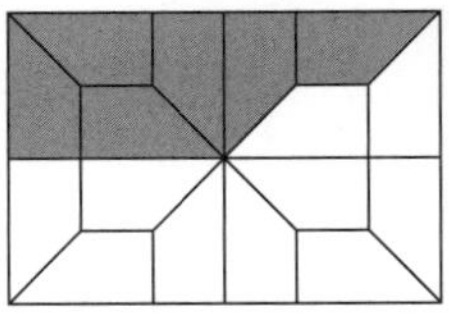

$\frac{6}{16}$

(b)

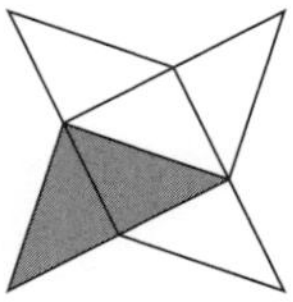

$\frac{2}{6}$

(c)

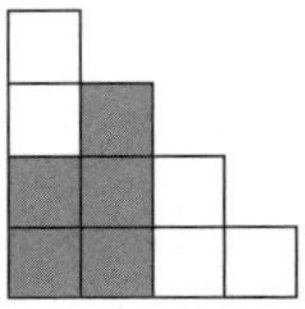

$\frac{5}{10}$

(d)

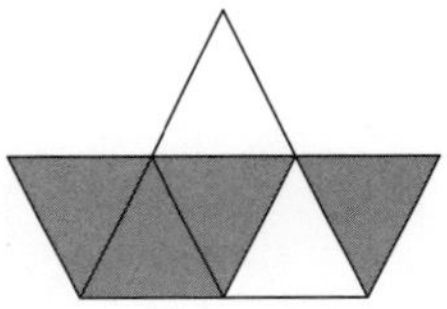

$\frac{4}{6}$

(e)

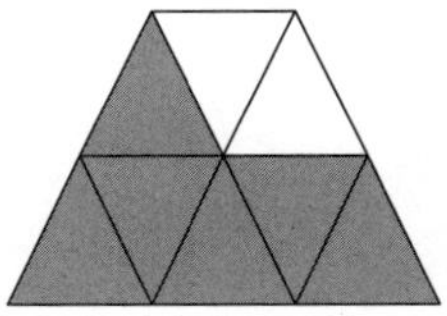

$\frac{6}{8}$

(f)

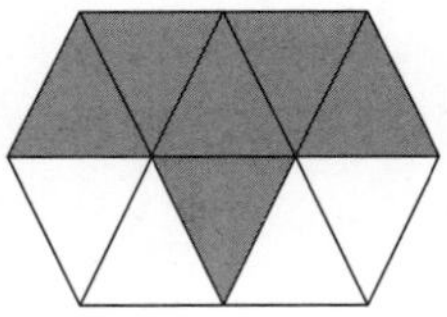

$\frac{6}{10}$

Chapter 10 Workbook Answers

Exercise 2 pp. 55–57

1

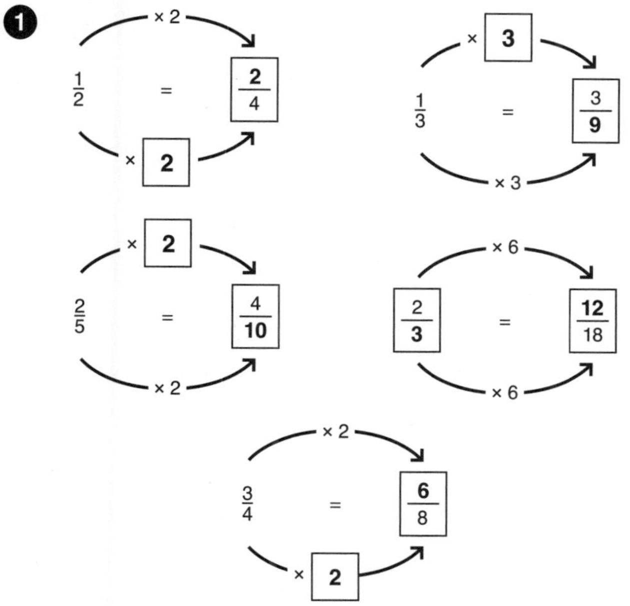

2 $\frac{2}{6} = \frac{3}{9} = \frac{4}{12}$

3 (a) $\frac{6}{8} = \frac{9}{12} = \frac{12}{16}$

(b) $\frac{15}{20}$

(c) $\frac{4}{14}$

(d) $\frac{6}{21}$

(e) $\frac{6}{10}$

4 Answers can vary. Examples:

(a) $\frac{2}{10}, \frac{3}{15}, \frac{4}{20}$

(b) $\frac{1}{1}, \frac{2}{2}, \frac{3}{3}$

5 Students can simplify each fraction in the answer chart and then determine which figure matches, rather than writing the fraction for each. Equivalent fractions that will match are given here for your benefit.

A	$\frac{2}{3} = \frac{6}{9} = \frac{8}{12}$	R	$\frac{1}{5} = \frac{4}{20}$	E	$\frac{1}{2} = \frac{4}{8} = \frac{3}{6}$
C	$\frac{1}{6} = \frac{2}{12}$	P	$1 = \frac{5}{5} = \frac{11}{11}$	N	$\frac{2}{5} = \frac{4}{10}$
T	$\frac{1}{4} = \frac{2}{8} = \frac{3}{12}$	S	$\frac{2}{9} = \frac{4}{18}$	O	$\frac{3}{7} = \frac{6}{14}$

PENTACERATOPS

Exercise 3 pp. 58–61

1

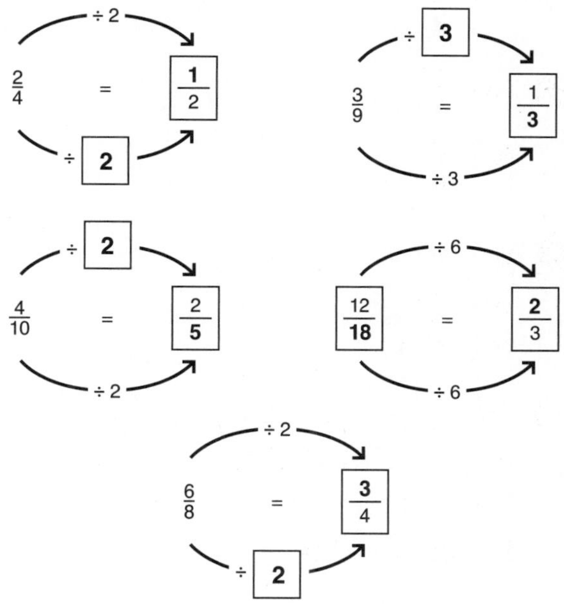

2 (a)

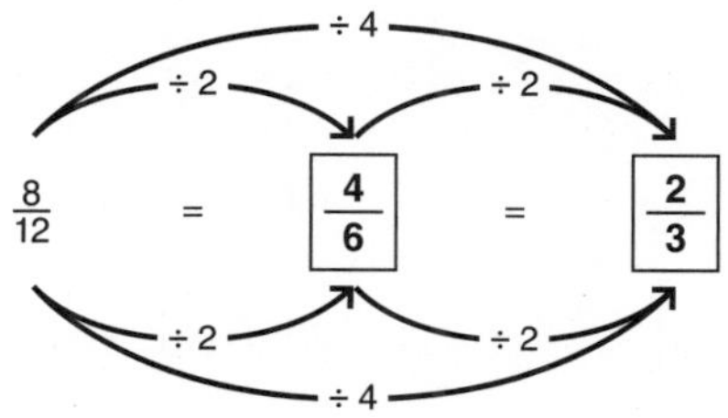

$\frac{2}{3}$

(b)

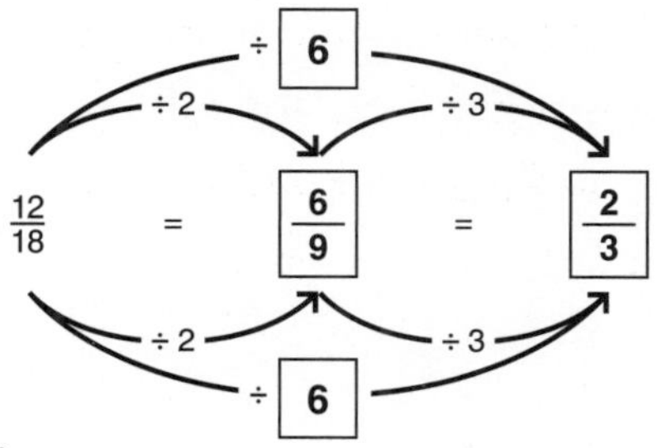

$\frac{2}{3}$

(c) $\frac{9}{12} = \frac{6}{8} = \frac{3}{4}$ $\frac{3}{4}$

3 (a) $\frac{1}{2}$ (b) $\frac{1}{3}$

(c) $\frac{4}{9}$ (d) $\frac{3}{7}$

Chapter 10 Workbook Answers

4 (a) $\frac{5}{7}$ (b) $\frac{1}{3}$

(c) $\frac{4}{5}$ (d) $\frac{3}{4}$

5 (a) $\frac{2}{3}$ (b) $\frac{2}{5}$

(c) $\frac{2}{3}$ (d) $\frac{1}{2}$

6 (a) 32

(b) $\frac{22}{45}$

(c) Yes

7 The first problem shows students that they should first simplify the fraction to its simplest form, then find the equivalent fraction with the given denominator.

(a) $\frac{2}{3}$ $\frac{8}{12}$ $\frac{\mathbf{8}}{\mathbf{12}}$

(b) $\frac{\mathbf{9}}{12}$ (c) $\frac{\mathbf{8}}{16}$

(d) $\frac{\mathbf{6}}{9}$ (e) $\frac{\mathbf{12}}{15}$

(f) $\frac{\mathbf{6}}{10}$ (g) $\frac{\mathbf{15}}{20}$

Exercise 4 pp. 62–64

1 Students should shade the contiguous parts starting from the left so that they can use the length of the shaded part to compare the fractions.

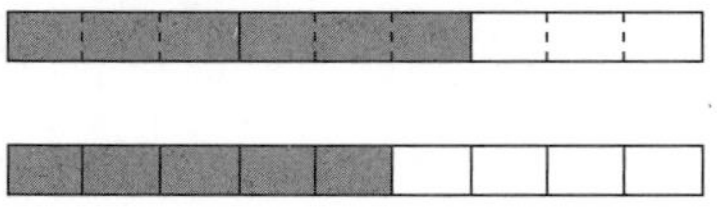

$\frac{2}{3} = \frac{\mathbf{6}}{\mathbf{9}}$

$\frac{5}{9}$

$\frac{2}{3} > \frac{5}{9}$

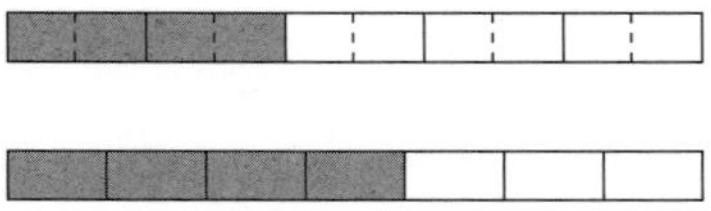

$\frac{2}{5} = \frac{4}{\mathbf{10}}$

$\frac{4}{7}$

$\frac{2}{5} < \frac{4}{7}$

2

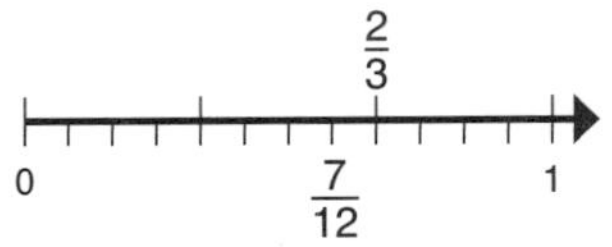

$\frac{2}{3} = \frac{\mathbf{8}}{12}$

$\frac{7}{12}$

$\frac{2}{3} > \frac{7}{12}$

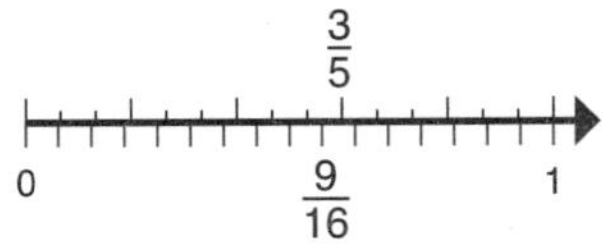

$\frac{3}{5} = \frac{9}{\mathbf{15}}$

$\frac{9}{16}$

$\frac{3}{5} > \frac{9}{16}$

3 (a) $\frac{\mathbf{4}}{6} = \frac{\mathbf{6}}{9} = \frac{\mathbf{10}}{15}$

$\frac{\mathbf{6}}{10} = \frac{\mathbf{9}}{15}$

$\frac{2}{3} > \frac{3}{5}$

(b) $\frac{8}{\mathbf{10}} = \frac{12}{\mathbf{15}}$

$\frac{6}{\mathbf{8}} = \frac{9}{\mathbf{12}} = \frac{12}{\mathbf{16}}$

$\frac{4}{5} > \frac{3}{4}$

4 (a) **>**

$\frac{7}{8} > \frac{6}{8}$

(b) **<**

$\frac{9}{12} < \frac{11}{12}$

(c) **>**

$\frac{6}{9} > \frac{5}{9}$

(d) **>**

$\frac{9}{15} > \frac{7}{15}$

(e) **<**

$\frac{8}{14} < \frac{8}{9}$

(f) **<**

$\frac{9}{12} < \frac{9}{11}$

(g) **<**

$\frac{3}{12} < \frac{5}{12}$

(h) **>**

$\frac{9}{12} > \frac{8}{12}$ or $\frac{6}{8} > \frac{6}{9}$

5 (a) $\frac{1}{2}, \frac{2}{3}, \frac{5}{6}$ $\frac{2}{3} = \frac{4}{6}, \frac{1}{2} = \frac{3}{6}, \frac{3}{6} < \frac{4}{6} < \frac{5}{6}$

(b) $\frac{5}{12}, \frac{2}{3}, \frac{3}{4}$ $\frac{3}{4} = \frac{9}{12}, \frac{2}{3} = \frac{8}{12}, \frac{5}{12} < \frac{8}{12} < \frac{9}{12}$

(c) $\frac{7}{12}, \frac{2}{3}, \frac{5}{6}$ $\frac{5}{6} = \frac{10}{12}, \frac{2}{3} = \frac{8}{12}, \frac{7}{12} < \frac{8}{12} < \frac{10}{12}$

(d) $\frac{3}{10}, \frac{6}{11}, \frac{2}{3}$ $\frac{2}{3} = \frac{6}{9}, \frac{3}{10} = \frac{6}{20}, \frac{6}{20} < \frac{6}{11} < \frac{6}{9}$

(e) $\frac{1}{2}, \frac{4}{7}, \frac{8}{11}$ $\frac{1}{2} = \frac{8}{16}, \frac{4}{7} = \frac{8}{14}, \frac{8}{16} < \frac{8}{14} < \frac{8}{11}$

Chapter 10 Workbook Answers

❻ (a) $\frac{1}{3} < \frac{5}{9} < \frac{2}{3}$

(b) $\frac{5}{8} < \frac{5}{7} < \frac{10}{11}$

(c) $\frac{5}{8} < \frac{7}{12} < \frac{3}{4}$

Exercise 5 pp. 65–67

❶ Students should shade the contiguous parts starting from the left so that they can use the length of the shaded part to compare the fractions.

(a)

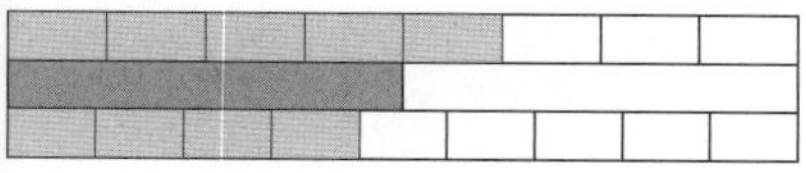

= > > $\frac{5}{8} > \frac{4}{9}$

< <

(b)

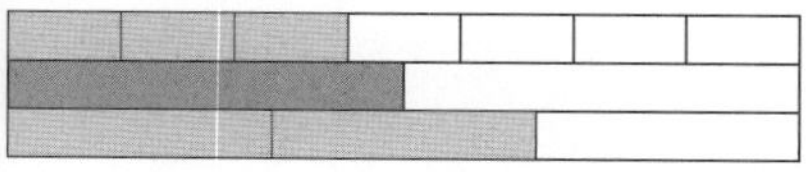

= = < < $\frac{3}{7} < \frac{2}{3}$

< > >

(c)

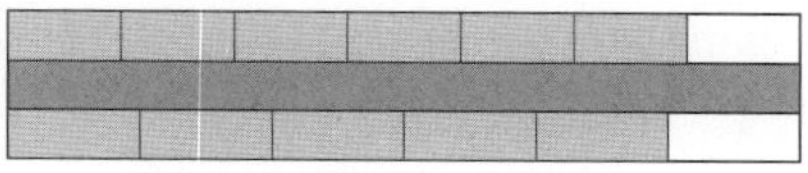

$\frac{1}{7} < \frac{1}{6}$, so $\frac{6}{7} > \frac{5}{6}$

In the next two problems, the numbers are in a deliberate order so students can notice a pattern by comparing the ones they circle to the ones next to them.

❷ $\frac{2}{6}$ $\frac{3}{8}$ $\frac{4}{10}$ $\frac{5}{12}$ $\frac{7}{16}$

❸ $\frac{3}{5}$ $\frac{4}{7}$ $\frac{5}{9}$ $\frac{6}{11}$ $\frac{7}{13}$

❹ Students should first compare each fraction to $\frac{1}{2}$, which will give them the answers for (a), (d), (e), and (f). For (b) and (c), they could list some equivalent fractions. Some students may think about how close they are to $\frac{1}{2}$. For example, for (b), $\frac{5}{8}$ is $\frac{1}{8}$ past $\frac{1}{2}$, and $\frac{7}{12}$ is only $\frac{1}{12}$ past $\frac{1}{2}$.

(a) < (b) >
(c) > (d) <
(e) > (f) >

❺ For all of these, the numerator is one less than the denominator, so they can be compared by comparing how close each is to 1.

(a) > (b) <
(c) < (d) <
(e) < (f) >

❻ (a) $\frac{2}{5}, \frac{5}{6}, \frac{6}{7}$

$\frac{2}{5} < \frac{1}{2}$, compare $\frac{5}{6}$ and $\frac{6}{7}$ to 1

(b) $\frac{3}{7}, \frac{7}{12}, \frac{3}{4}$

$\frac{3}{7} < \frac{1}{2}, \frac{3}{4} = \frac{9}{12}$

(c) $\frac{2}{5}, \frac{5}{9}, \frac{13}{12}$

$\frac{2}{5} < \frac{1}{2}$, $\frac{5}{9}$ is a bit more than $\frac{1}{2}$, $\frac{13}{12}$ is greater than 1.

(d) $\frac{3}{10}, \frac{3}{7}, \frac{9}{11}, \frac{8}{8}$

$\frac{3}{10}$ and $\frac{3}{7}$ are less than $\frac{1}{2}$ and have the same numerator, $\frac{8}{8} = 1$.

(e) $\frac{3}{7}, \frac{1}{2}, \frac{7}{8}, \frac{8}{9}$

$\frac{3}{7} < \frac{1}{2}$, compare $\frac{7}{8}$ and $\frac{8}{9}$ to 1.

Chapter 10 Workbook Answers

7 If your student struggles with these, suggest that they make the last fraction as close to 1 as possible (with a numerator 1 less than the denominator.)

(a) $\frac{4}{7} < \frac{7}{8} < \frac{8}{9}$

(b) $\frac{2}{7} < \frac{4}{9} < \frac{3}{4}$

(c) $\frac{3}{8} < \frac{7}{9} < \frac{6}{7}$

Exercise 6 pp. 68–70

1 B

B has 5 out of 6 parts are shaded.
$\frac{5}{6}$ is not equivalent to $\frac{3}{4}$

A has 3 out of 4 parts shaded, or $\frac{3}{4}$.
C and D have 9 out of 12 parts shaded: $\frac{9}{12} = \frac{3}{4}$.

2 (a)

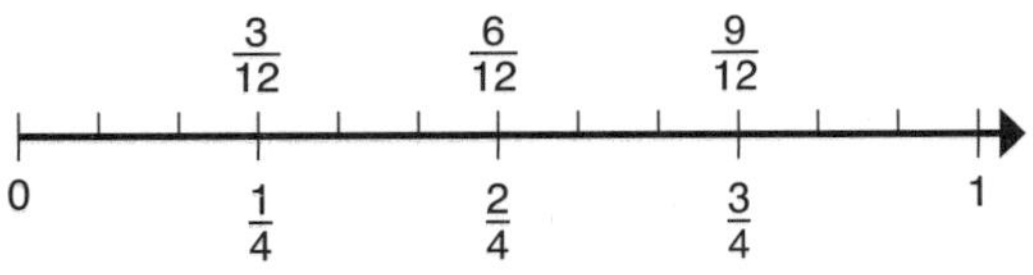

(b)

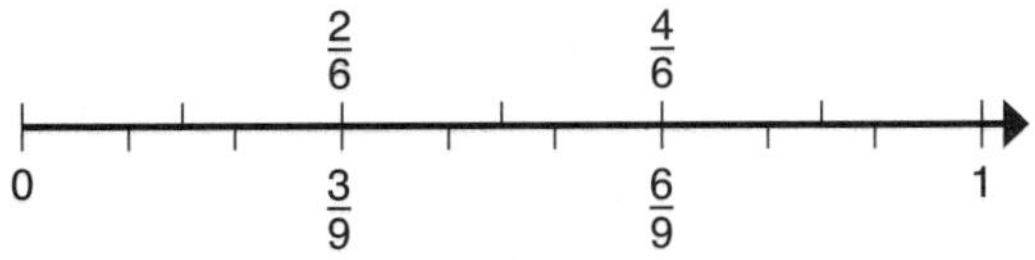

(c)

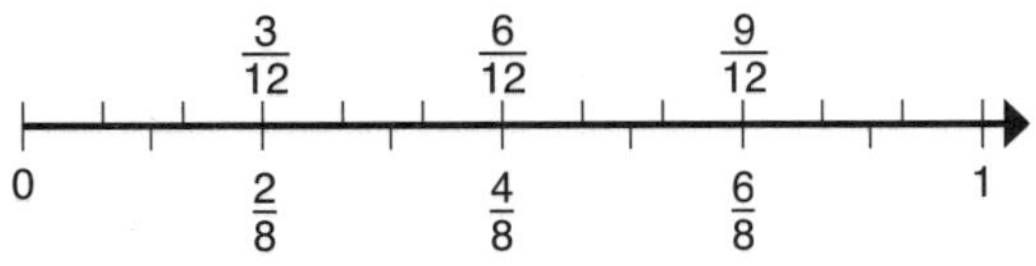

3 $\frac{6}{4}$ $\frac{8}{5}$ $\frac{10}{9}$ $\frac{20}{16}$

4 Answers can vary, though students will most likely list the next four:

(a) $\frac{4}{6}, \frac{6}{9}, \frac{8}{12}, \frac{10}{15}$ (b) $\frac{6}{10}, \frac{9}{15}, \frac{12}{20}, \frac{15}{25}$

5 (a) $\frac{6}{12}$ (b) $\frac{3}{6}$

(c) $\frac{5}{10}$ (d) $\frac{8}{16}$

6 (a) $\frac{3}{4}$ (b) $\frac{4}{5}$

(c) $\frac{3}{4}$ (d) $\frac{5}{8}$

7 More flour was used for the bread.
$\frac{3}{10} = \frac{6}{20}$ (bread)
$\frac{1}{4} = \frac{5}{20}$ (scones)

8 (a)

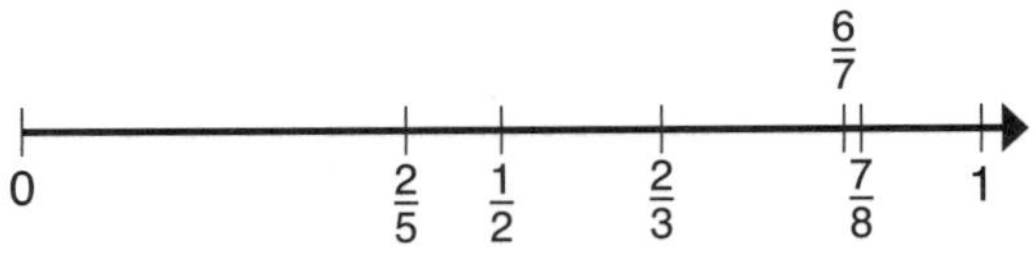

(b)

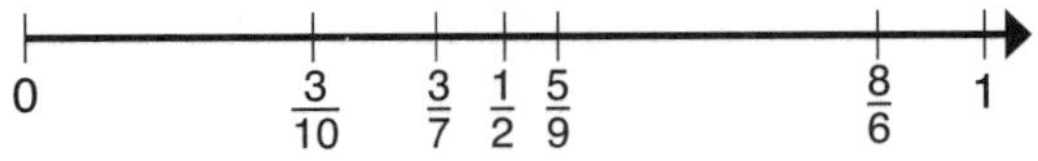

9 (a) $\frac{1}{3}$ (b) $\frac{1}{4}$

10 $\frac{1}{3}$

11 June 4

Exercise 7 pp. 71–73

1 $\frac{7}{10}$ $\frac{7}{12}$ $\frac{5}{5} = 1$

2 (a) $\frac{7}{8}$

(b) $\frac{6}{7}$

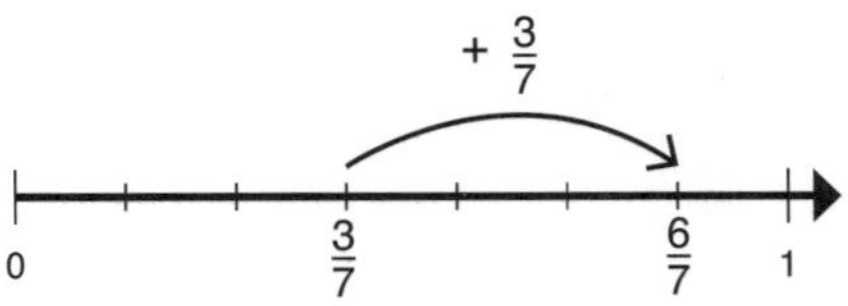

(c) $\frac{11}{16}$

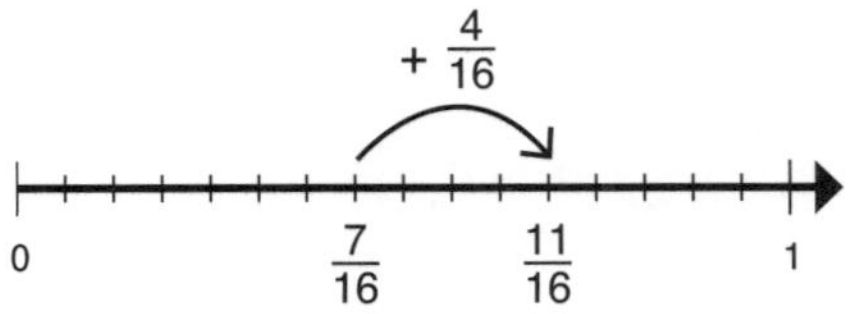

Chapter 10 Workbook Answers

3 (a) $\frac{4}{9}$

(b) $\frac{3}{10}$

(c) $\frac{1}{6}$

4 (a) $\frac{3}{8}$

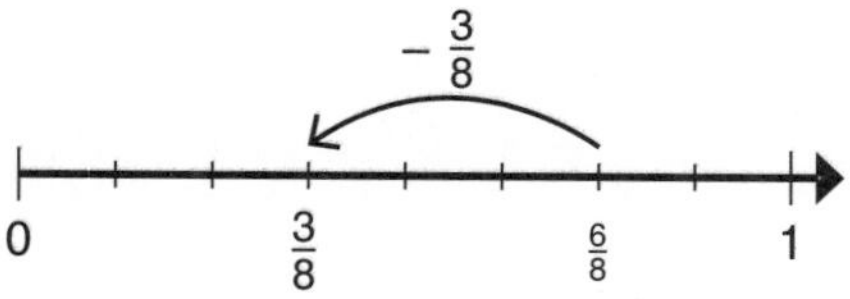

(b) $\frac{3}{7}$

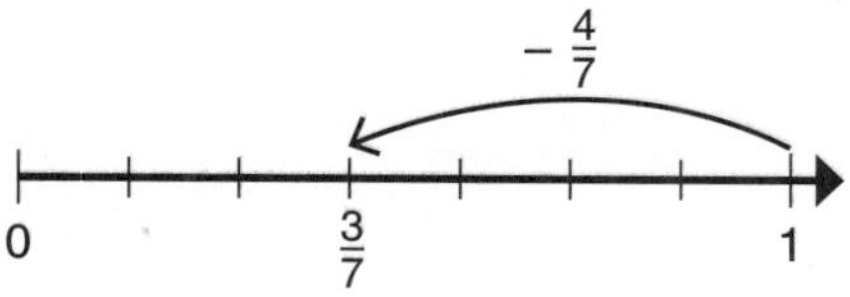

(c) $\frac{5}{12}$

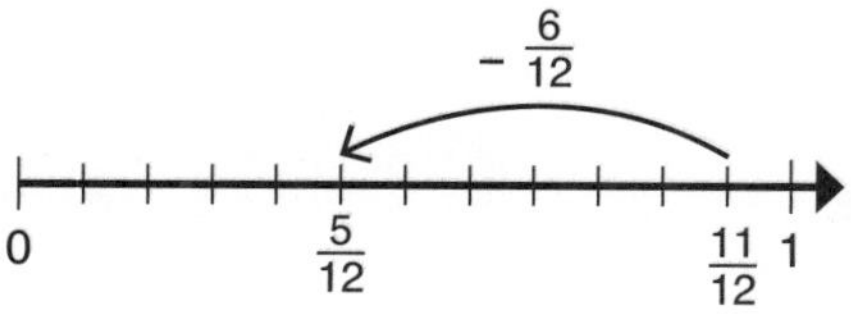

(d) 0

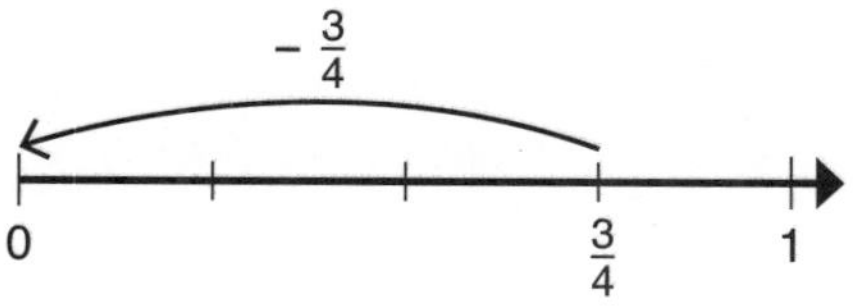

5 (a) $\frac{4}{7}$ (b) $\frac{6}{6}$ or 1

(c) $\frac{1}{9}$ (d) $\frac{5}{16}$

(e) $\frac{7}{12}$ (f) $\frac{7}{9}$

(g) $\frac{4}{4}$ or 1 (h) $\frac{4}{15}$

6 **$\frac{7}{8}$ cup**

$\frac{4}{8} + \frac{2}{8} + \frac{1}{8} = \frac{7}{8}$

7 **$\frac{3}{10}$ m**

$\frac{10}{10} - \frac{4}{10} - \frac{3}{10} = \frac{3}{10}$

Exercise 8 pp. 74–76

1 (a) $\frac{4}{6} = \frac{2}{3}$

(b) $\frac{5}{10} = \frac{1}{2}$

(c) $\frac{3}{9} = \frac{1}{3}$

(d) $\frac{8}{12} = \frac{2}{3}$

2 (a) $\frac{6}{8} = \frac{3}{4}$

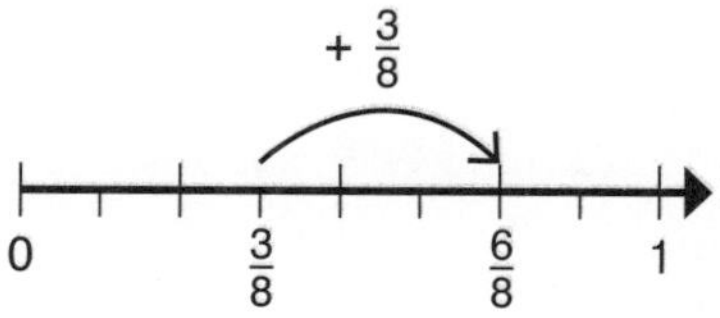

(b) $\frac{8}{12} = \frac{2}{3}$

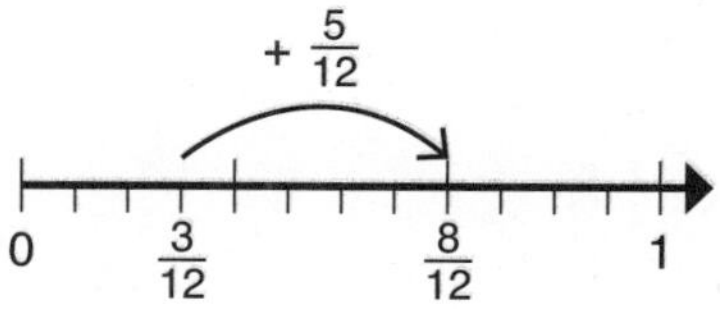

(c) $\frac{4}{8} = \frac{1}{2}$

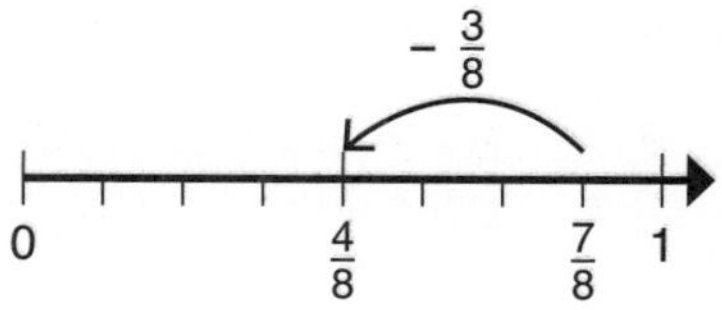

(d) $\frac{4}{16} = \frac{1}{4}$

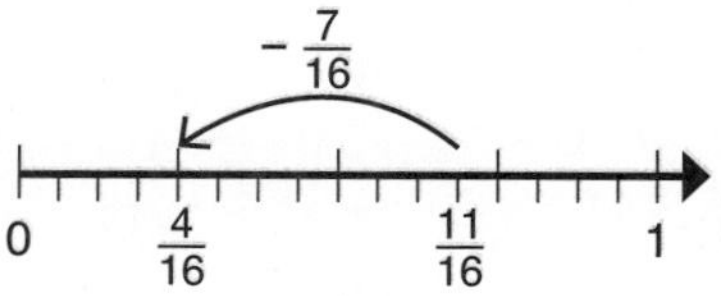

3 (a) $\frac{1}{4} + \mathbf{\frac{1}{4}} = \frac{2}{\mathbf{4}} = \frac{1}{2}$ (b) $\mathbf{\frac{3}{14}} + \frac{7}{\mathbf{14}} = \frac{10}{\mathbf{14}} = \frac{5}{7}$

(c) $\mathbf{\frac{5}{6}} - \frac{2}{\mathbf{6}} = \frac{3}{6} = \frac{1}{\mathbf{2}}$ (d) $\frac{13}{20} - \mathbf{\frac{9}{20}} = \frac{4}{\mathbf{20}} = \frac{1}{5}$

4 (a) **$\frac{4}{5}$ mile**

$\frac{5}{10} + \frac{3}{10} = \frac{8}{10} = \frac{4}{5}$

(b) **$\frac{1}{5}$ mile farther**

$\frac{5}{10} - \frac{3}{10} = \frac{2}{10} = \frac{1}{5}$

Chapter 10 Workbook Answers

5 S $\frac{1}{2}$ O $\frac{3}{4}$ K $\frac{3}{7}$

E $\frac{1}{4}$ D $\frac{2}{3}$ A $\frac{6}{7}$

R $\frac{5}{9}$ A $\frac{3}{5}$ C $\frac{1}{3}$

D $\frac{4}{5}$ C $\frac{2}{5}$ F $\frac{7}{8}$

A DECK OF CARDS

Exercise 9 pp. 77–80

1 6,249 7,747 1,864

2,685 31 R 1 4,655

16 70 R 4 1,776

1,375 5,518 2,811

2 (a) 4

$\frac{2}{9} + \frac{4}{9} = \frac{2}{3}$

(b) 2

$\frac{1}{6} + \frac{2}{6} = \frac{1}{2}$

(c) 5

$\frac{3}{10} + \frac{5}{10} = \frac{4}{5}$

(d) 8

$\frac{4}{14} + \frac{8}{14} = \frac{6}{7}$

(e) 7

$\frac{5}{18} + \frac{7}{18} = \frac{2}{3}$

(f) 9

$\frac{3}{16} + \frac{9}{16} = \frac{3}{4}$

3 (a) $\frac{7}{10} - \frac{3}{10} = \frac{2}{5}$

(b) $\frac{7}{8} - \frac{5}{8} = \frac{1}{4}$

(c) $\frac{11}{12} - \frac{7}{12} = \frac{1}{3}$

4 (a) >

$1 > \frac{7}{9}$

(b) <

$0 < \frac{3}{8}$

(c) >

$\frac{8}{12} > \frac{5}{12}$

(d) =

$\frac{1}{3} = \frac{1}{3}$

(e) =

$\frac{1}{2} = \frac{1}{2}$

(f) >

$\frac{10}{12} > \frac{9}{12}$

(g) >

$\frac{5}{8} > \frac{1}{2}$

and $\frac{1}{5} < \frac{1}{2}$

so $\frac{5}{8} > \frac{1}{5}$

(h) >

$\frac{6}{9} > \frac{4}{9}$

5 **$\frac{2}{5}$ is greater**

$\frac{7}{21} = \frac{1}{3} = \frac{2}{6}$

$\frac{2}{5} > \frac{2}{6}$

6 Divide each chocolate bar into 5 pieces.

$4 \times 5 = 20$ pieces

$20 \div 5 = 4$

Each person can have 4 pieces.

Each person gets $\frac{4}{5}$ of a bar.

7

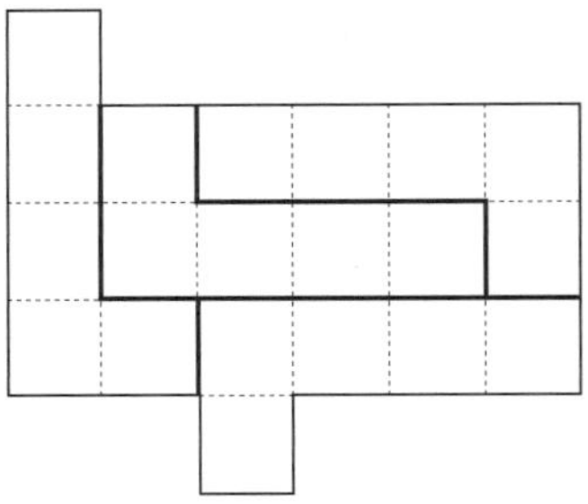

Chapter 11 Measurement

	Lesson	Page	Objectives
	Chapter Opener	79	
1	Meters and Centimeters	80	Express length in compound units of meters and centimeters. Convert between length expressed in centimeters only and length expressed in meters and centimeters.
2	Subtracting from Meters	81	Subtract centimeters, or meters and centimeters, from a whole number of meters.
3	Kilometers	83	Understand the kilometer as a unit of measurement. Convert between length expressed in meters and length expressed in kilometers and meters.
4	Subtracting from Kilometers	84	Subtract meters, or kilometers and meters, from a whole number of kilometers.
5	Liters and Milliliters	86	Understand the milliliter as a unit of measurement. Convert between liquid volume expressed in milliliters and liquid volume expressed in liters and milliliters.
6	Kilograms and Grams	88	Review the kilogram and the gram as units of measurement. Convert between mass expressed in grams and mass expressed in kilograms and grams.
7	Word Problems	89	Solve word problems involving measurement expressed in compound units.
8	Practice	90	
	Review 3	100	

Materials

Materials

- 1-L beaker
- Containers (cups, bottles)
- Meter stick
- Platform scale (in kilograms)
- Tape measure

Optional

- 100-mL beaker
- 500-mL beaker
- Centimeter cube
- Metric weight set
- Teaspoon

Mental Math Sheets

(singaporemath.com/higprintouts)

Mental Math		After Lesson
16	Subtract from 100	2
17	Subtract from a multiple of 100	2
18	Subtract from meters	2
19	Subtract from meters and centimeters	2 (enrichment)
20	Subtract from a multiple of 1,000	4
21	Subtract from kilometers	4
22	Subtract from kilometers and meters	4 (enrichment)
23	Subtract from meters, kilometers, liters, or kilograms	8

Notes

Measurement Systems

In the Dimensions Math® curriculum, students learn to measure and perform calculations with measurements in two distinct measurement systems: the metric system and what this guide will call the "U.S. customary system" (sometimes called the "imperial system"). All countries have either fully adopted or legally sanctioned the International System of Units, or SI, the modern form of the metric system. Currently, only the United States of America, Liberia, and Myanmar still use the "imperial system" of measurement. In the U.S., the metric system is designated as the preferred system of weights and measures for U.S. trade and commerce. The metric system is used predominantly in science even in the U.S. Students in the U.S. do still need to learn the outdated and cumbersome customary system. However, the metric system is given a predominant place in this curriculum.

In Dimensions Math® 2, students learned to estimate, measure, and compare lengths, weights or masses, and capacities in both systems of measurement. They learned to measure in centimeters, meters, kilograms, grams, and liters, which are part of the metric system. They also learned to measure in inches, feet, pounds, and were briefly introduced to gallons, quarts, and cups. In this chapter, students will learn that the kilometer is used for longer distances and is equal to 1,000 meters. They will also learn that milliliters are used for measuring amounts of liquid less than a liter and that 1,000 milliliters is equal to 1 liter. There is no standard abbreviation for liters or milliliters since they are not part of the International System of Units. This curriculum uses L for liters and mL for milliliters.

Mass and weight are different attributes of an object. Mass is a measure of an object's resistance to acceleration when a net force is applied, and is dependent on the amount of matter in the object (not the pull of gravity). Mass is measured using a balance to compare a known mass to an unknown mass. The kilogram and gram are units of mass. Weight is a measure of the gravitational pull between two objects and is generally measured using a scale where the gravitational pull is calibrated. An object has the same mass even when the gravitational pull is less, such as on the moon, but not the same weight. (When mass is measured on a scale, the scale is calibrated for use on Earth only.) The pound and the ounce (which students will learn in Dimensions Math® 4A) are units of weight. The metric unit for weight is the Newton; on Earth, a mass of 1 kilogram weighs 9.8 Newtons.

In this curriculum, a formal distinction will not be made between mass and weight. This can be done in science lessons. The verb "weigh" will be used even when finding the mass of an object, since even in countries where only the metric system is used, daily speech includes "weighing" an object to find its mass.

Compound Units

In Dimensions Math® 2, students only measured in a single unit, such as finding the length of an object to the nearest centimeter or inch. In this chapter, they will learn to express measurements in compound units, such as 4 m 20 cm or 6 L 200 mL. They will learn to convert between a smaller unit of measurement and a compound unit or larger unit of measurement, such as expressing 4,020 g as 4 kg 20 g. This chapter will only cover metric measurements. This is because the metric system is based on the base-ten system of numeration and so the only units of conversion in this chapter are 100 and 1,000. Students can convert using place-value concepts, rather than specifically thinking in terms of multiplying or dividing by 100 or 1,000. In Dimensions Math® 4A, they will learn to convert between units in the U.S. customary system, which involves multiplying and dividing by numbers such as 12 and 16.

Students will not spend much time actually measuring length, since it is assumed they are familiar with meters and centimeters. They will measure in liters and milliliters, since milliliters are introduced in this chapter. If you do not have beakers, such as those pictured in the textbook, you can create some using straight-sided jars and marking the sides similar to a beaker after adding the appropriate amount of water (most measuring cups include metric measures, but the sides are not usually vertical, and they may show fractional or decimal quantities). A quart is a little less than 1 liter, and a pint is a little less than 500 mL. Sometimes sports water bottles, which usually hold about 500 mL, are marked on the side, so you could use that for a 500 mL container.

In Dimensions Math® 2A, students used a balance and metric weights (set of masses) to weigh objects in grams. In this chapter they will use a platform scale to weigh objects in kilograms and grams. You can use a kitchen scale, and will have to make sure your student is reading the correct scale, since in the U.S. it is usually marked in both kilograms and pounds. Once they understand the movement of the needle, they will not likely have trouble reading the measurements on the images of platform scales in the textbook.

If you do not have a platform scale, Lesson 6 could be done without one if your student understands the needle rotates similar to a hand on a clock, and the amount of rotation depends on how much the object pushes the weighing pan down.

Calculations with Compound Units

Students learned mental math strategies for subtracting from 100 and from 1,000 in Dimensions Math® 3A. They only subtracted two-digit or three-digit numbers with 0 in the ones place from 1,000 or from thousands, such as finding the value of 4,000 – 590 mentally (unless you did the optional enrichment suggested in the Home Instructor's Guide). They will apply these strategies to mentally subtracting centimeters or meters and centimeters from a whole number of meters, or subtracting meters or kilometers and meters from kilometers. The advantage to using compound measures in the metric system to solidify mental math strategies is that the hundreds or thousands digits are already "split" out from the three-digit or four-digit number. Students who master these strategies will be able to subtract any number of up to three digits from hundreds and any number of up to four digits from thousands mentally. If your student is not proficient with mental math, they can convert meters to centimeters or kilometers to meters and subtract using the standard algorithm. (Any student who feels unsure of an answer when using mental math strategies should feel free to use the standard algorithm.)

This guide includes some optional extensions which involve subtracting compound units from compound units. Although strategies for adding or subtracting greater numbers where there is more than one renaming are not specifically taught in this curriculum, students who are more proficient at mental math and flexible with math thinking may be able to apply strategies they learn here to whole numbers on their own. For example, strategies for solving a problem such as 51 m 5 cm – 23 m 90 cm mentally can be applied to solving 5105 – 2390 mentally.

In Lesson 7, students will solve word problems involving compound units. The word problems are not any more challenging than word problems they have already encountered; the only difference is the use of compound units for measurements. Although they may not need to draw a bar model to solve any of the problems in the lesson, a few of the problems in the review will require a bar model to solve at this level. Students are expected to convert the measurements to the smaller unit and use the standard algorithm to add or subtract, but some students may be able to solve some of the expressions mentally.

The solutions in this guide for this chapter will include units in the expression. It is good practice to include the units, and you can encourage your student to do so, but it is not essential at this level except for expressions that involve compound units, for example, 3 km – 1 km 260 m. It is up to you whether you want to include units and write, for example, 850 g × 6 instead of just 850 × 6.

Activities

- After Lesson 1 or 2
  Materials: Paper, tape measure
  Purpose: Measure length in compound units.
  Procedure: Have your student fold paper airplanes and measure how far they fly, recording the distance in compound units. After Lesson 2, they could find the difference between the longest and shortest distances, or between the longest distance for different models of folded paper airplanes.
  Variation: Do several trials for one airplane and graph the results.
  Variation: Measure the distance for some other type of experiment, such as rolling a marble or toy car down an incline.

- After Lesson 3
  Materials: Map application
  Purpose: Become familiar with distances in kilometers, estimate distances.
  Procedure: Most map applications have a way to set the distance units in miles or in kilometers. Help your student use a map application to find the distance between some familiar places in kilometers and compare that to miles.

- After Lesson 7
  Materials: Paper, crayons or markers
  Purpose: Drawing maps, creating word problems.
  Procedure: Your student may enjoy drawing maps similar to the ones in Lesson 7 (or a treasure map). Have them include distances, and determine if they are reasonable.
  For example, a curved path between two points would have a greater distance than a straight or less curved path between the same two points. If the map has trails to hike or walk that could be done in a day, the distances should probably be within 10 km total distance. Your student might also like to write some word problems based on the map, or you can make up some for them to solve.

Chapter Opener (p. 85)

This Chapter Opener introduces students to the idea that we can measure length in meters and centimeters, and convert between centimeters only and compound units of meters and centimeters.

The following activity will cover this opener and also lead into Lesson 1.

Have your student measure their height using a meter stick. You can mark their height on a wall with masking tape or pencil, or use butcher paper and outline their bodies and find the length from a heel to the top of the head. They will find that their height is more than 1 meter. Help them with repositioning the meter stick to determine the height past 1 meter. Tell them they can write the measurement as 1 meter and then some centimeters, for example, 1 m 45 cm. Remind them that 1 meter is the same as 100 centimeters.

Then, have your student measure their height with a tape measure that is marked in centimeters. Make sure they know which markings denote centimeters. Sewing tapes often do not indicate the meters, just the total centimeters. Cased tape measures (in the U.S.) will generally give the measurement in total number of centimeters, but may only include the tens every ten centimeters. Have your student write how many centimeters their height is, for example, 145 cm. Compare the two recorded measurements. Since 100 cm is equal to 1 m, we know that 145 cm is the same as 1 m and 45 cm, and can write this as 1 m 45 cm. Point out that expressing longer lengths this way gives a better feel for how long the length or distance is, since (if they did Dimensions Math® 2A) they have an idea of how long a meter is.

You can also have them measure their height in inches, record that, and then use a ruler or the feet markings on a tape measure to write their height in feet and inches. Similar to not indicating meters, sewing tapes do not indicate feet, but cased tapes usually do, so they could determine the feet and inches using those markings.

If you live in the U.S. and this is the first time your student has used meters or centimeters, help them become familiar with these measurements. They can estimate and measure some lengths less than a meter in centimeters, then estimate lengths longer than a meter to an approximate number of meters, and then measure them to the closest meter.

Lesson 1 Meters and Centimeters (pp. 86–89)

Think (p. 86)

Have your student read the problem and find the answer if they can. Have them answer Sofia's question at the bottom of the page.

Learn (p. 87)

This uses a bar model to show how to convert between the smaller units to compound units. One part is 1 meter, which is equal to 100 centimeters. You could also use a number bond, splitting 128 cm into 100 and 28 cm. Your student may not have too much difficulty with this concept, since it is similar to converting from dollars and cents to cents only and vice versa, which they may have done in Dimensions Math® 2B. Point out what Mei is saying about compound units at the bottom of the page.

Do (pp. 88–89)

❶ ❷ The number of meters is just the number of hundreds, or "units" of 100 (the digit in the hundreds place) in the quantity given in centimeters.

❸ The number bond shows that Mei is thinking in terms of, splitting apart the hundreds from the tens and ones.

❺ We can convert from meters and centimeters to centimeters only by expressing the meters as centimeters and adding the centimeters.

❻ ❼ Students do not have to write addition equations or show the split with number bonds. Pay particular attention to ❼ (c). If your student gets this incorrect, such as writing 75 cm instead of 705 cm, have them write it first as 700 cm + 5 cm. This is similar to money conversions.

❽ Students should be able to list the lengths in order without rewriting the ones in compound units as centimeters only.

Answers

(a) 1 m 28 cm
(b) 130 cm

❶ 4 m

❷ 500 cm

❸ 65 cm
1 m 65 cm

❹ 50 cm
2 m 50 cm

❺ 20 cm
120 cm
300 cm
345 cm

❻ (a) 3 m 20 cm
(b) 4 m 43 cm
(c) 9 m 82 cm

❼ (a) 270 cm
(b) 586 cm
(c) 705 cm

❽

Zebra	1 m 50 cm
Gazelle	1 m 65 cm
Antelope	180 cm
Moose	210 cm

Lesson 2 Subtracting from Meters (pp. 90–93)

Think (p. 90)

Have your student read the problem, write an expression, and find the answer. You may want to write the problem on a separate sheet of paper. It is not necessary for your student to come up with different methods on their own. They may simply automatically convert 3 m to 300 m to subtract. You can discuss Mei's questions after looking at the methods in Learn.

Answers

2 m 25 cm
2 m 25 cm

❶ 38 cm and 62 cm
45 cm and 55 cm
71 cm and 29 cm
76 cm and 24 cm
58 cm and 42 cm
34 cm and 66 cm

❷ (a) 65 cm
(b) 2 m 65 cm
(c) 2 m 65 cm
(d) 3 m 5 cm

❸ (a) 64 cm (b) 1 m 30 cm
(c) 3 m 13 cm (d) 1 m 75 cm
(e) 3 m 58 cm (f) 4 m 50 cm

❹ (a) 45 cm
(b) 71 cm
(c) 42 cm
(d) 25 cm

Learn (p. 91)

Discuss the three methods. They rely on being able to mentally subtract from 100, which was reviewed in Dimensions Math® 3A. If your student cannot subtract from 100 mentally, you may want to use ❶ to discuss how to do this, and then return to these methods. Even without being able to mentally subtract a number from 100, though, your student may know that 75 and 25 make 100 from experience with coins.

Alex splits 3 m into 2 m and 1 m (100 cm), subtracts 75 cm from 100 cm to get 25 cm, and adds in the 2 m. The textbook shows his steps using an arrow diagram. Do not require your student to draw this type of diagram, or even the number bond such as what is shown in Alex's thought bubble. This is just a way of explaining the thought process without words. Students are expected to find the answers mentally.

Emma determines what makes 100 with 75 (mentally subtracting 75 from 100). She subtracts 1 m from 3 m and, knowing that she subtracted 25 cm too much, adds that back in. This method is easiest when the number of centimeters is close to 100 or is multiple of 10.

Sofia converts 3 m to 300 cm and subtracts 75 from that, then converts the answer back to compound units. We are not told what method she uses to subtract, but if she uses mental math, she also mentally subtracts 75 from 100.

Do (pp. 92–93)

1. Students should realize they need to find pairs of numbers that make 100. If necessary, remind them that they need to find pairs of numbers where the digits in the tens place add to 9 and the digits in the ones place add to 10. Dion reminds them why: 100 = 9 tens + 10 ones.

   If subtracting from multiples of 100 is new to your student, write some expressions such as 100 – 38. Help your student understand that the tens digit in the answer is the digit that makes 9 (tens) with 3 (tens). The ones digit in the answer is the digit that makes 10 with 8.

2. The answer to (a) is used to find the answer to (b): to subtract 35 from 3 m, we use the fact that 100 – 35 = 65. Then (c) introduces a new idea: subtracting compound units from a whole number of meters. We can do this in steps, first subtracting the meters, and then the centimeters in the same way as in (b). In (d), Dion sees that 95 cm is almost 1 meter, so he subtracts 4 m, and adds back in the 5 extra centimeters he subtracted doing this.

3. Students can use any strategy they want, and do not have to justify their answers with equations or number bonds unless they get an incorrect answer, since they should be solving these mentally.

4. Each of these has a missing part. Students learned as early as Dimensions Math® 1A than in order to find the missing part, we can subtract the other part from the whole.

Enrichment

If your student finds this lesson easy, you can extend it to subtracting from compound units. They can then use this for some of the calculations in the word problems if they want, rather than converting the compound units to the smaller unit and using the algorithm to subtract.

Refer back to 2 (a). If necessary, have your student find the answer again.

Write the expression 1 m 15 cm – 35 cm. Help your student to see they can solve this by using the answer to 1 m – 35 cm; they just need to add 15 cm to that answer.

Refer back to the answer to 2 (b). Then write the expression 3 m 15 cm – 35 cm. They can solve this by subtracting 35 cm from 3 m, then adding 15 cm.

Refer back to the answer to 2 (c). Then write the expression 4 m 15 cm – 1 m 35 cm. They can subtract 1 m first, then 35 cm, from 3 m, then add 15 cm.

Write the expression 4 m 35 cm – 1 m 15 cm and have your student find the answer. They should realize they can subtract meters from meters and centimeters from centimeters, since 35 cm is greater than 15 cm.

You can use the **Mental Math Sheet** 19 for more practice.

Lesson 3 Kilometers (pp. 94–97)

Think (p. 94)

Have your student write an expression and find the answer for each of these. Unless they are already familiar with kilometers, they will likely find the answer in meters only.

Learn (p. 95)

Alex introduces students to kilometers as a unit for measuring longer distances. There are 1,000 m in 1 km. So we can say the distance from Sofia's house to the library is 1 km. You may want to tell your student that the prefix kilo- means "one thousand." Your student may be more familiar with miles. You can tell them that kilometers are used in nearly every other country, rather than miles, and a kilometer is a little over half of a mile, or about six tenths of a mile. Ask them if a distance in miles will be more or fewer kilometers. It will be more kilometers, a bit less than twice as many. A distance of 6 miles is about 10 kilometers. If you know some distances in kilometers that your students has traveled, you can discuss them.

In (b) and (c), students are introduced to converting a length in meters only to the compound units of kilometers and meters. Using compound units makes it easier to visualize longer distances.

Do (pp. 96–97)

❶ Students are introduced to the difference between travel distance and direct distance. In (b), students are introduced to converting from compound units to meters only, which simply involves thinking of kilometers as thousands.

❹ ❺ Pay particular attention to the first three problems in each of these.

Answers

(a) 1,000 m
(b) 1 km 300 m
(c) 1 km 100 m
1 km 100 m

❶ (a) 1,400 m
400 m
(b) 80 m
1,080 m

❷ 500 m
3 km 500 m

❸ 50 m
4,050 m

❹ (a) 6 km 700 m
(b) 6 km 70 m
(c) 6 km 7 m
(d) 1 km 275 m
(e) 8 km 997 m
(f) 4 km 22 m

❺ (a) 5,300 m
(b) 5,030 m
(c) 5,003 m
(d) 1,375 m
(e) 8,008 m
(f) 6,028 m

Lesson 4 Subtracting from Kilometers (pp. 98–101)

Think (p. 98)

This lesson assumes students can subtract from 1,000 mentally, which they did learn for numbers such as 750 (no ones) in Dimensions Math® 3A. If your student does not know how to subtract 750 from 1,000 mentally, you may want to discuss ❶ first and teach the strategy, or you can let your student use the algorithm for now.

Have your student read the problem, write an expression, and solve it. You can cover up the bottom of the page or not; your student should know even without the line diagram that they need to subtract.

Learn (p. 99)

Discuss the three methods. They are similar to those used to subtract from meters, except that now we are subtracting from 1,000 rather than 100. The number bonds and arrow diagrams are explaining the thought processes for the mental calculations.

Mei splits 2 km into 1 km and 1,000 m, subtracts 750 m from 1,000 m to get 250 m, and adds the 1 km.

Dion first determines what makes 1,000 with 750. He subtracts 1 km from 2 km and, knowing that he is subtracting 250 too much, adds that back in.

Emma converts 2 km to 2,000 m and subtracts 750 from that. (If she uses mental math to do this, she likely subtracts from 1,000.) Then she converts the answer back to compound units.

Answers

1 km 250 m
1 km 250 m
1 km 250 m
1 km 250 m

❶ 380 m and 620 m
405 m and 595 m
670 m and 330 m
462 m and 538 m
701 m and 299 m
60 m and 940 m

❷ (a) 390 m
(b) 2 km 390 m

❸ 1 km 975 m

❹ (a) 2 km 700 m
(b) 4 km ⟶ 3 km 150 m

❺ (a) 740 m
(b) 940 m
(c) 3 km 170 m
(d) 1 km 670 m
(e) 3 km 580 m
(f) 9 km 500 m

❻ (a) 150 m
(b) 850 m
(c) 995 m
(d) 250 m

<u>Do</u> (pp. 100–101)

❶ Students need to find pairs of numbers where the digits in the hundred and the tens place add to 9 and the digits in ones place add to 10. Emma reminds them why:
1,000 = 9 hundreds + 9 tens + 10 ones.
If one number is a two-digit number, the hundreds digit can be thought of as being 0, so the hundreds digit in other number of the other number in the pair must be 9. If there are no ones, then the tens digits must add to 10, as in 380 and 620.

If subtracting from 1,000 is new to your student, or they need more practice when there is a digit in the ones place, write some expressions such as 1,000 – 462. Help your student understand that the hundreds digit in the answer is the digit that makes 9 (hundreds) with 4 (hundreds). The tens digit in the answer is the digit that makes 9 (tens) with 6 (tens). The ones digit in the answer is the digit that makes 10 with 2. In particular, write some problems where one of the digits in the number being subtracted is 0, such as 380, 405, or 60. You can use **Mental Math Sheet** 20 for more practice.

❷ The answer to (a) is used to find the answer to (b).

❹ To subtract a compound unit, we can subtract in steps, first subtracting the kilometers, then the meters.

❺ ❻ Students can use any strategy they want, and do not have to justify their answers with equations or number bonds, unless they get an incorrect answer.

Enrichment

If your student finds this lesson easy, you can extend it to subtracting from compound units. They can then use this for calculations for the word problems at this level, especially when the numbers are multiples of 10 or 100, or the number of meters in the number being subtracted is close to 1,000, such as 995.

To subtract from compound units, we can subtract from the whole number of kilometers as in the lesson, then add the meters. For example:

9 km 30 m – 4 km 420 m

9 km – 4 km = 5 km
5 km – 420 m = 4 km 580 m
4 km 580 m + 30 m = 4 km 610 m

Give your student a few examples. You can use the **Mental Math Sheet** 22 for more practice. Generally, students might apply this strategy to numbers that are multiples of 10 or 5 or easy to calculate with mentally, and use the standard algorithm for calculations that involve more renaming.

Lesson 5 Liters and Milliliters (pp. 102–106)

Think (p. 102)

If you do the activities, this lesson may take more than one day, but the problems in Do should be relatively easy and not take long.

Think introduces the milliliter as a unit of measure, as well as the abbreviation that will be used in this curriculum, mL. Students should be familiar with liters already if they did Dimensions Math® 2B. They likely have already seen markings for milliliters on measuring cups. Show your student a liter beaker, if you have one, and have them look at the markings for milliliters. Tell them that liquid volumes less than a liter can be measured in milliliters. 1 L is the same as 1,000 mL.

You can tell your student that the prefix "milli-" means one thousand and, in the metric system, it is used to denote one thousandth of a given base unit, in this case, 1 liter: one milliliter is equal to one thousandth of a liter. (Since students have not formally learned of fractions with denominators greater than 24, in ❶ Dion says that milli- is used for "1 out of 1 thousand." However, your student should probably be able to deduce the meaning of "one thousandth.")

Answers

❶ 1,000 mL
1 L

❸ 250 mL

❹ (a) 1,200 mL
(b) 1 L 200 mL

❺ (a) 4,550 mL
(b) 4 L 550 mL

❻ 2,050 mL

❼ (a) 3,500 mL
(b) 3,050 mL
(c) 3,005 mL
(d) 4,025 mL
(e) 6,008 mL
(f) 4,250 mL

❽ (a) 2 L 400 mL
(b) 2 L 40 mL
(c) 2 L 4 mL
(d) 6 L 25 mL
(e) 6 L 205 mL
(f) 1 L 750 mL

❾ (a) 1 L – 850 mL = 150 mL
(b) 2 L – 1 L 350 mL = 650 mL

If your student is more familiar with gallons, quarts, and cups, tell them that most of the world uses milliliters and liters for liquid measurement, and milliliters and liters are used in science. You can have your student look at measuring cups, which are usually marked in milliliters as well as fluid ounces or fractions of a cup. They should see that 250 mL is a little more than one-fourth cup (which may be marked as 8 fluid ounces).

You may want to mention that many countries also use deciliters. The prefix deci-is used for one tenth in the metric system. One liter is the same as 10 deciliters, or one deciliter is equal to one tenth of a liter.

Have your student do some of the activities in Think, using whatever resources you have available. They will have to estimate the capacity since the markings are often for every 50 mL.

You may also want to do ❷ at this time, while you have containers and water. The purpose of ❷ is to point out that we can use compound units of liters and milliliters to express capacities greater than 1 liter.

Learn (p. 103)

Discuss the contents of this page. Help your student read the volumes on the beakers pictured here. Students did not use the term volume in previous levels when they learned to measure capacity, so that term is introduced here. This lesson just covers liquid volume. Since students will later learn that volume is measured in cubic units, specifically use the term "liquid volume." Students will learn later that 1 milliliter of liquid has the same volume as 1 cubic centimeter.

Point out what Emma and Alex are saying at the bottom of the page. You can show your student a measuring teaspoon and a 1-cm cube, such as a unit cube from base-ten blocks.

Do (pp. 104–106)

❹ ❺ ❻ In these problems, students convert from milliliters to compound units of liters and milliliters, and then from compound units to milliliters only. Since the conversion unit is the same as for meters and kilometers, this should be easy, so number bonds and addition equations are not shown.

❾ Your student may notice in (a) that they can find the answer by seeing the difference between the water level and the 500 mL mark in the second beaker, and may do the same in (b), which would be incorrect since the total for the three beakers is not 2 L. Ask your student to write a subtraction expression for both of these. The main point of this problem is for them to realize they can subtract milliliters, or liters and milliliters, from a whole number of liters with the same strategies they used in subtracting from kilometers. There will be more practice in the exercise for this lesson.

Lesson 6 Kilograms and Grams (pp. 107–110)

Think and Learn (p. 107–108)

Students learned about kilograms and grams in Dimensions Math® 2B. Think and Learn is a review and an introduction to the use of a platform scale and the use compound units of kilograms and grams.

Tell (or remind) your student that a kilogram is a little over 2 pounds, and that most countries in the world use kilograms, not pounds. Have them weigh themselves in pounds and then kilograms (they need to ignore the tenths on the weighing scale) or just tell them their weight in pounds and approximate weight in kilograms (divide by 2). Tell them grams are much smaller units; 1,000 grams is equal to 1 kilogram. Show them a 1-cm cube (or unit cube from base-ten blocks, or a paperclip) and tell them it weighs about 1 gram.

Show your student a platform scale, if you have one. If your scale also has markings for pounds as well make sure they know which scale to read. Ask them what the interval between each tick mark is. Then have them measure and record the weight of objects in compound units to the closest 100 g, including some over 1 kilogram (but less than the maximum number of kilograms your scale can measure). Discuss pages 107–108. Make sure they can read the scales, which are different for the two pictures on page 108. The interval is 100 g for both scales, but the maximum mass of the objects they can weigh differs.

Answers

2 2 kg 400 g   1 kg 200 g

3 3,045 g

4 the bag of sugar

5 (a) 3,630 g
(b) 7,455 g
(c) 5,593 g
(d) 6,055 g
(e) 4,002 g
(f) 8,008 g

6 (a) 2 kg 400 g
(b) 6 kg 115 g
(c) 2 kg 764 g
(d) 3 kg 305 g
(e) 4 kg 27 g
(f) 7 kg 3 g

7 1 kg – 610 g = 390 g
2 kg – 1 kg 125 g = 875 g

Do (pp. 109–110)

These problems should not be difficult, since the conversion unit is the same as in the previous two lessons.

1 Skip this if you do not have a metric weight set.

7 Have your student write a subtraction expression for each of these.

Lesson 7 Word Problems (pp. 111–115)

Think (p. 111)

Have your student read the problem. Discuss how the bar model relates to the information in the word problem and why the bar for the distance between the hotel and the bakery is longer than the one for the distance from the hotel to Alex's house (the bakery is farther from Alex's house). Make sure your student knows that the question mark on the side of the two bars means that we need to find the total value for both of them, since we need to find the total distance. Have them answer Dion's question (we need to find the distance between the hotel and Alex's house first) and then solve the problem.

Learn (p. 112)

To do the calculations, we can convert from compound units to the smaller unit, and then add or subtract. If you did the enrichments in this guide, your student might instead calculate mentally in compound units.

Do (pp. 113–115)

None of the problems are more challenging than what students have seen already in this curriculum, other than the use of compound units. Discuss any problems your student has difficulty with, in particular relating the information in provided bar models to the information in the word problems. You can have your student show what they need to find on each model for the problems on page 115, using a question mark for the quantity. If your student needs more practice interpreting word problems, write the problems on a separate sheet of paper and then guide your student in drawing their own bar models. Answers should be in compound units when appropriate.

Answers

1 km 950 m
4,700 m
4 km 700 m
4 km 700 m

1 (a) **1 m 30 cm**
200 cm – 90 cm = 130 cm
(b) **40 cm**
130 cm – 90 cm = 40 cm

2 **1 kg 560 g**
3 × 520 g = 1,560 g

3 (a) **1 km 250 m**
2,200 m – 950 m = 1,250 m
(b) **3 km 150 m**
2,200 m + 950 m = 3,150 m

4 9 kg 615 g

5 **1 kg 150 g**
1,500 g – 350 g = 1,150 g

6 **140 mL**
1,250 mL – 550 mL = 700 mL
700 mL ÷ 5 = 140 mL

7 **4 kg 725 g**
5 × 945 g = 4,725 g

Lesson 8 Practice (pp. 116–118)

Kilograms to grams, liters to milliliters, and kilometers to meters all involve a conversion factor of 1,000. Meters to centimeters involves a conversion factor of 100. One way to remember is to look at the prefixes. Kilo- and milli- both mean 1 thousand, and centi- means 1 hundred. Students know that 100 cents is 1 dollar, and that might help them to remember to use 100 when converting between centimeters and meters.

It is unlikely students will need to draw bar models for any of the word problems in this practice if they have mastered earlier content, but they can if they need to. Encourage them to calculate mentally when they can, but they should feel free to use the algorithms at any time.

❷ ❸ You can let your student write a little 1, 2, 3, and 4 above the "cards" to indicate what order they would put them in. They should by now be able to list them in order without first expressing them all in the same form (compound units or single unit), but can if they need to.

❺ Students should be able to calculate the answer mentally, since they are subtracting from a whole number of kilometers.

❼ Students may recall strategies for adding or subtracting numbers close to 100, and use mental calculation to find the answer.

Answers

❶ (a) 1 m 59 cm
(b) 4 m 8 cm
(c) 198 cm
(d) 2 km 34 m
(e) 8,009 m
(f) 5 L 1 mL
(g) 2,432 mL
(h) 3 kg 215 g
(i) 8,082 g

❷ 54 cm, 4 m 5 cm, 4 m 50 cm, 540 cm

❸ 5,600 g, 6 kg 5g, 6,050 g, 6 kg 500 g

❹ (a) 27 cm
(b) 1 m 91 cm
(c) 1 m 95 cm
(d) 380 m
(e) 3 km 910 m
(f) 2 km 150 m
(g) 595 mL
(h) 3 L 965 mL
(i) 5 kg 880 g
(j) 6 kg 995 g

❺ **3 km 580 m**
6 m – 2 km 420 m = 3 km 580 m

❻ (a) **2 L 155 mL**
1,500 mL + 655 mL = 2,155 mL
(b) **845 mL**
1,500 mL – 655 mL = 845 mL

❼ **Sebastian is taller by 39 cm.**
135 cm – 96 cm = 39 cm

(11) As with all word problems involving more than one step, solutions may vary from the ones shown in this guide. Students might, for example, first subtract 900 g from 3 kg, and then 700 g from that answer.

Enrichment

At this level, students will only learn commonly used units measurements (kilometer, meter, centimeter, millimeter, liter, milliliter, kilogram and gram). You can have your student look at a metric system chart, such as the one shown here, and see how regular the naming convention is. The meter, liter, or gram is the base unit. A prefix relates smaller or larger units to the base unit. The prefixes deci-, centi-, and milli- are used for units that are one tenth, one hundredth, or one thousandth as large as the base unit (or one ten, one hundred, one thousand times smaller), and the prefixes deca-, hecto- and kilo- are used for units that are one ten, one hundred, or one thousand times as large as the base unit. For example, a decaliter is equal to ten liters.

Answers (continued)

(8) **65 cm**

585 cm ÷ 9 = 65 cm

(9) **1 km 900 m**

2 × 950 m = 1,900 m

(10) **2 km 60 m**

4 × 515 m = 2,060 m

(11) **1 kg 400 g**

900 g + 700 g = 1,600 g

3 g – 1 kg 600 g = 1 kg 400 g

Kilo	1,000 times larger	kilometer kiloliter kilogram
Hecto	100 times larger	hectometer hectoliter hectogram
Deca	10 times larger	decameter decaliter decagram
Base		meter liter gram
Deci	10 times smaller	decimeter deciliter decigram
Centi	100 times smaller	centimeter centiliter centigram
Milli	1,000 times smaller	millimeter milliliter milligram

Review 3 (pp. 119–122)

This review covers content from Dimensions Math® 3A as well as 3B.

❶ Estimations may vary depending on how the numbers are rounded to get the estimate. Only actual values are provided.

❷ Students can write the answer to division problems as quotient R remainder (without using =).

❼ Students should be able to answer (e) by looking at the graph and visualizing the bars moved next to each other. If they can't, they can use estimation and try various combinations.

❽ Most students will multiply each distance by 2 and then add, but some students might add first, which may be easier to calculate mentally:

1,800 + 2,450 = 4,250
2 × 4,250 m = 8,500 m

Answers

❶ (a) 6,201 (b) 7,823
(c) 8,260 (d) 3,457
(e) 7,885 (f) 3,695

❷ (a) 261 (b) 315
(c) 15 R 5 (d) 14 R 1
(e) 65 R 4 (f) 2,412
(g) 6,744 (h) 114 R 3

❸ B and D

❹ (a) $\frac{3}{4}$
(b) D
(c) 4 eighths

❺ (a) > (b) > $(\frac{8}{16} > \frac{7}{16})$
(c) > $(\frac{3}{5} > \frac{3}{15})$ (d) > $(\frac{4}{6} > \frac{4}{7})$
(e) > $(\frac{5}{7} > \frac{5}{8})$ (f) < $(\frac{1}{2} < \frac{3}{4})$

❻ (a) 2 L 500 mL
(b) **1 L 750 mL**
2,500 mL – 750 mL = 1,750 mL

❼ (a) 500 m
(b) Meadow, Waterfalls, Mountain Views, Lakeside, Forest Trail.
(c) Mountain View and Lakeside
(d) Lakeside
(e) Mountain View and Meadow

❽ (a) **8 km 500 m**
2 × 1,800 m = 3,600 m
2 × 2,450 m = 4,900 m
3,600 m + 4,900 m = 8,500 m
(b) **650 m**
2,450 m – 1,800 m = 650 m

9 Students will most likely have to draw a bar model to solve this problem at this level. A suggested model is provided in the answers; your student's model can vary. Students are not required to precede equations with the number of units and an arrow, but it can be an aid in thinking through the solution.

10 A bar model is the best method to use to arrive at a solution. If necessary, remind students that they can think of either bar as the "unit" and need to make them equal. Since they are finding the greater number, the first solution at the right makes the longer bar the unit, which will lead to fewer calculations. Students might instead automatically think of the shorter bar as the unit and solve using the alternate method. If they do, you might want to discuss the first method.

Answers (continued)

9 **28 more seashells**

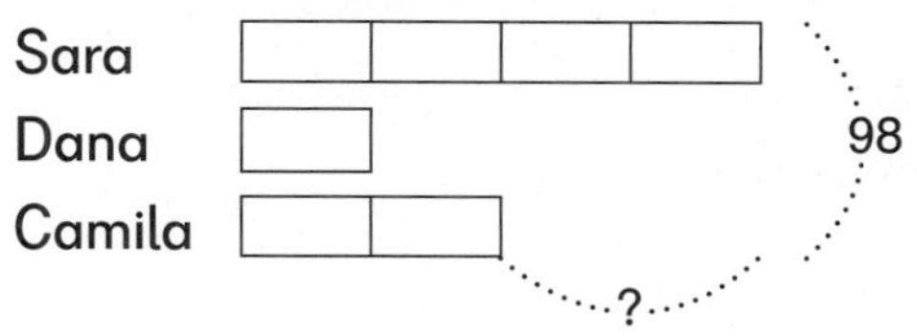

1 unit ⟶ $98 \div 7 = 14$
2 units ⟶ $2 \times 14 = 28$

10 **485**

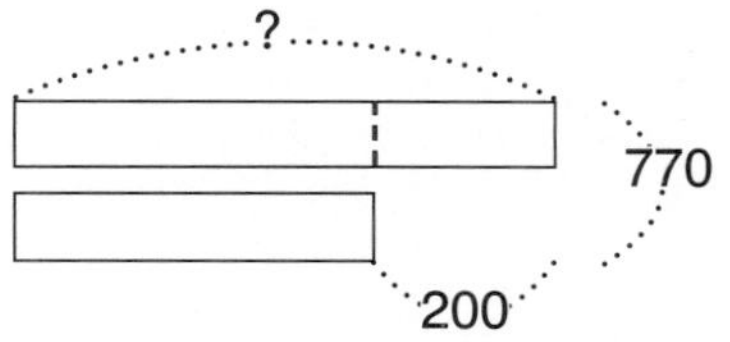

2 units ⟶ $770 + 200 = 970$
1 units ⟶ $970 \div 2 = 485$

or

2 units ⟶ $770 - 200 = 570$
1 units ⟶ $570 \div 2 = 285$
$285 + 200 = 485$

11 **586 g**

768 g ÷ 8 = 96 g
980 g ÷ 2 = 490 g
96 g + 490 g = 586 g

Chapter 11 Workbook Answers

Exercise 1 pp. 81–84

1 (a) m
(b) cm
(c) m
(d) cm

2 (a)
200 cm
600 cm
1,000 cm

(b) 1 m
2 m
5 m
9 m

3 15 cm
815 cm
815 cm

4 40 cm
40 cm
7 m 40 cm

5 3 cm
2 m 3 cm
2 m 3 cm

6 203 cm, 2 m 30 cm, 3 m 2 cm, 320 cm

7 (a) 530 cm
(b) 608 cm
(c) 235 cm
(d) 727 cm

8 (a) 8 m 70 cm
(b) 5 m 25 cm
(c) 6 m 2 cm

9 (a) 60 cm
(b) 2 m 90 cm
(c) 4 m 50 cm

10 (a) $>$
(b) $=$
(c) $>$
(d) $<$

11 **1 m 28 cm**
261 cm − 5 cm = 256 cm
256 cm ÷ 2 = 128 cm
128 cm = 1 m 28 cm
Word problems are specifically covered in Lesson 6, so you may want to consider this problem as optional.

12 (a) 1,025 cm
(b) 61 m 85 cm
In the lesson, the total centimeters is always less than 1,000. When it is more than 1,000 cm, the concept is the same. If 1 m is 100 cm, then 10 meters is 10 hundreds centimeters, and 61 hundreds centimeter is 61 meters.

13 **40 blocks**
Height of 1 block first:
40 cm ÷ 8 = 5 cm
Number of 5-cm blocks in 2 m:
2 m = 200 cm
200 cm ÷ 5 = 40
Or:
Find how many 40 cm are in 2 m by thinking 200 = 20 tens = 4 tens × 5.
Since 40 cm is 8 blocks, multiply the number of 40 cm units by 5:
5 × 8 = 40

Chapter 11 Workbook Answers

Exercise 2 pp. 85–87

1
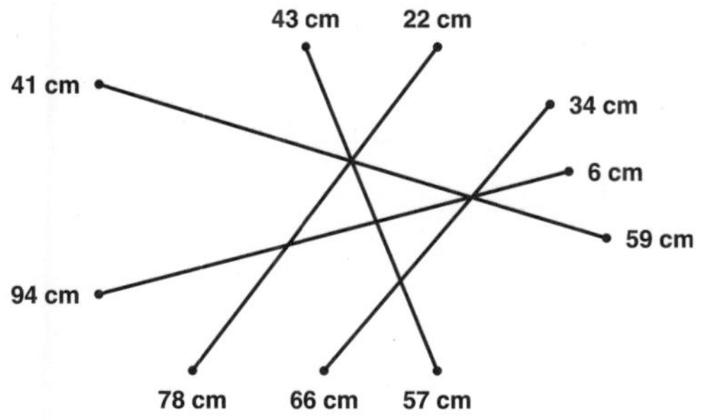

There are 3 small triangles, and 2 larger triangles each composed of 2 of the smaller triangles.

2 (a) 59 cm   59 cm
(b) 78 cm   78 cm

3 (a) 94 cm
(b) 5 m 94 cm
(c) 34 cm
(d) 9 m 34 cm
(e) 14 m 22 cm

4 (a) 57 cm
(b) 5 m
(c) 57 cm
(d) 57 cm

5 (a) 2 m
(b) 1 m 2 cm
(c) 1 m 2 cm

6 (a) 25 cm
(b) 18 cm
(c) 1 m 65 cm
(d) 1 m 18 cm
(e) 7 m 97 cm

7 (a) 65 cm   (b) 14 cm
(c) 92 cm   (d) 72 cm

8 (a) 4 m 80 cm
(b) 3 m 7 cm
(c) 1 m 94 cm
(d) 9 cm

9 (a) 71 cm
(b) 38 cm
(c) 82 cm
(d) 63 cm

Other than Think, the textbook lesson does not include word problems, which are covered in Lesson 6. You may want to omit or save the next two problems for later if you think your student will find them difficult. They are, however, no more challenging than word problems your student has seen already with regard to determining what expression to write.

10 **2 m 52 cm**
8 m – 5 m 48 cm = 2 m 52 cm

11 **3 m 35 cm**
7 m – 3 m 65 cm = 3 m 35 cm

Exercise 3 pp. 88–90

1 (a) m
(b) km
(c) km
(d) km
(e) m

2 (a)   (b) 1 km
2,000 m   2 km
5,000 m   6 km
7,000 m   9 km

Chapter 11 Workbook Answers

3 848 m
8,848 m
8,848 m

4 34 m
3 km 34 m
3 km 34 m

5 (a) 5,300 m (b) 2,205 m
(c) 9,819 m (d) 6,080 m
(e) 1,010 m (f) 7,007 m

6 (a) 8 km 700 m
(b) 9 km 147 m
(c) 5 km 65 m
(d) 6 km 2 m

7 (a) > (b) >
(c) > (d) =

8 (a) 835 m
(b) 3,080 m
(c) **1 km 5 m**
245 m + 760 m = 1,005 m
(d) **1 km 190 m**
760 m + 430 m = 1,190 m
1,190 m < 1 km 260 m
The trail through the meadow is shorter.

Exercise 4 pp. 91–93

1 (a) 10 m
(b) 200 m
60 m
6 m
266 m

2

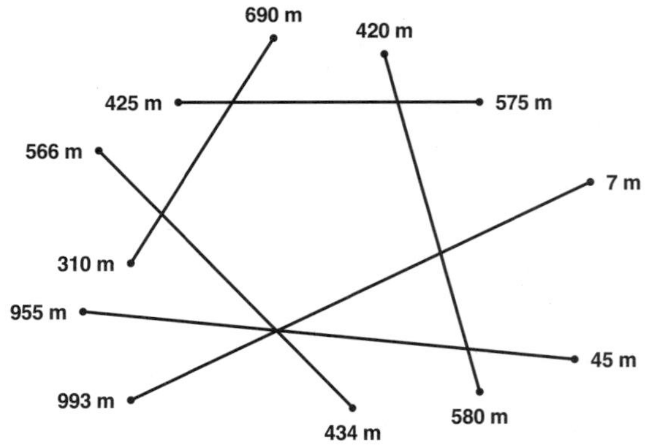

One of the pentagons is composed of the smaller pentagon and the triangle.

3 (a) 310 m 310 m
(b) 7 m 7 m

4 (a) 580 m
(b) 2 km 580 m
(c) 3 km
(d) 2 km 580 m

5 (a) 350 m (b) 348 m
(c) 991 m (d) 973 m
(e) 651 m

6 (a) 651 m
(b) 300 m
(c) 950 m
(d) 1 km 995 m
(e) 2 km 530 m
(f) 6 km 953 m

7 (a) **570 m**
1 km − 430 m = 570 m
(b) **755 m**
1 km − 245 m = 755 m
(c) **2 km 240 m**
3 km − 760 m = 2 km 240 m
(d) **1 km 740 m**
3 km − 1 km 260 m = 1 km 740 m

Chapter 11 Workbook Answers

(e) **1 km 995 m**
245 m + 760 m = 1,005 m
3 km − 1 km 5 m = 1 km 995 m

Exercise 5 pp. 94–96

1. (a) L
(b) mL
(c) mL
(d) L
(e) mL

2. (a) 3,000 mL
(b) 1 L
6 L

3. (a) 700 mL
(b) 300 mL
(c) 350 mL

4. (a) 2,250 mL
(b) 2 L 250 mL

5. (a) 4 L
(b) 4 L 200 mL
(c) 4 L 20 mL
(d) 4 L 2 mL

6. (a) 770 mL
(b) 1 L 770 mL
(c) 3 L 770 mL

7. (a) 5,734 mL
(b) 8,032 mL
(c) 3 L 705 mL
(d) 6 L 43 mL

8. (a) 655 mL
(b) 955 mL
(c) 2 L 997 mL
(d) 4 L 620 mL
(e) 4 L 925 mL

9. Fill the 5-L container.
Pour from the 5-L container into the 3-L container.
Pour the remaining 2 L from the 5-L container into the bucket.
Repeat.

Exercise 6 pp. 97–100

1. (a) g
(b) kg
(c) kg
(d) g
(e) kg
(f) g

2. (a) 4,000 g
(b) 1 kg
7 kg

3. (a) 6,260 g (b) 6,026 g

4. (a) 4 kg 900 g
(b) 4 kg 9 g

5. (a) 570 g (b) 570 g

6. (a) 400 g (b) 3 kg 300 g
(c) 2 kg 655 g

7. 1 kg 460 g

8. 8 kg 5 g, 8 kg 58 g, 8,085 g, 8,580 g, 8,805 g, 8 kg 850 g

9. (a) 1 kg 100 g
(b) 6,960 g

Chapter 11 Workbook Answers

10 (a) >
(b) >
(c) < 4,050 g < 4 kg 750 g
(d) < Subtracting 789 will result in a value less than subtracting 250 from 4 g.
(e) < The left hand side will be less than 1, and the right hand side will be greater than 1.
(f) < Subtracting 3 kg will result in a value less than subtracting 2 kg.
(g) < When kilograms are subtracted, both sides will have 4 kg; subtracting 856 g will result in a value less than subtracting 568 from 4 g.

Students may also simply find the final values for (d)–(g), rather than applying mathematical reasoning.

11 (a) **7 triangles**
3 triangles = 1 hexagon
3 hexagons = 3 × 3 triangles
= 9 triangles
9 triangles = 1 square 2 triangles
Take away 2 triangles from both sides: 7 triangles = 1 square
(b) **4 triangles**
3 triangles = 2 hexagons
Replace 2 hexagons each with 3 triangles. Left hand side of balance will now have 8 triangles.
8 triangles = 2 squares
4 triangles = 1 square

12 **3 kg 200 g**
Replace the B block with 4 A blocks.
5 A blocks balance 4 kg.
1 A block: 4,000 g ÷ 5 = 800 g
4 × 800 g = 3,200 g
If your student cannot divide 4,000 by 5, having not formally learned to divide by a 4-digit number, they should think of a different approach, using the skills they do have. They can divide the value of each A block by 5, and add.

Exercise 7 pp. 101–104

1 = 4,300 mL – 2,450 mL
= 1,850 mL
= 1 L 850 mL
1 L 850 mL

2 = 5,100 g = 5 kg 100 g
5 kg 100 g

3 = 207 cm
207 cm ÷ 9 = 23 cm
23 cm

4 **25 g**
3 × 60 g = 180 g
380 g – 180 g = 200 g
200 g ÷ 8 = 25 g

5 (a) **355 m longer**
760 m + 430 m = 1,190 m
1,190 m – 835 m = 355 m
(b) **7 km 770 m**
One method for solving this problem is to add km and m separately.
1 km + 3 km + 3 km = 7 km
260 m + 430 m + 80 m = 770 m

(c) **3 km 40 m**
4 × 760 m = 3,040 m

(d) **590 m farther**
1,260 m + 430 m + 760 m = 2,450 m
3,040 m − 2,450 m = 590 m

(e) **345 m**

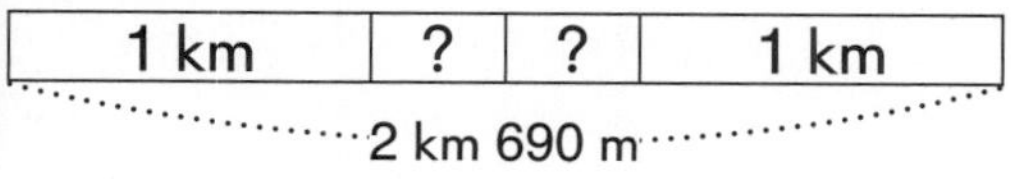

2 km 690 m − 2 km = 690 m
690 m ÷ 2 = 345 m

6 **25 cm**
200 cm ÷ 8 = 25 cm

7 **335 mL**

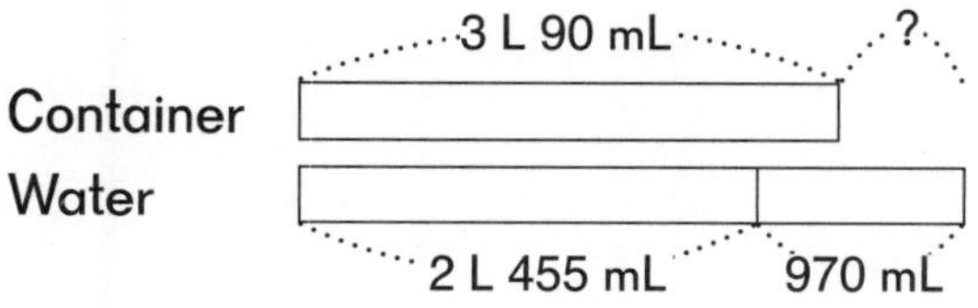

2,455 mL + 970 mL = 3,425 mL
3,425 mL − 3,090 mL = 335 mL
Or:
3,090 mL − 2,455 mL = 635 mL
970 mL − 635 mL = 335 mL

Students are unlikely to use the second method, but if they draw a bar model they might. It is provided here to illustrate that using bar models can lead to creative solutions.

8 **535 g**

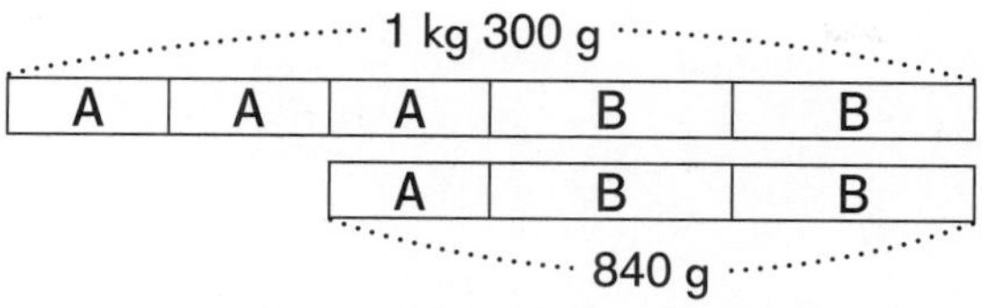

If students draw a bar model, they may simply draw one in the order the information is given, align them at the left, and then be unable to determine a method of solution. Suggest they slide one bar to the right so that the Bs align, or flip their model so the Bs are first. Redrawing models is a good problem solving strategy. This problem is similar to the balance ones on page 100, but more abstract since there is no image. You can suggest they draw a picture of a balance and see if they can solve the problem from that.

1,300 g − 840 g = 460 g (two As)
460 g ÷ 2 = 230 g (one A)
840 g − 230 g = 610 g (two Bs)
610 g ÷ 2 = 305 g (one B)
305 g + 230 g = 535 g
Or:
Two As and two Bs:
840 g + 230 g = 1,070 g
One A and one B:
1,070 g ÷ 2 = 535 g

Some students may think of the second method since the problem asks for the weight of A and B together. They might have no difficulty dividing 1,070 by 2 and may divide mentally; if they can't, they may have to resort to the first method.

Chapter 11 Workbook Answers

Exercise 8 pp. 105–108

1 (a) g
(b) m
(c) L
(d) mL
(e) km
(f) cm
(g) kg

2 (a) 446 cm
(b) 4,046 m
(c) 6,207 g
(d) 2,002 mL
(e) 4 kg 689 g
(f) 8 km 20 m
(g) 80 m 20 cm

3 4,250

4 **96 g**
780 g ÷ 8 = 96 g

5 **Javier Sotomayer, 36 cm**
245 cm − 209 cm = 36 cm

6 6 × 750 mL = 4,500 mL
4,500 mL − 3,450 mL = 1,050 mL
1 L 50 mL

7 Students can use mental math or the algorithm for any of these.
(a) **The grocery store and post office**
5,000 m + 2,800 m = 7,800 m
(b) **280 m**
3,080 m − 2,800 m = 280 m
(c) **5 km 900 m**
5 km − 3 km 450 m = 1 km 550 m
1 km 550 m + 1 km 550 m + 2 km 800 m
= 4 km + 1 km 10 m + 800 m
= 5 km 900 m
(d) **4 km 630 m**
5 km + 3 km 80 m = 8 km 80 m
8,080 m − 3,450 m = 4,630 m
(e) **Gas station to post office to park.**
1 km 550 m + 2 km 800 m
+ 2 km 800 m = 7 km 150 m
This problem might be challenging. Add kilometers to narrow down the choices: the kilometers should add to 5 or 6 km.

8 **49 g**

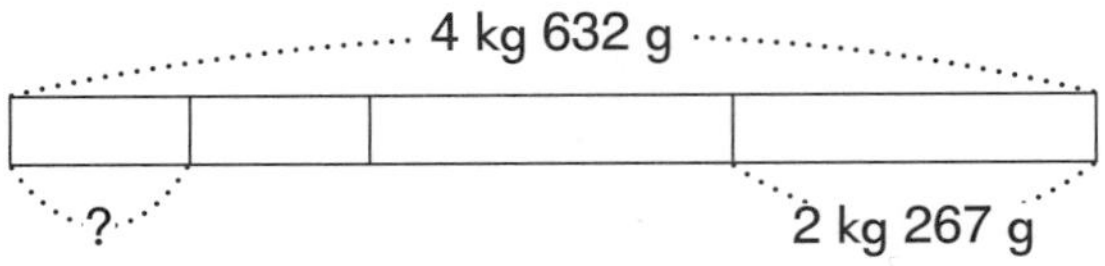

2,267 g + 2,267 g = 4,534 g
4,632 g − 4,534 g = 98 g
98 g ÷ 2 = 49 g

9 **285 mL**

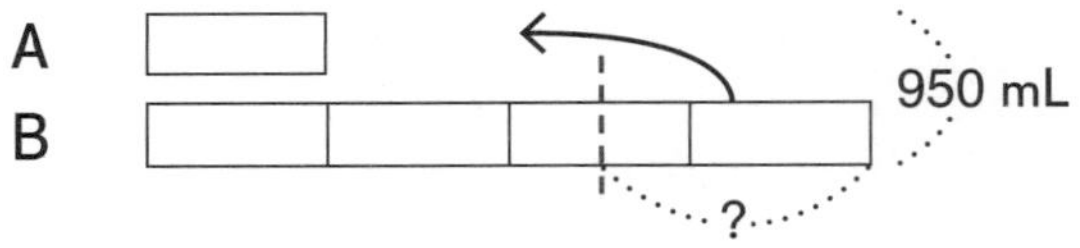

For both containers to have the same amount, half the difference needs to be transferred.
1 unit ⟶ 950 mL ÷ 5 = 190 mL
3 units ⟶ 3 × 190 mL = 570 mL
570 mL ÷ 2 = 285 mL

10 **17 cups**
The first cup is 16 cm. Each cup adds 4 cm.
Height from the additional cups:
80 cm − 16 cm = 64 cm
Number of additional cups:
64 cm ÷ 4 cm = 16
Total cups: 1 + 16 = 17

Chapter 11 Workbook Answers

Exercise 9 pp. 109–114

1 (a) 940

(b) 20

(c) **2**

Students should be able to find the answer without finding the quotient. The digit in the hundreds place is less than 7.

(d) Answers can vary.

Example: 4,600 + 800 = 5,400

(e) **5**

Students can just look at the digits in the tens and ones places.

(f) **9**

To subtract 42, 600 tens will have to be renamed as 599 tens. There are no hundreds to subtract.

(g) **1**

The number is odd, so the remainder is 1.

2 (a)

$$\begin{array}{r} 6{,}487 \\ +\ 2{,}908 \\ \hline 9{,}395 \end{array}$$

(b)

$$\begin{array}{r} 6{,}487 \\ -\ 2{,}908 \\ \hline 3{,}579 \end{array}$$

(c)

$$\begin{array}{r} 629 \\ \times\ \ \ 7 \\ \hline 4{,}403 \end{array}$$

(d)

$$\begin{array}{r} 87 \\ 8\overline{)696} \\ 64 \\ \hline 56 \\ 56 \\ \hline 0 \end{array}$$

3 (a)

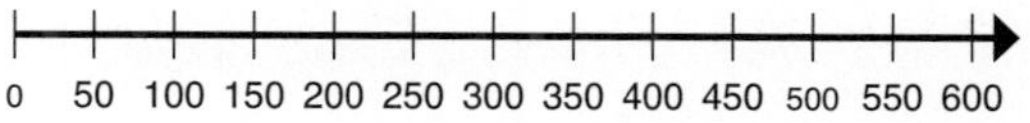

(b)

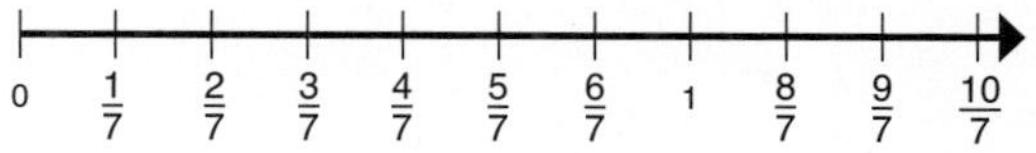

(c)

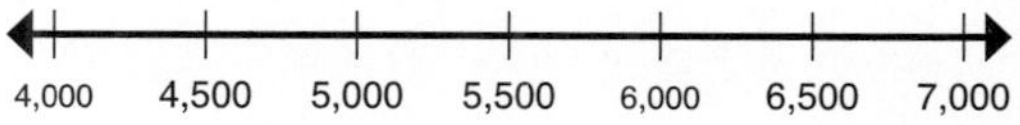

(d)

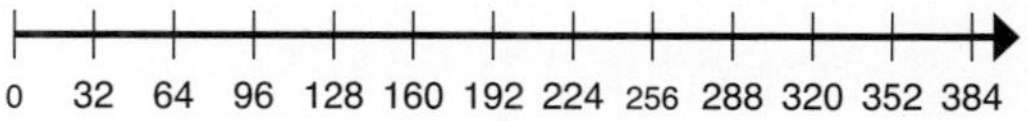

Interval: 256 ÷ 8 = 32

4 (a) 32

(b) 96

(c) 620

5 (a) $\frac{5}{8}$ (b) $\frac{3}{4}$

(c) $\frac{1}{2}$

6 (a)

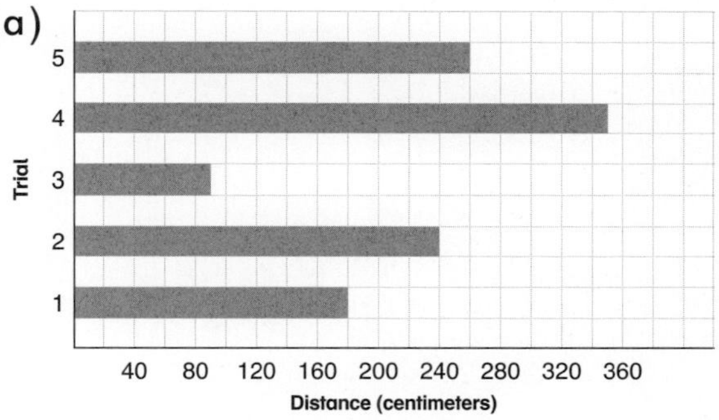

(b) Trial 3, Trial 1, Trial 2, Trial 5, Trial 4

(c) **2 m 60 cm**

350 cm – 90 cm = 260 cm

7 $\mathbf{\frac{1}{5}}$

$\frac{7}{10} - \frac{5}{10} = \frac{2}{10} = \frac{1}{5}$

8 4

9 **even**

Any number multiplied by 2 is even. 2 is a factor in the expression.

Chapter 11 Workbook Answers

10 Answers can vary. Examples:

Unit fractions: $\frac{1}{5}$, $\frac{1}{3}$ and

non-unit fractions: $\frac{4}{5}$, $\frac{3}{9}$, $\frac{2}{6}$, $\frac{3}{5}$

Simplest form: $\frac{1}{5}$, $\frac{1}{3}$, $\frac{4}{5}$, $\frac{3}{5}$ and

not simplest form: $\frac{3}{9}$, $\frac{2}{6}$

Greater than one-half: $\frac{4}{5}$, $\frac{3}{5}$ and

less than one-half: $\frac{1}{5}$, $\frac{1}{3}$, $\frac{3}{9}$, $\frac{2}{6}$

11 **tying the package**
$\frac{2}{3}$ is the only fraction greater than $\frac{1}{2}$.

12 (a) 7,260 g
(b) 2,312 cm

13 A: **3 L 100 mL**
B: **2 L 700 mL**
C: **3 L 900 mL**

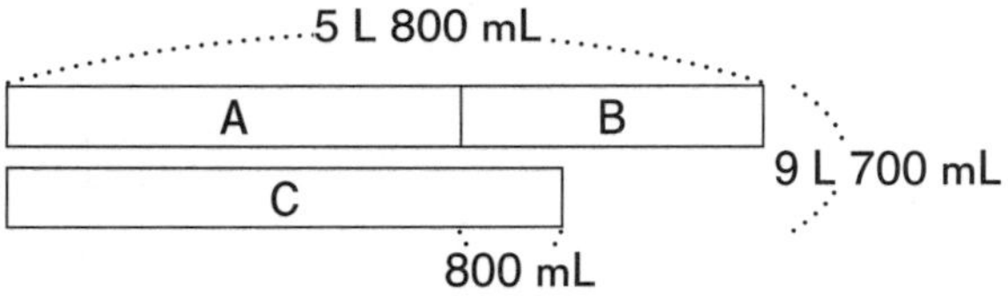

Students will not know in advance if B should be drawn longer than A, but that does not affect using the model to arrive at a method of solution.

C: 9,700 mL − 5,800 mL = 3,900 mL
A: 3,900 mL − 800 mL = 3,100 mL
B: 5,800 mL − 3,100 mL = 2,700 mL

14 **215 m**

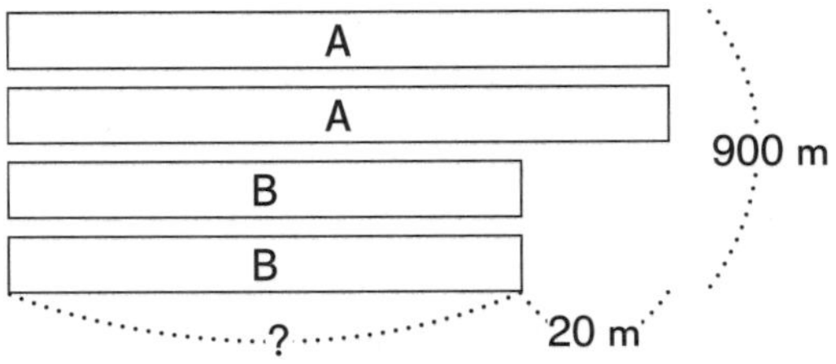

2 × 20 m = 40 m
4 units (B) ⟶ 900 m − 40 m = 860 m
1 unit ⟶ 860 m ÷ 4 = 215 m
Check: 215 + 215 + 235 + 235 = 900

15 **$480**
Students should remember from their hands-on experience with 1-L beakers that there are four 250 mL cups in 1 L.
4 × 60 L = 240
There are 240 cups of 250 mL in 60 L.
240 × $2 = $480

16 **blue**
6th from the right is 35th from the left.
The pattern repeat every 3 flags.
35 ÷ 3 is 11 R 2
The flag is second in the repeating unit of the pattern.

17 Answers can vary. Students should find an answer without using fraction tiles.
Example:
$\frac{1}{3} = \frac{4}{12}$ and $\frac{1}{2} = \frac{6}{12}$ so $\frac{1}{3} < \mathbf{\frac{5}{12}} < \frac{1}{2}$
$\frac{1}{3} = \frac{3}{9}$; $\frac{4}{9} < \frac{1}{2}$ so $\frac{1}{3} < \mathbf{\frac{4}{9}} < \frac{1}{2}$

Some other possible answers (simplest forms): $\frac{2}{5}$, $\frac{3}{7}$, $\frac{3}{8}$, $\frac{4}{11}$, $\frac{5}{11}$, $\frac{5}{13}$, $\frac{6}{13}$, $\frac{5}{14}$, $\frac{7}{16}$

Chapter 12 Geometry

	Lesson	Page	Objectives
	Chapter Opener	107	
1	Circles	108	Identify the center, diameter, and radius of a circle. Find the diameter of a circle given its radius or the radius of a circle given its diameter.
2	Angles	109	Understand that angles are figures where two lines meet at a point. Identify the sides and vertex of an angle. Identify angles in geometric figures.
3	Right Angles	110	Identify right angles. Compare the size of angles.
4	Triangles	111	Classify triangles based on the length of their sides.
5	Properties of Triangles	112	Determine the number of equal angles in a given triangle. Construct triangles with 0, 2, or 3 equal sides using set squares and circle dot paper.
6	Properties of Quadrilaterals	114	Identify equal sides, equal angles, and right angles on quadrilaterals. Identify rhombuses.
7	Using a Compass	116	Use a compass to draw circles of a given radius or diameter. Use a compass to identify equal sides of a figure. Use a compass to construct triangles with given whole number side lengths.
8	Practice	118	

Materials

Materials

- Cardboard strips and brad fastener
- Compass
- Geoboard and rubber bands
- Ruler
- Set squares

Optional

- Short lengths of pipe cleaner or thin wire
- Straws
- Tangrams

Printouts

(singaporemath.com/higprintouts)

- Alternate Set Squares
- Centimeter Graph Paper
- Circle
- Circle Dot Paper
- Geoboard
- Graph Paper
- Lesson 12-4
- Lesson 12-5
- Set Squares
- Square Dot Paper
- Tangram Pieces
- Triangle Sides

Notes

Attributes

In mathematics, the word attribute is used to describe a characteristic or feature of an object that allows it to be grouped with other similar objects. Shapes can be described and classified according to their attributes.

In Dimensions Math® 1A, students investigated the attributes of some basic three-dimensional shapes (cuboid, cube, cylinder, cone, and pyramid). They identified the two-dimensional shapes on the flat faces of these solids (squares, rectangles, triangles, and circles). They combined simple shapes to make more complex shapes.

In Dimensions Math® 2B, students identified straight and curved sides, closed and open shapes, polygons, quadrilaterals, pentagons, hexagons, semicircles, and quarter-circles. They reviewed the attributes of cuboids, cubes, cones, and cylinders, and they identified spheres.

In this chapter, students will examine some length attributes of circles and angle and length attributes of triangles and quadrilaterals.

Circles

The chapter starts with the idea that the distance from the center of a circle to its edge is the same for every point on the edge. This idea is central to the extensive use of circles in constructing geometric figures, whether by hand or using a dynamic geometry software program. Students will use the fact that all radii of a circle are equal in order to make simple constructions of triangles of given side lengths using a compass and ruler in Lesson 7. Lesson 7 is optional if your student has trouble manipulating a compass. However, one useful use of a compass is to compare lengths. Compasses can be opened to match one length and then moved (without changing the opening) to see if the opening matches another length. This allows a more precise and quicker comparison of the lengths of different lines than measuring with a ruler.

Angles

In Lesson 2, students will be introduced to angles. They will learn that any two lines that meet at a point form an angle. If the lines cross, they will form four angles at the intersection. A more formal definition of an angle, which students will not learn yet, is "a figure formed by two rays that have the same endpoint." The purpose of the lessons at this level is not to start a formal study of geometry, but simply to get students familiar with various attributes of geometric figures, in this case the angles of rectangles, triangles and other polygons.

In order to understand what is meant by the size of an angle, students will think of angles being formed as if one side were rotated away from the other side by a certain amount. However, they need to understand that an angle is not the process of turning; it is a fixed, static figure.

The amount of "turning" needed to go from one line to the other determines the size of the angle. The size of the angle is not determined by the length of the sides. The following two angles have the same size:

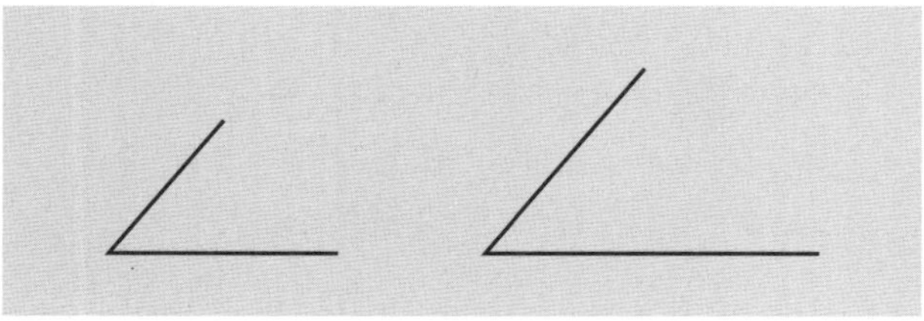

Students will be using set squares extensively in the Dimensions Math® curriculum. These are plastic triangles that you can find in geometry kits. It is best to use ones that do not have rounded corners. If you do not have appropriate set squares, use the **Set Square** printout to make set squares using thin cardboard or thick paper, such as a file folder.

Students will learn to recognize right angles and determine if an angle is smaller than or greater than a right angle, but will not formally learn the terms "acute angle" or "obtuse angle" at this level.

Most of the internal angles of the shapes in the textbook are smaller than a straight line. In the workbook exercises, there will be internal angles that are larger than a straight line. Students need to recognize these as angles as well, even though they will not formally learn about reflex angles in Dimensions Math® 4B. For example, the following figure has an internal angle that is larger than a straight line:

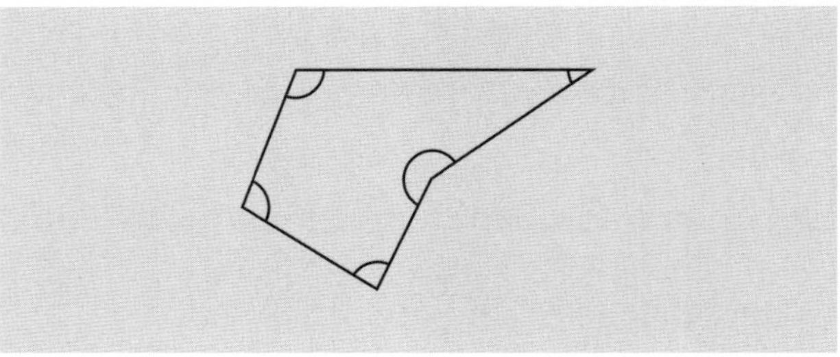

Angle Properties of Polygons

Students will classify triangles based on attributes involving side lengths and angles. They will learn that triangles have the same number of equal angles as equal sides. They will not learn the names given to triangles based on the lengths of the sides until Dimensions Math® 4B. This guide, however, will use their names:

- equilateral triangle: 3 equal sides
- isosceles triangle: 2 equal sides
- scalene triangle: 0 equal sides

Students will also examine side and angle properties of quadrilaterals. They will now know that the "special corners" in rectangles are called right angles. They will learn that a rhombus is a quadrilateral with four equal sides. They already should know that a square is a special type of rectangle, and will learn that a square is also a special type of rhombus. However, they will not formally classify quadrilaterals until Dimensions Math® 4B, where they will also learn to identify parallelograms and trapezoids.

Chapter Opener (p. 123)

One tangram set is composed of seven figures that together to form a square:

Your student can create the shapes shown on page 123, if they want, and/or make their own figures. You can make several copies of the **Tangram** printout and cut out the shapes if you do not have any tangram sets.

As your student makes pictures, discuss various attributes of the tangram shapes, particularly those that allow them to fit together to form a square, such as:

- There is one figure that has four equal sides but is not a square.
- All the triangles in the set have two equal sides.
- The smallest triangles have two sides the same length as the side of the square, and one side the same length as the side of the other quadrilateral.
- The middle-sized triangle has one side that is twice as long as one of the sides of the smallest triangles, and the other two sides are each half as long as one of the sides of the largest triangles.
- Certain corners of some of the figures together form a straight line (such as two of the corners on the largest triangles).
- Certain corners of some of the figures together form the corner of a square (such as the corners on the largest and the smallest triangles).

You can find other figures made from tangrams online or in publications, as well as dissection puzzles, where the objective is to replicate a pattern (given only as an outline) using all seven pieces without overlap.

Lesson 1 Circles (pp. 124 – 127)

Think (p. 124)

Use the **Circle** printout. Your student will find that the answer is 7 cm for (a) and 14 cm for (b). You can use other paper circles but at this level, if they are measuring, the radius should be a whole number of centimeters. However, it should be obvious just from folding that the distance from across the circle through the center is twice as much as the distance just to the center.

Answers

2

1. 3 cm
   6 cm
2. (a) 60 ft
   (b) 60 in
3. (a) 16 cm
   (b) 6 in
4. (a) 14 cm
   (b) 6 in
5. **32 cm**
   $4 \times 8 = 32$

8 in

13 in (If your copy has 12 in for the diameter of the wheel, It should be corrected to 26 in)

Learn (p. 125)

Tell your student that a circle is a flat figure where the edge is always the same distance from the center. (A geometric definition of a circle is the set of points in a plane at a given distance from a given point in that plane.) Discuss the definitions for radius and diameter. Point out that the plural of radius is radii (pronounced rādēī). Since a diameter is composed of two radii, it is twice as long as a radius.

Do (pp. 126–127)

1. 2. Students should realize that they can multiply the radius by 2 to find the diameter, or divide the diameter by 2 to find the radius.

3. Students should note that the diameter is the same as the side of a square circumscribed about a circle (the edge of the circle touches the midpoint of each side of the square).

4. Students should realize that the side of a quarter-circle is the same as the radius of the full circle.

Activity

You may want to give your student a compass and show them how to use it. Let them practice drawing circles with it prior to Lesson 7. You can even have them practice making circles of a given radius or diameter.

Lesson 2 Angles (pp. 128 – 131)

Think (p. 128)

Tell your student that the corners of rectangles and circles, as well as other polygons (closed flat figures with straight sides), are called angles. Point out that the corners are different sizes: they are more or less "pointy." You can use the tangram shapes as examples.

As they do the activity given in Think, they should realize that the cardboard strips form an angle along the inside edges. An angle is a geometric figure. As with activities where they found rectangles or other geometric figures in their environment, they are only finding approximations of the geometric figure itself.

Learn (p. 129)

An angle needs to have two sides and a vertex for there to be a "space between the sides." Students can think of the size of an angle as the amount of "opening," as if one side had been rotated away from the other about the vertex in order to form the angle.

Show your student that opening the strips even more than a straight line also makes an angle:

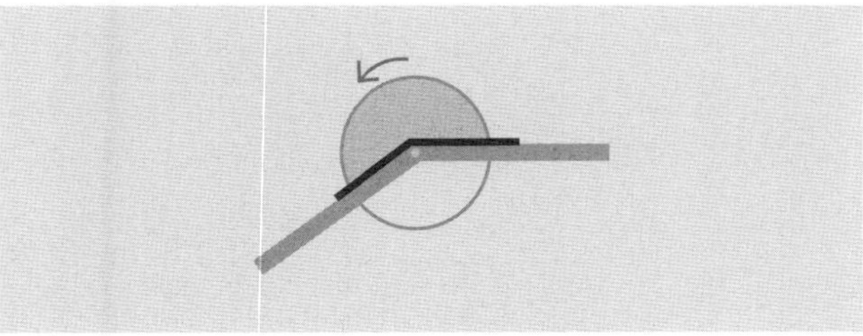

Answers

1. (a) 4 angles and 4 sides
   (b) 3 angles and 3 sides
2. (b) and (c)
5. Each shape has the same number of sides as it does angles.

Do (pp. 130–131)

3, 4. Students should realize that it does not matter how long they draw the sides: the size of the angle (the amount of "opening") is the same. This might be somewhat of an abstract concept for some students.

5. In Dimensions Math® 2B, students already learned that the number of corners of a polygon is the same as the number of sides. The only new concept here is that the corners are now called angles. If you do not have a geoboard, you can make several copies of the **Geoboard** printout and have your student use a ruler to connect the dots. Their shapes should be polygons, and so their lines should not cross. The shapes they make could be concave. The number of internal angles is still the same as the number of sides:

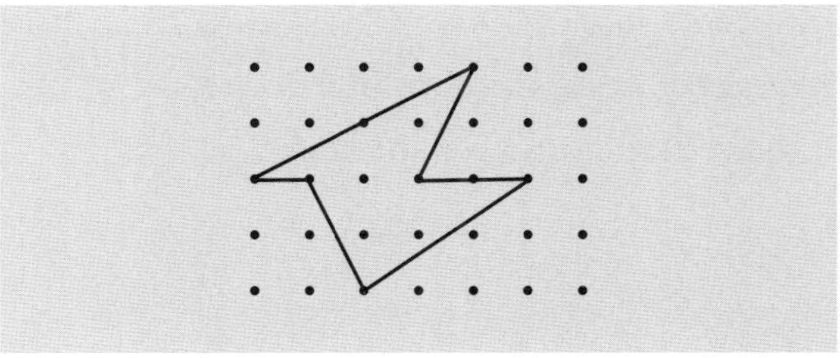

Lesson 3 Right Angles (pp. 132 –136)

Think (p. 132)

The piece of paper has to be carefully folded so that the edges line up in order to form a right angle. You can also cut out the circle from the **Circle** printout and have your student fold it into a quarter-circle. After they use their folded shape to find right angles in their environment, it will be easier to use the right angle on a set square or index card to check the size of an angle compared to a right angle. However, using a circle or torn piece of paper will help prepare students for the idea later that the measure of a right angle is the same as the measure of a quarter-turn around a circle.

Learn (p. 133)

Students need to realize that the size and classification of the angle (whether a right angle, smaller than a right angle, or larger than a right angle) is dependent on the amount of "opening", not the length of the sides, nor the orientation of the angle.

Ask your student to determine which angle is smallest and which is largest in the second row, and which is smallest in the third row. They should be able to do this by looking at the difference in size compared to a right angle, whether from the overlap of the green quarter-circle in the second row or from the space between the side of the strips and the quarter-circle in the third row.

Answers

❶ (b) Both of the other two angles are smaller than a right angle.
(c) None of the angles are larger than a right angle.

❸ Angle a is larger.
Angle b has longer sides.

❹ All of the tangram pieces have a right angle except one (the dark blue one in the textbook image).

❺ (a) Angle d.
(b) f, c, d, e, g

❻ (a) B
(b) C
(c) A

❼ F, J, N, R

Do (pp. 134–136)

❷ ❸ These problems reinforce the idea that the size of the angle does not depend on the length of the sides.

❺ ❻ ❼ Students can use a set square, the right angle they made in Lesson 3, or the corner of an index card to check which angles are right angles, larger than a right angle, or smaller than a right angle. For ❺ (b), they might be able to put them in order by visual inspection only, except perhaps angles e and g.

Lesson 4 Triangles (pp. 137 – 139)

Think (p. 137)

You can cut out the strips from the **Triangle Sides** printout to use instead of straws. Your student can form the triangles on paper and trace them. If you do have straws, cut them into lengths of 10 cm, 8 cm, 6 cm, and 5 cm. You can use short pieces of pipe cleaner or thin wire to connect the sides. Each triangle should be different. Your student should form at least some of their own triangles, enough to have several of each type. For all the possible triangles, you can also cut out the triangles from the **Lesson 12-4** printout, which includes all 18 possible triangles. Have your student group the triangles. Save them for the next lesson.

Answers

1 (a) A: 5 cm, 4 cm, 3 cm
0 equal sides
B: 4 cm, 4 cm, 4 cm
3 equal sides
C: 3 cm, 4 cm, 4 cm
2 equal sides

(b) A

2

2 equal sides   0 equal sides

3 (a) 3 equal sides
(b) 2 equal sides
(c) 0 equal sides
(d) 2 equal sides

Learn (p. 138)

Your student should realize there are only three possible groups when grouping triangles according to number of equal sides.

For the lengths used here, there is only one possible combination that can't be used to make a triangle: two 5-cm lengths and one 10-cm length, which your student may have discovered on their own. The sum of the lengths of two of the sides has to be greater than the length of the third side, or else it is not possible to form a triangle. This may be self-evident to your student from their experience creating triangles in Think, but you can have them experiment with other lengths, or you can find some interactive activities online where they can adjust the side lengths of a triangle.

Do (p. 139)

3 In this problem, students are introduced to the use of hash marks as a form of mathematical notation to indicate equal sides of geometric figures. Usually, one hash mark is used if there is only one set of equal sides, then two hash marks for another set of equal sides on the same figure, but (b) shows two hash marks for the equal sides just to familiarize students with them. Hash marks only refer to equal sides in a single specific figure, unless stated otherwise.

Lesson 5 Properties of Triangles (pp. 140 – 142)

Think (p. 140)

Cut out the triangles from the **Lesson 12-5** printout. There are two copies of each triangle. You may want to label the angles on the reverse side. Ask your student to determine which angles in each triangle are equal to each other, and to find a way to show that the angles are equal to each other. They can use any method they want, such as flipping or rotating one copy to lay an angle on top of the other or folding the triangle to make the angles match.

Learn (p. 140)

This shows one method for determining which angles are equal: folding the paper triangle so that the angles can be placed on top of each other.

Students should notice that for the triangle with two equal sides, the angles opposite those sides are equal. For the triangle with three equal sides, all the angles are equal.

You can have your student use the triangles from the **Lesson 12-4** printout to see if this is true for other triangles. They might notice that in the case of all triangles with three equal sides, all the angles are equal, regardless of the size of the triangle.

Answers

2

3

1 (a) 3

(d) The triangle made with the smaller of the two set squares

2 (a) Orientation can vary.

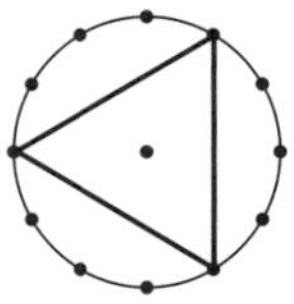

(b) Answers can vary. Examples:

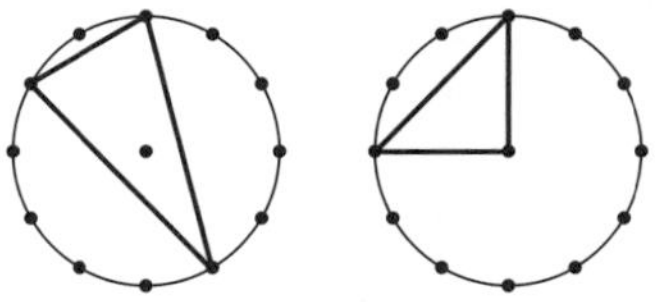

(c) Answers can vary. Examples:

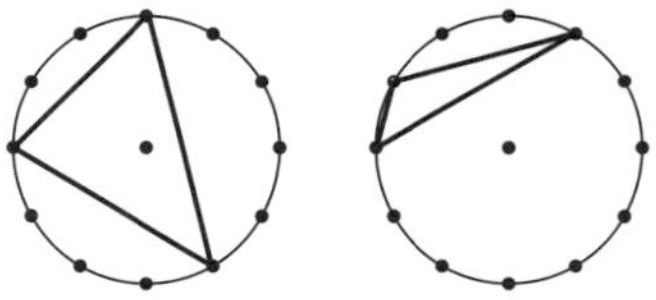

3 Other possible triangles:

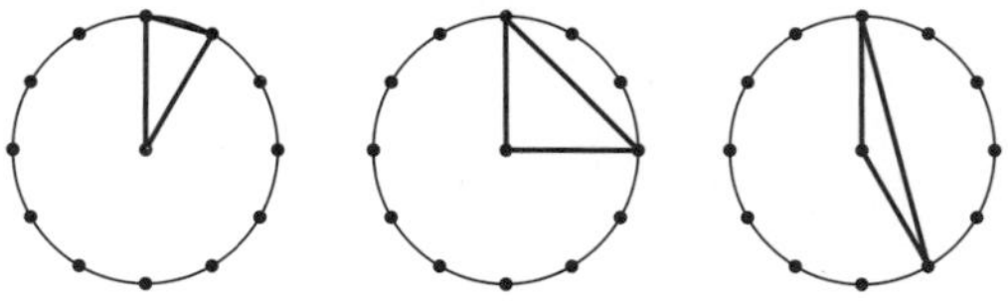

They all have 2 equal sides.

Do (pp. 141–142)

1 You can print two copies of the **Set Square** printout or use actual set squares if you have two sets. Only thee different triangles are possible, since no sides of the scalene set square matches a side of the isosceles set square. In order to have more possible triangles, you can instead use the **Alternate Set Squares** printout, which has two sets

of set squares with the same size angles of standard set squares, but one of the sides of the scalene set square is the same as one of the sides of the isosceles set square.

2. Use several copies of the **Circle Dot Paper** printout. This is an easy way for students to draw triangles with equal sides. If there are an equal number of intervals around the circle between the two endpoints of lines drawn between the dots on the edge of the circle, then the lines are equal in length. All lines drawn from the center to one of the points on the edge are equal in length. The textbook shows an example for each; students should attempt to draw a different example. You can ask your student to try to find more than one that is different from the example in the textbook, not just with a different orientation, where possible.
   (a) Only one triangle is possible.
   (b) For drawings not using the center dot, there are only two possible triangles, since there needs to be an even number of intervals between the end points of the sides. One of them will be the same as the triangle in (a). All triangles with 3 equal sides have 2 equal sides. For drawings using the center, there are 5 possible triangles.
   (c) None of the triangles can use the center dot as one of the vertices. There are eight possible triangles.

3. Ask your student why the triangles all have two equal sides. The two sides are both radii of the circle, and all radii are equal.

Enrichment

Ask your student to draw triangles using the circle dot paper where one side is a diameter of the circle:

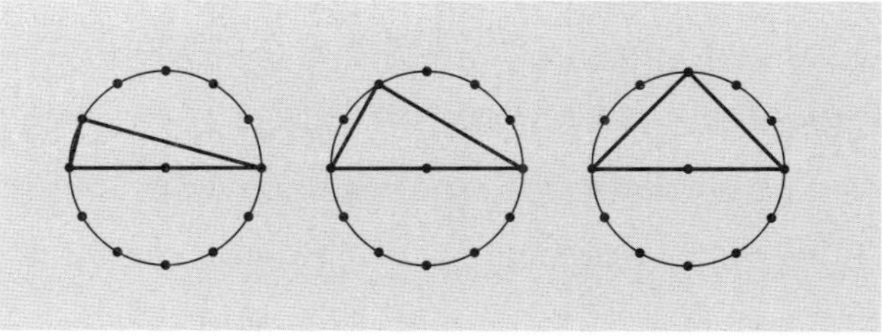

Ask them if they notice anything special about one of the angles. All triangles inscribed in a circle where one of the sides is a diameter has a right angle.

Ask your student to draw some triangles where one of the angles is greater than a right angle, if they did not already.

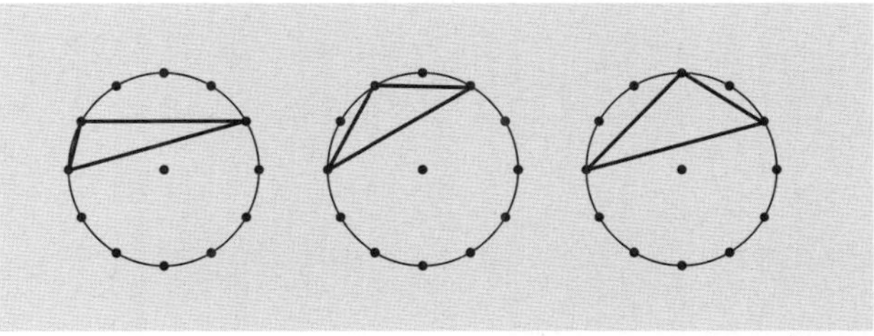

Ask them to compare the triangles to those that do not have an angle greater than a right angle. They should notice that one of the sides is always less than the length of the diameter, or that the center of the circle is not within the triangle.

Lesson 6 Properties of Quadrilaterals (pp. 143 –146)

Think (p. 143)

If you don't have a geoboard, you can use the **Geoboard** printout and have your student form quadrilaterals by connecting the dots using a ruler. They should make or draw a variety of quadrilaterals and then answer the questions for their own quadrilaterals as well as for the quadrilaterals on page 143. All of the quadrilaterals in Think are convex figures. Your student might draw or create a concave figure, such as the following:

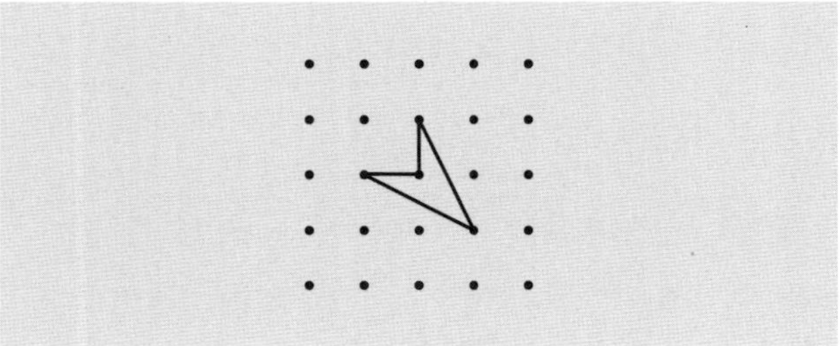

This example does have an external right angle. The internal angle at the same vertex is greater than a straight line (a reflex angle). All your student needs to say at this point is that the internal angle is greater than a right angle.

Learn (p. 144)

The attributes of one of the figures from the previous page with respect to the size of the angles compared to a right angle and the length of the sides compared to each other are listed at the top of the page. Ask your student to describe some of the other quadrilaterals on the previous page, as well as some of the ones they created, in the same way.

Answers

1 right angle,
2 angles greater than a right angle,
1 angle smaller than a right angle,
2 equal sides

4 right angles

3 A, B, C, E
E is also a square.

Ask your student to answer Dion's question. If necessary, remind them that quadrilaterals must have straight sides, that a flat figure with straight sides and no opening (closed figure) is called a polygon, and that quadrilaterals are polygons.

Students may already know that all four "corners" of a rectangle look the same, and a figure where they do not all look the same is not a rectangle. They now know that these corners are right angles. A rectangle is defined as a quadrilateral with four equal angles. A square is a type of rectangle.

At the bottom of the page, students learn that a quadrilateral with four equal sides is called a rhombus, and a square is a type of rhombus.

You can have your student draw some rhombuses on the **Square Dot Paper** printout and cut them out. Ask them to compare the angles. They should find that the opposite angles are equal. Ask them if they can define a rhombus by saying that opposite angles are equal. They cannot, since opposite angles of a rectangle are also equal. (Students will learn later that rhombuses and rectangles are both parallelograms, and opposite angles of all parallelograms are equal.) A rhombus is defined as a quadrilateral with equal sides. A square is a rhombus because it has equal sides, and a rectangle because it has equal angles.

Do (pp. 145–146)

1. Ask your student to describe the properties of their quadrilaterals.

2. Instead of standard set squares, you can use the **Alternate Set Square** printout so that a greater variety of quadrilaterals can be formed. Only one rhombus is possible, and it is also a square. The answer to Sofia's question is that the opposite angles are equal.

3. Students can check for right angles using the right angle of a set square or index card. The answer to Emma's question is that E is a square.

   You can tell your student, if you want, that F is called a "kite." It has two pairs of equal sides, as does a rectangle, but the equal sides are not opposite each other as in a rectangle, but rather adjacent. A square is a type of kite.

4. Students can use either the **Square Dot Paper** printout or graph paper, where the vertices of their quadrilaterals are at the intersections of the lines on the graph paper. The answer to Mei's question is that they cannot all be greater than a right angle. In fact, a quadrilateral can have no more than two angles greater than a right angle.

Extension

Have your student draw a figure on the **Square Dot Paper** printout using the dots as the vertices and then describe it in a way that you can draw one just like it. It should not be too simple, such as a rectangle or square, nor too difficult, such as one with many sides. In order to describe any adjacent sides where the angle between them is not a right angle, they will have to say something like "count over two dots to the right and three dots down for the next vertex." Then reverse roles.

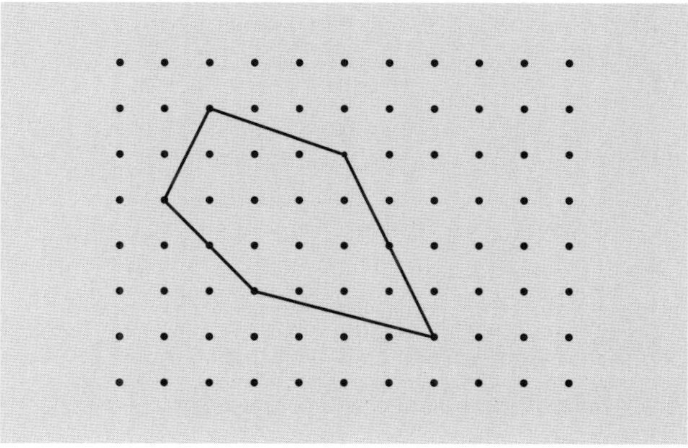

Lesson 7 Using a Compass (pp. 147–150)

Think and Learn (pp. 147–148)

This lesson is optional. Show your student how to use a compass, if you have not already. You can use the **Centimeter Graph Paper** printout to draw circles with the given radius or diameter, which should be easier than using a ruler. The compass should be opened to the same length as the radius, so students need to find the radius when given the diameter.

Since this is new material, you can go directly to the explanations in Learn and demonstrate how to draw the given triangle for (c). It may make it easier for your student to understand if you draw the entire circle around the two endpoints of the 3-cm line:

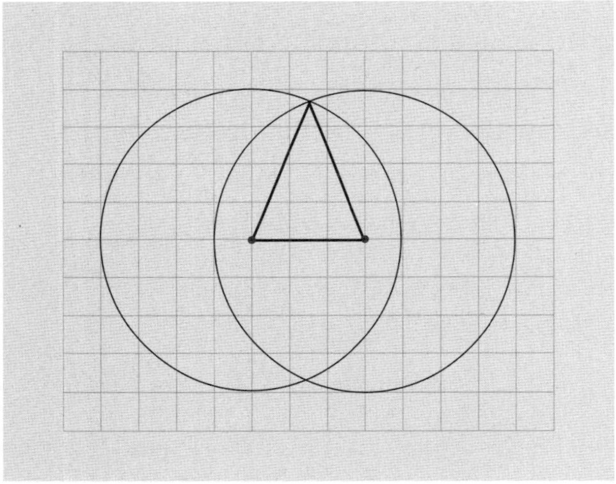

The circles will overlap. Since they both have a diameter of 4 cm, a line drawn from the endpoints of the 3-cm line (the centers of each circle) to the intersection of both circles are radii and are both 4 cm. If we have an idea of what the final figure will look like, we don't need to draw the entire circles, just part of them where they are likely to intersect, as shown on page 148.

Answers

1 (a)

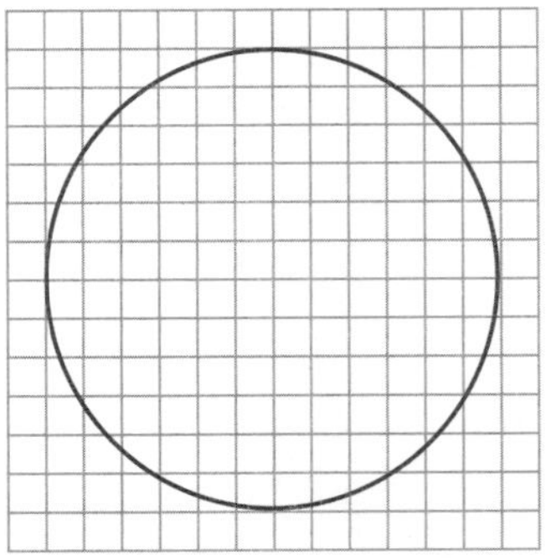

(b)

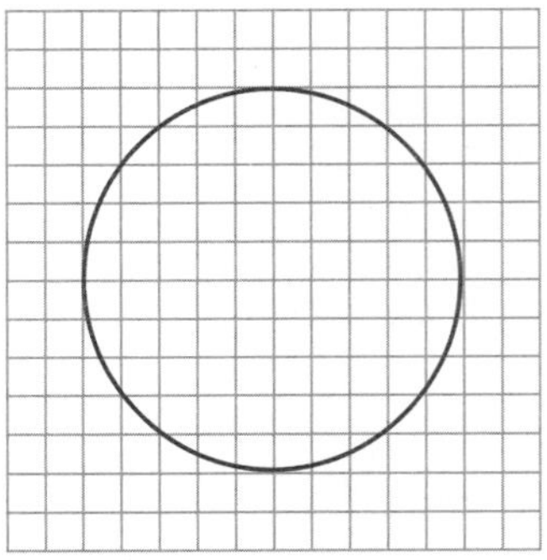

(c)

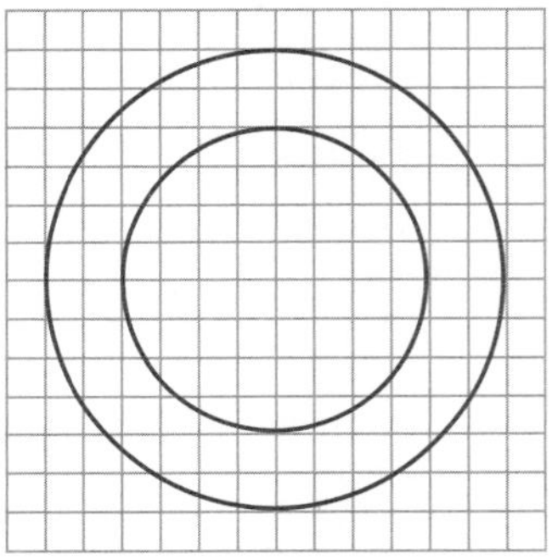

2

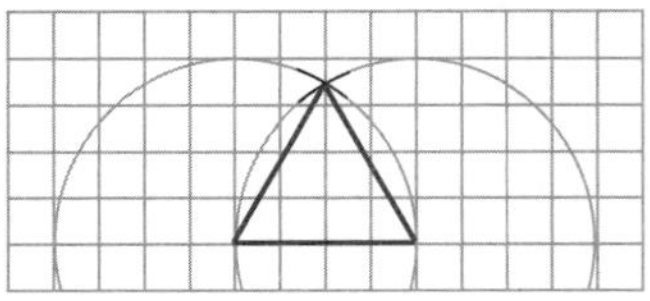

3 (a) The angle between the shorter two sides is a right angle.

(b)

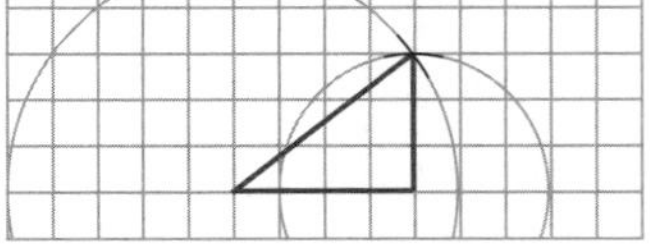

The triangle is the same but with a different orientation.

Do (pp. 149–150)

The answers here show what the figures would look like on centimeter graph paper.

5 The answer here shows where the centers of the circles would be. The figure on the right shows partial circles. One figure that is often confusing for students later is the overlap of quarter circles in a square, such as that shown below. By allowing your student to draw circle designs, you are helping them prepare for later lessons in later grades on the area and perimeter of figures made using circles.

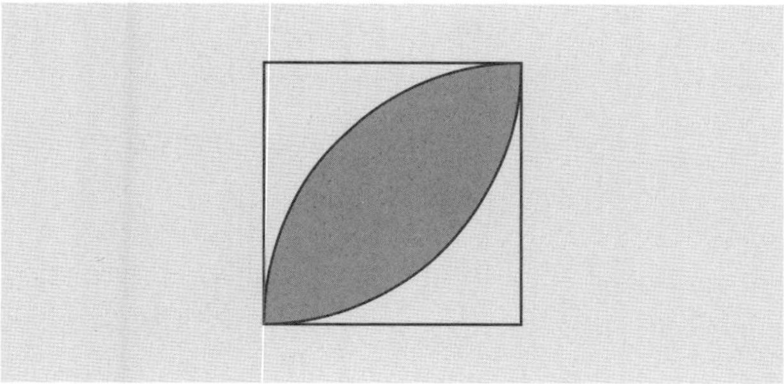

Answers (continued)

4 The orientation can vary.

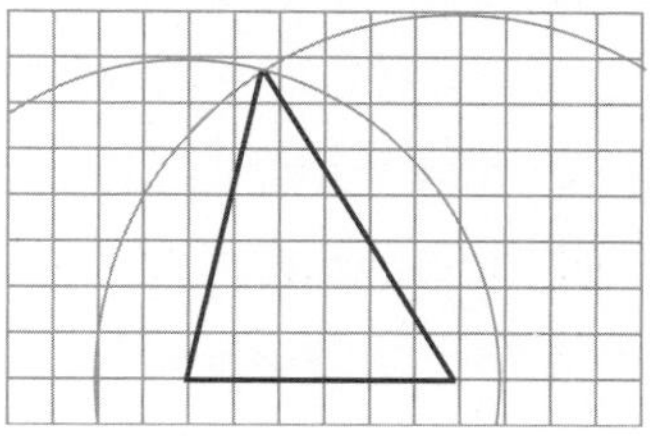

5

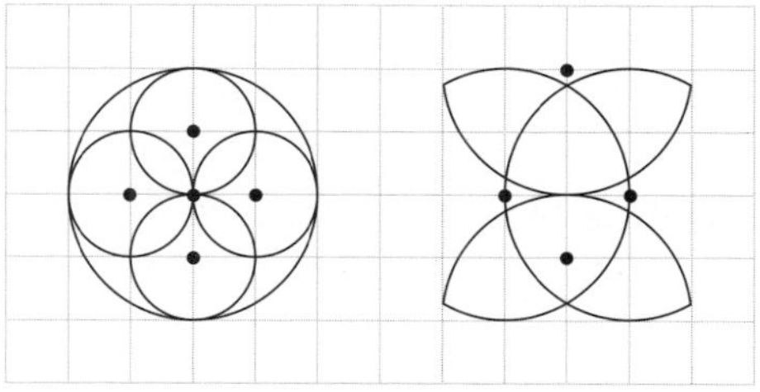

Extension

A compass is a good tool for comparing length. This idea is used in the last two problems in the workbook exercise.

Refer back to the figures on page 146 of the textbook and ask your student if they can think of a way to determine if any of the sides are equal with a compass, without a ruler. Help them see that if they open the compass to match the length of one side, they can then move the compass to see if the same opening matches the length of another side.

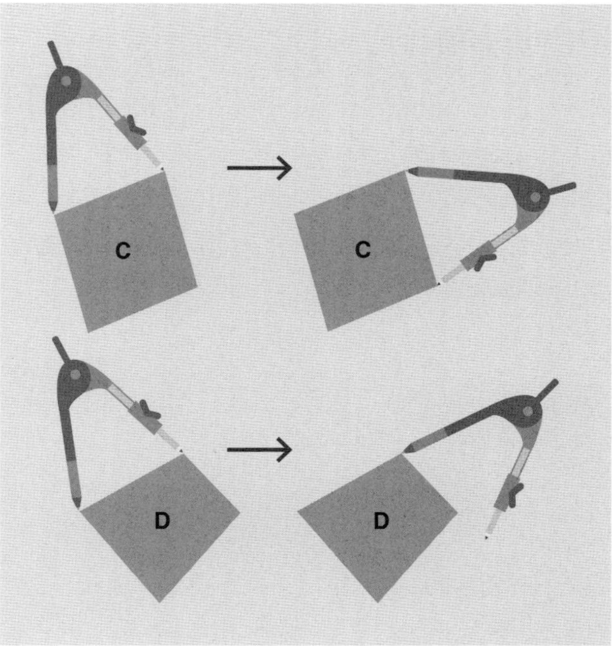

Practice (pp. 151–154)

Students should use a set square or corner of an index card to determine if angles are equal to, greater than, or smaller than a right angle.

10 Students should realize that the blue radius and the length from the edge of each circle to the center along the red line are the same.

11 Students should realize that the rectangle has a length equal to 8 radii, and a width equal to 4 radii.

If your student did Lesson 7, ask them to draw some triangles with given sides up to 10 cm.

Extension

Ask your student to construct a figure that is composed of triangles. For example, the following figure (a trapezoid) is composed of three equilateral triangles with sides three units long.

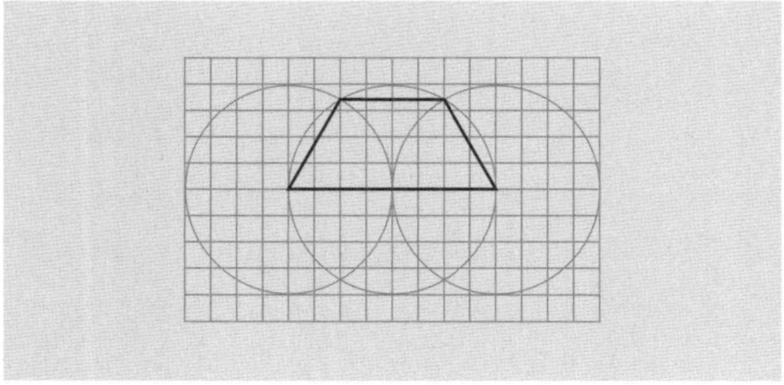

Enrichment

Workbook Exercises 5 and 6 include some "toothpick challenges." You can find additional toothpick challenges online if your student is interested.

Answers

1 (a) radius: 79 m diameter: 158 m
(b) radius: 71 cm diameter: 142 cm

2 b, c, a, d

3 (a) 2
(b) 3
(c) 0

4 (a) 0 right angles
8 angles larger than a right angle
0 angles smaller than a right angle
(b) 3 right angles
2 angles larger than a right angle
0 angles smaller than a right angle
(c) 0 right angles
2 angles larger than a right angle
2 angles smaller than a right angle
(d) 2 right angles
5 angles larger than a right angle
0 angles smaller than a right angle

5 (a) N, O
(b) J, L, N
(c) M

6 (a) P, Q, R, S, V
(b) Q, R
(c) Q, S

8 A rectangle can be a rhombus if it is a square.

9 14 cm

10 16 cm 4×4 cm = 16 cm

11 length: 24 cm 8×3 cm = 24 cm
width: 12 cm 4×3 cm = 12 cm

Chapter 12 Workbook Answers

Exercise 1 pp. 115–118

1 (a)

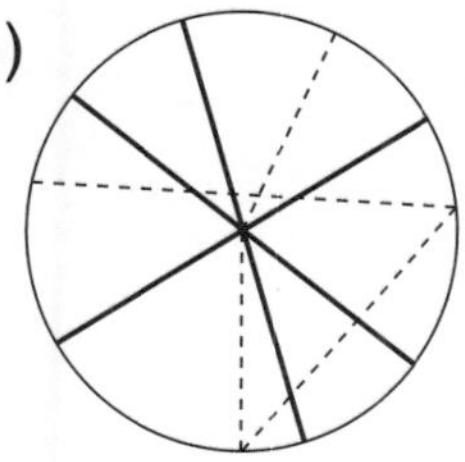

(b)

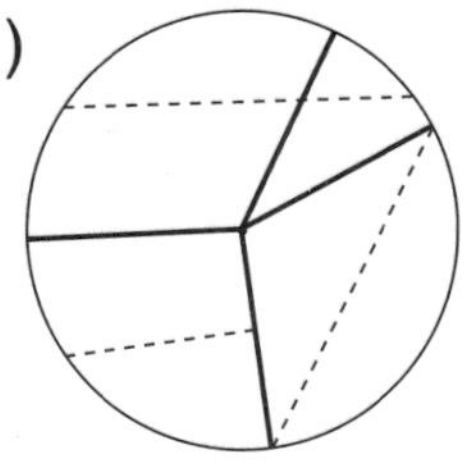

2 (a) radius: 5 cm
diameter: 10 cm

(b) radius: 2 cm
diameter: 4 cm

(c) radius: 3 cm
diameter: 6 cm

3 (a) 30 cm (b) 18 cm

4 17 cm

5 (a) 9 cm (b) 29 cm

6 36 cm

7 (a) **3 cm**
24 cm ÷ 8 = 3 cm

(b) **144 cm**
6 × 24 cm = 144 cm

(c) **36 cm**
24 cm ÷ 2 = 12 cm
3 × 12 cm = 36 cm

8 (a) **18 cm**
12 cm ÷ 2 = 6 cm
3 × 6 cm = 18 cm

(b) **56 cm**

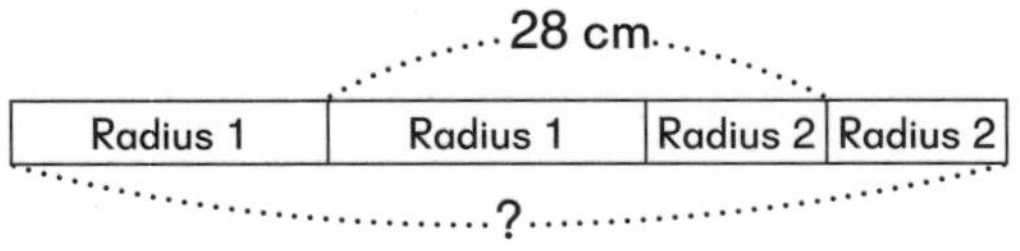

2 × 28 cm = 56 cm

9 **4 cm**

If your student struggles with this problem, suggest that they think of what would happen if they slide the smaller circle to the right so that the edges of the circles line up and there is no overlap. It would have to be slid the same length as the overlap. You can show this with paper strips, marking the total length of both, then sliding one over the other.

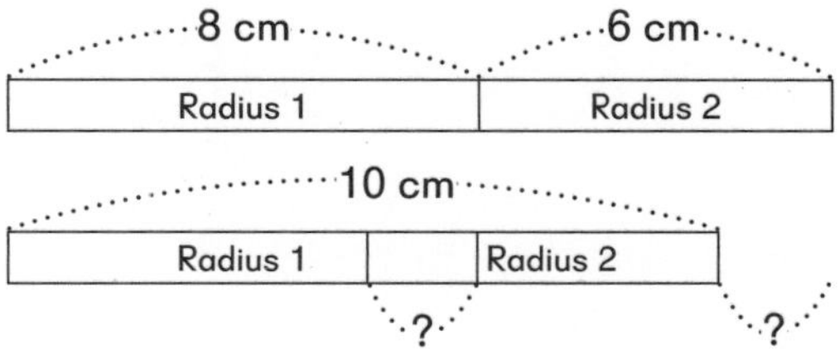

From this, they can see that the overlap is the sum of the two radii minus the given length.

8 cm + 6 cm = 14 cm
14 cm − 10 cm = 4 cm

Exercise 2 pp. 119–120

1 Make sure your student understands that this does not depict one angle which changes. It depicts several angles one after the other that are formed between the two strips each time they are opened a bit farther. An angle is not an object that changes over time.

(a) z

(b) center

(c) sides

Chapter 12 Workbook Answers

❷

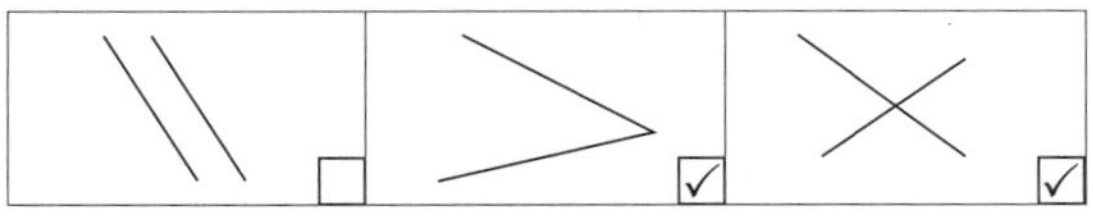

❸

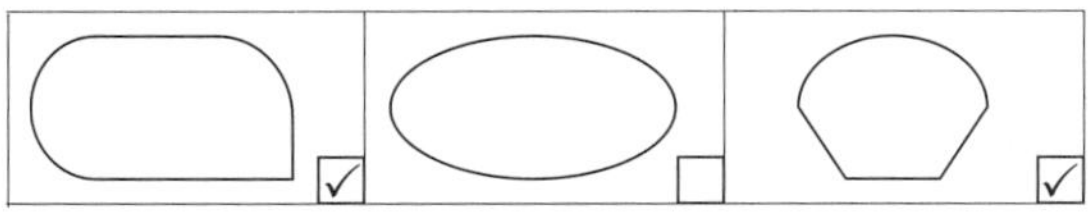

❹

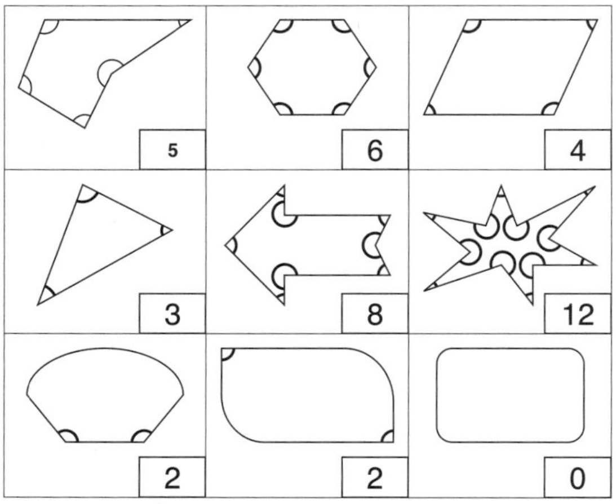

Make sure your student understands that they are to mark angles on the inside of the figure (even when they are larger than a straight line).

❺ Answers can vary. The number of inside angles should be the same as the number of sides. A closed figure does not have lines that cross each other.

Exercise 3 pp. 121–124

❶ 4 right angles

1 right angle   0 right angles

❷ (a) x

(b) y

(c) z

(d) same size

(The orientation does not affect whether an angle is a right angle.)

❸ a, b, g

❹

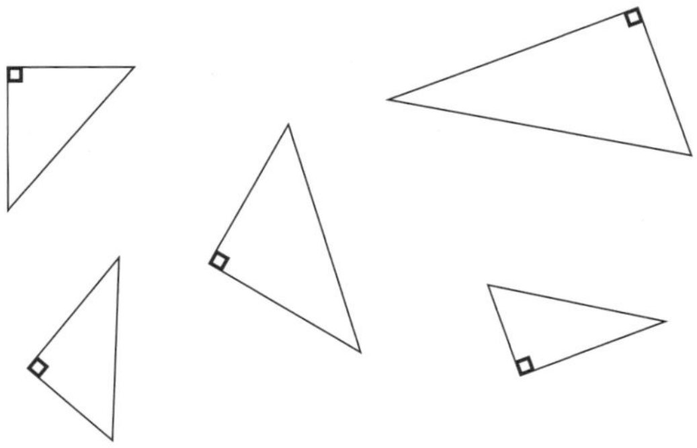

This answer key will show right angles marked with a small square. Students will learn to mark right angles this way in Dimensions Math® 4B, and so will more likely mark them with a curve. You can, if you want, let them know now that right angles are generally marked with a square, but it is not necessary.

❺ (a) k, o

(b) l, n

(c) n, l, m, k, o

❻

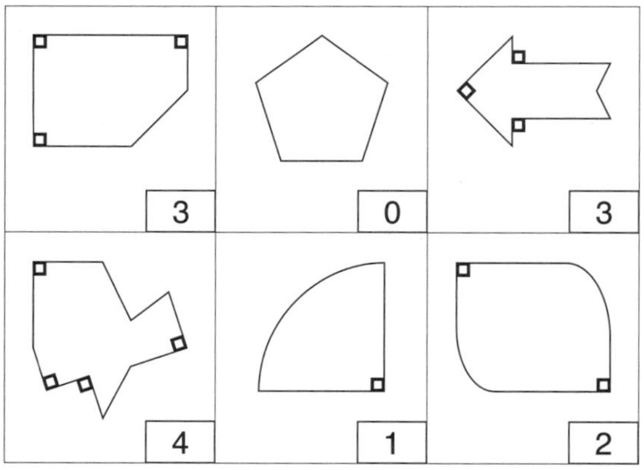

Chapter 12 Workbook Answers

7 Make sure your student knows that the path needs to make some kind of turn at each intersection. (Later, they will learn that the straight line at the intersection is an angle, so theoretically they could skip some turns.)

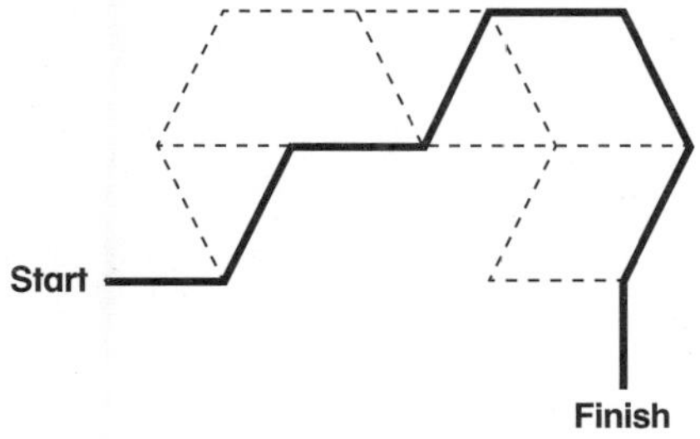

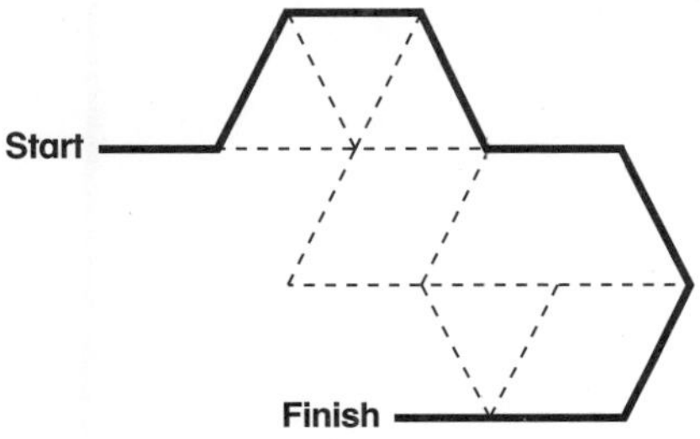

8 4

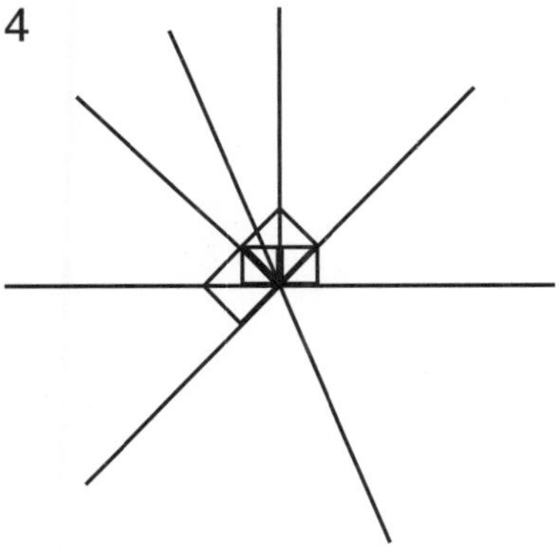

If your student does not see any right angles, tell them to imagine separate pairs of lines that are coming out from the center. They can use a set square.

Exercise 4 pp. 125–126

1 All the sides are 3 cm, 4 cm, 5 cm, or 6 cm long.

(a) J, L
(b) I, M
(c) H, K, N
(d) H
(e) I, K

2

3 equal sides	Exactly 2 equal sides	0 equal sides
B, H	C, E, G	A, D, F

3 (a) no (b) yes
(c) yes (d) no

The third side has to be shorter than the sum of the other two sides.

Exercise 5 pp. 127–129

1 (a) 0, 2, or 3
(b) 2
(c) 0
(d) 3
(e) 0 or 2

If your student thinks a right triangle could have 3 equal sides, have them attempt to prove it by using a ruler to try to "cut off" a corner of a sheet of paper such that all three sides are the same length. The cut side will always be longer than the other two sides.

2

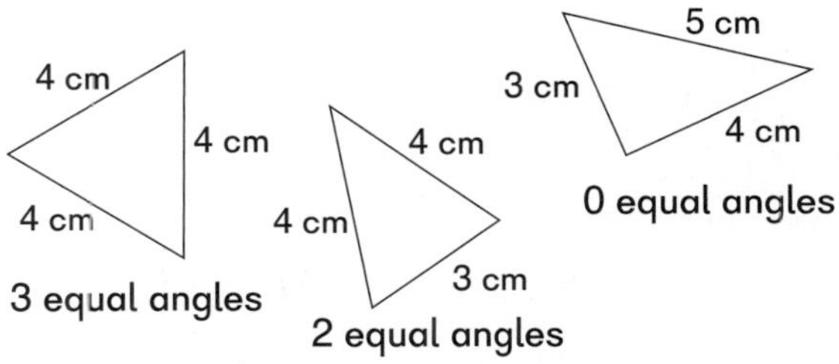

Chapter 12 Workbook Answers

3 Answers will vary. The interlocking circles allow for a greater variety of triangles. Examples:

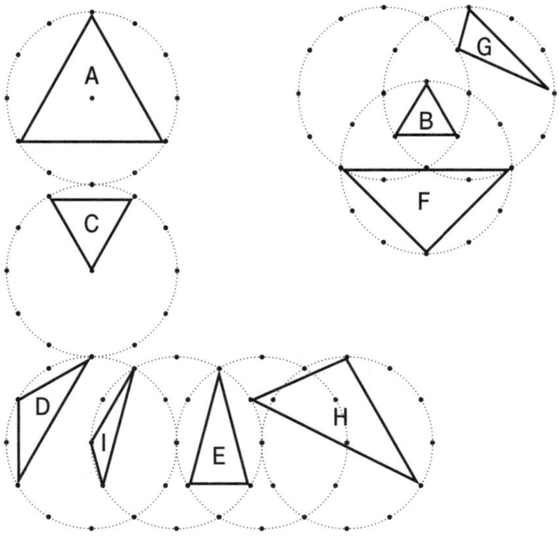

3 equal sides	Exactly 2 equal sides	0 equal sides
A, B, C	D, E, F	G, H, I

4 (a)

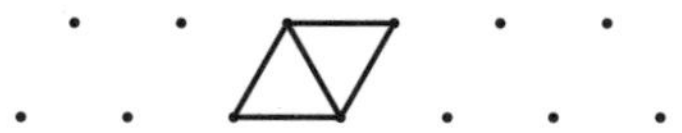

(b)

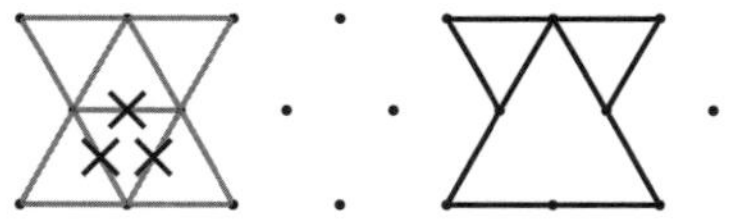

(c)

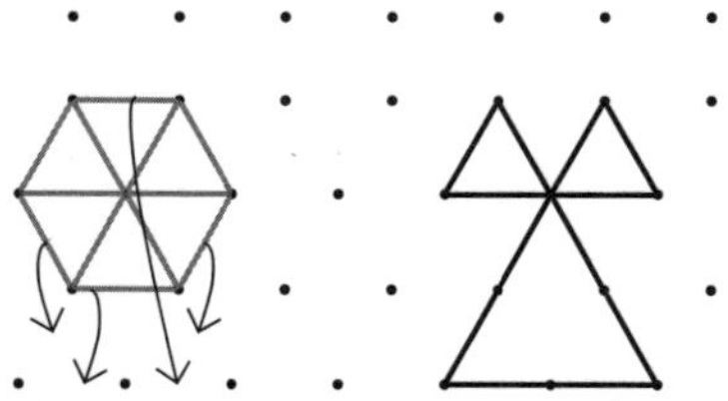

Exercise 6 pp. 130–133

1

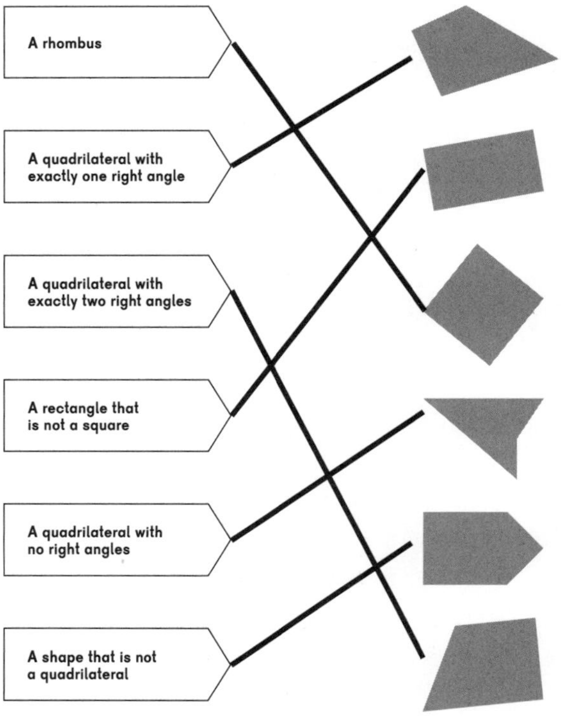

2

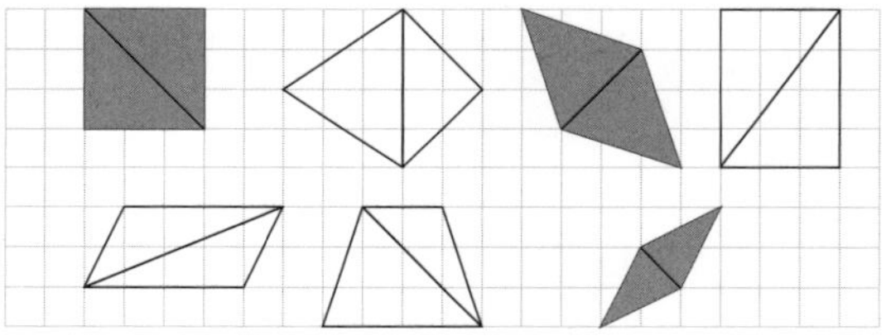

3 Answers will vary. Examples:

(a)

(b)

(c)

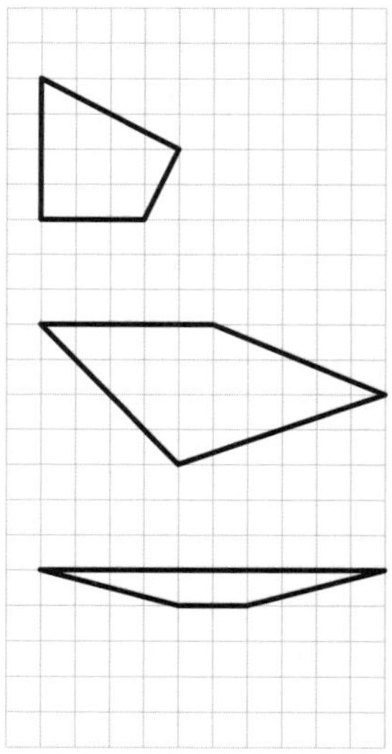

Chapter 12 Workbook Answers

4 Orientation can vary. Examples:

(a) 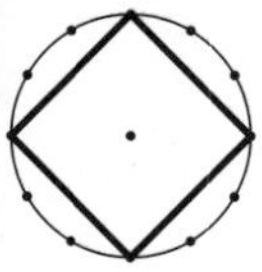

(b) 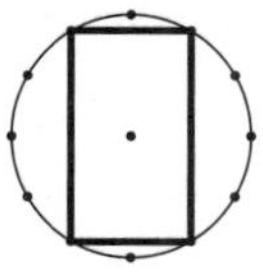

(c) Answers can vary. Examples:

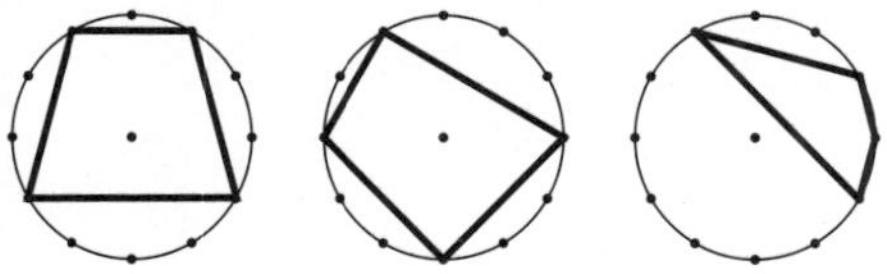

(d) 

(e) 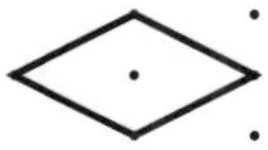

(f) 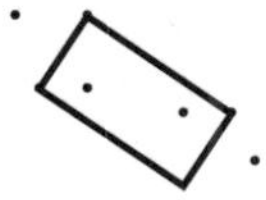

5 (a) 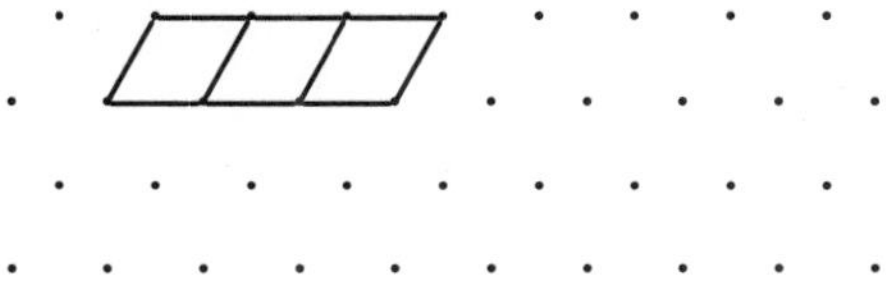

(b) 

(c) 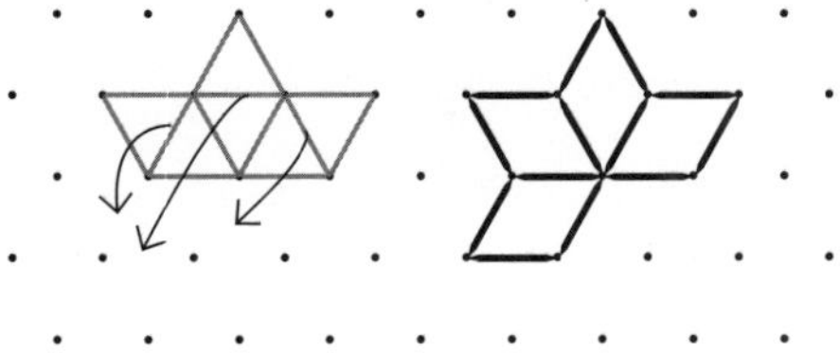

Exercise 7 pp. 134–138

1 Check drawings.

2 (a) 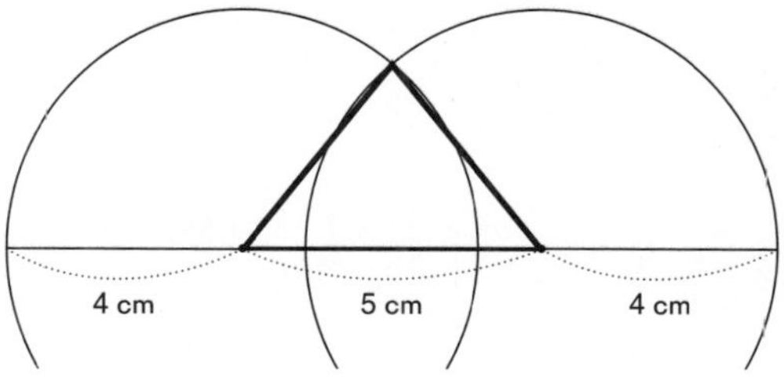

(b) 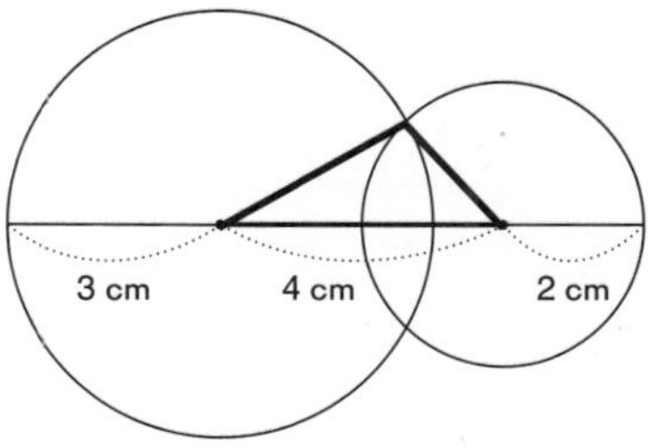

3 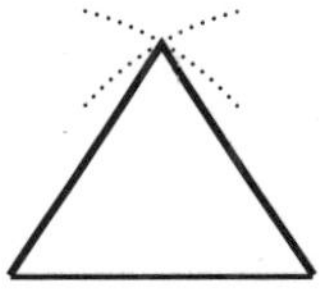

4 (a) 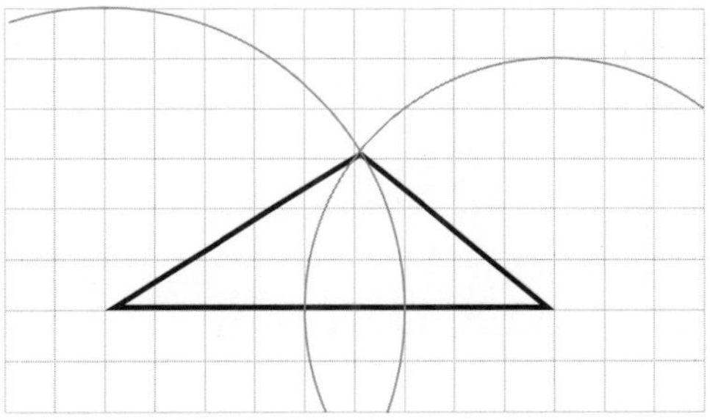

(b) 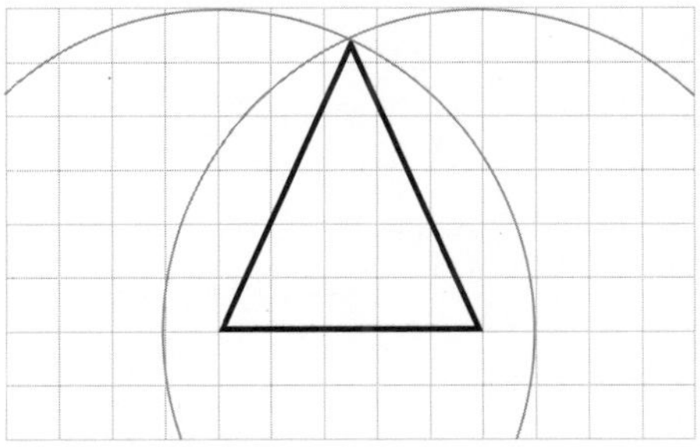

Chapter 12 Workbook Answers

5

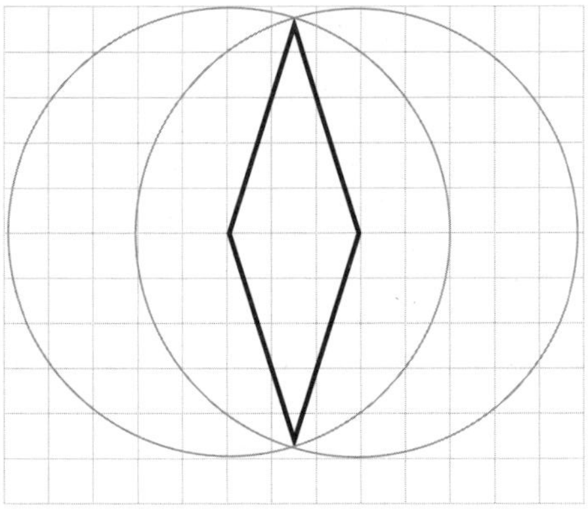

6 (a) Q, S, U

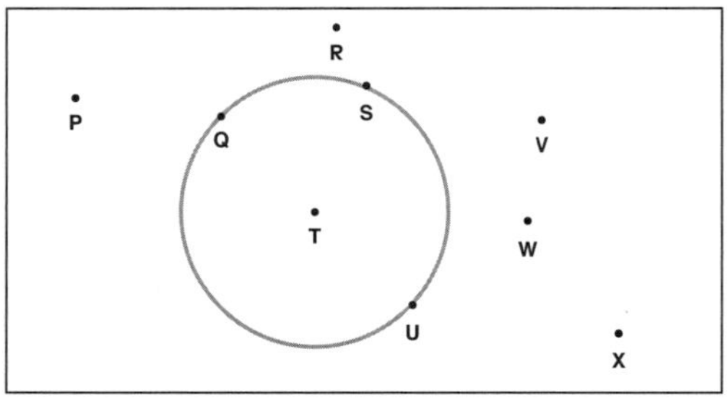

(b) R, U, X

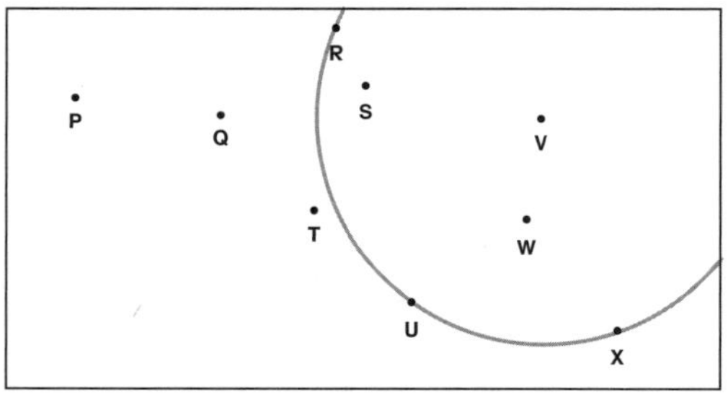

(c) P, W

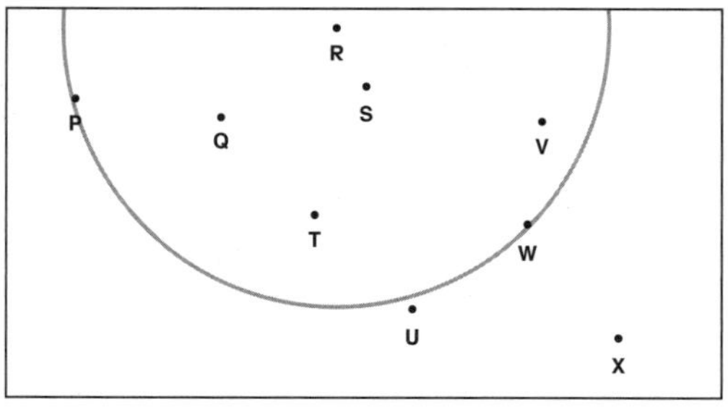

(d) U

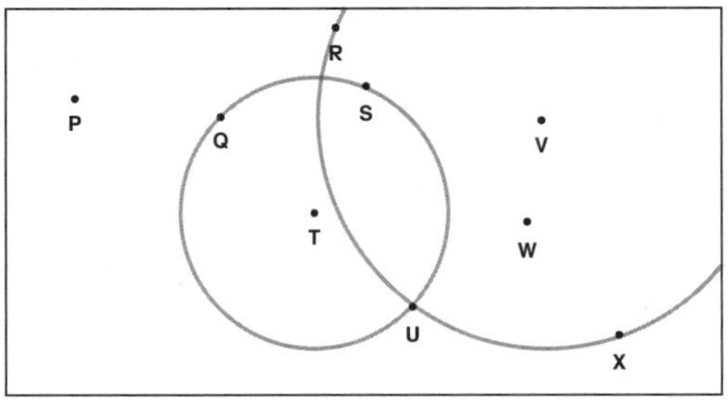

7 (a) 2 (b) 0

Exercise 8 pp. 139–142

1 **14 cm**

28 ÷ 2 = 14

2 **23 cm**

46 ÷ 2 = 23

3 (a)

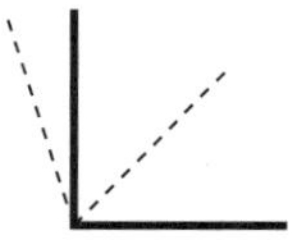

(b)

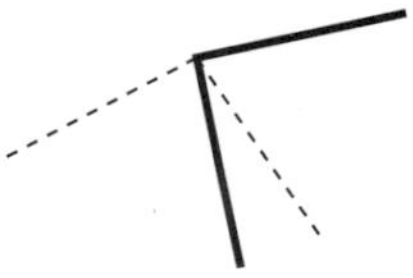

4 (a) True

(b) False

Example: A rhombus that does not have right angles

(c) True

(d) True

(e) False

Example: A rectangle

Chapter 12 Workbook Answers

5 (a)

	Sides	Angles	Angles smaller than a right angle	Right angles	Angles larger than a right angle
A	4	4	2	0	2
B	3	3	2	1	0
C	5	5	0	0	5
D	4	4	0	4	0
E	6	6	1	2	3
F	6	6	2	1	3
G	4	4	3	0	1
H	10	10	0	3	7

(b) A, D, G

(c) A, D

6 Answers can vary. Examples:

(a)

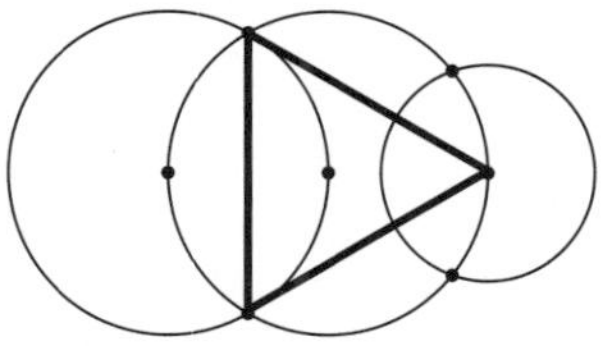

(b)

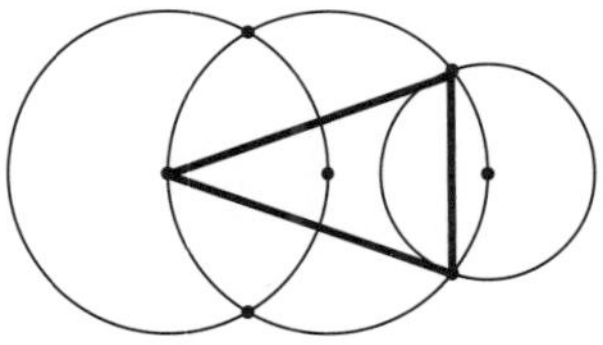

(c)

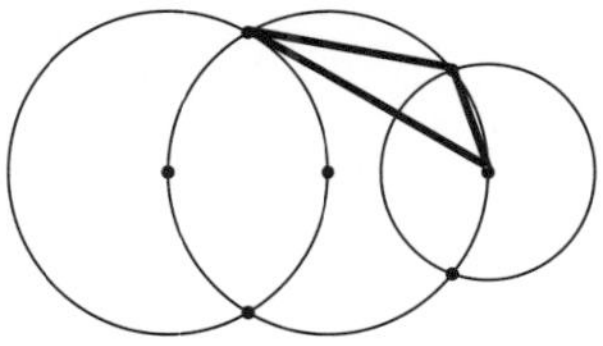

(d)

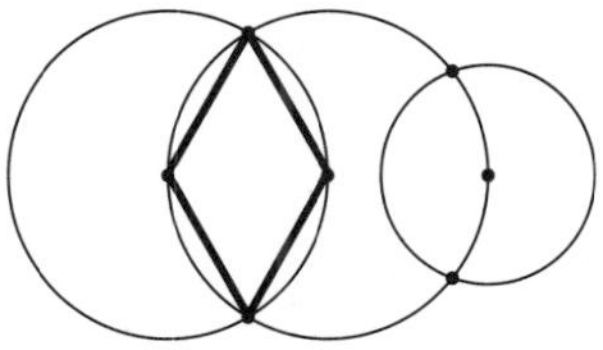

7 10 rectangles

Make sure your student understands that, in this case, position matters; a rectangle in a different position is to be considered a different rectangle.

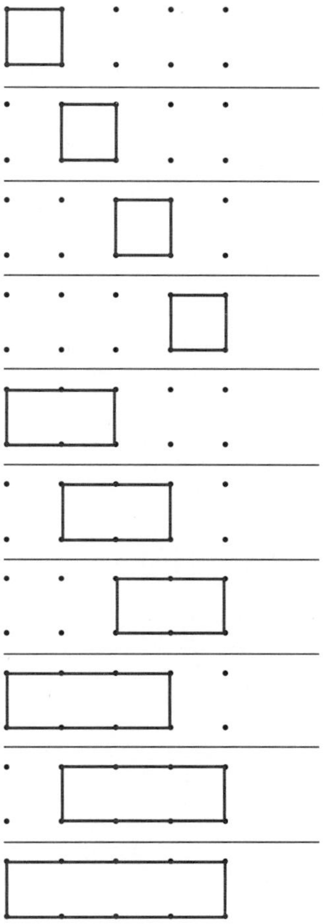

This problem is similar to problems students might see where they need to count the number of figures in a drawing. For example, there are 10 rectangles in the following figure:

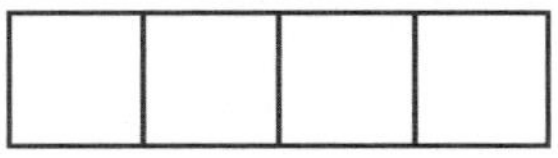

Chapter 12 Workbook Answers

8. 6 rhombuses

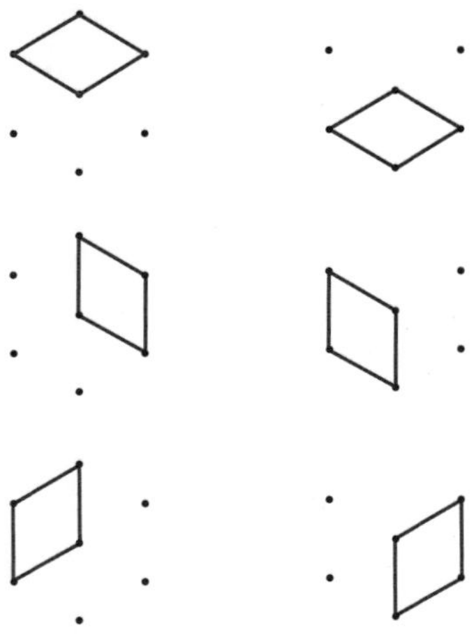

9.

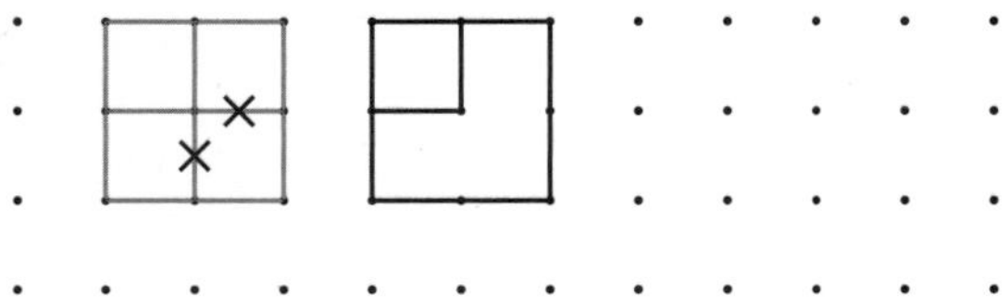

10.

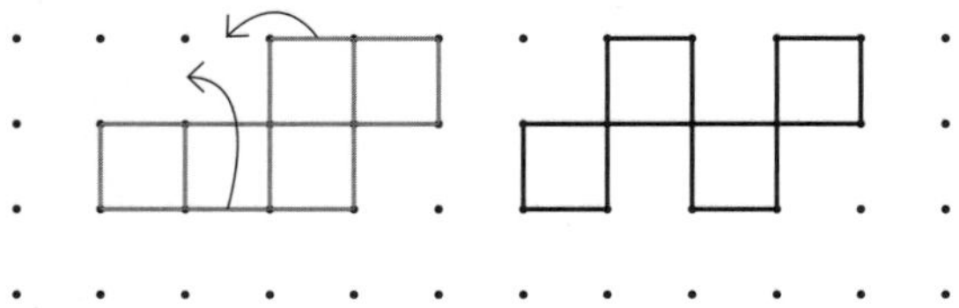

Chapter 13 Area and Perimeter

	Lesson	Page	Objectives
	Chapter Opener	131	
1	Area	132	Understand the meaning of area. Understand that area is measured in square units. Find and compare the areas of simple figures in square units by counting unit squares.
2	Units of Area	133	Find the area of figures in standard square units, such as square centimeters or square inches. Understand the use of the superscript in the abbreviation for square units, such as cm^2.
3	Area of Rectangles	134	Use multiplication to find the area of rectangles.
4	Area of Composite Figures	135	Find the area of composite shapes formed from rectangles.
5	Practice A	136	
6	Perimeter	137	Understand the meaning of perimeter. Find the perimeter of simple geometric figures by adding the length of each side.
7	Perimeter of Rectangles	138	Use multiplication as well as addition to find the perimeter of rectangles.
8	Area and Perimeter	139	Understand how perimeter changes when the area changes. Determine when figures have the same perimeter but different areas, or the same area but different perimeters.
9	Practice B	141	

Materials

Materials

- Ruler
- Toothpicks

Optional

- Centimeter cubes
- Dice
- One-inch square tiles

Printouts

(singaporemath.com/higprintouts)

- Area of Figures
- Centimeter Graph Paper
- Graph Paper
- Inch Graph Paper
- Lesson 13-1
- Pentominoes

Notes

Area

In this chapter, students will be formally introduced to the concept of area. Area is the amount of space inside a closed two-dimensional object, such as a polygon. At this level, students will learn that area is the "size of a closed surface" and that area is measured in square units. A square unit is a square with any unit length, such as centimeters or inches. Area can be measured in square centimeters, square inches, square meters, or square feet, for example. At this level, students will only find the area when it is a whole number of square units. Later, they will find the area where the number of square units is a fraction or a decimal.

Square units are abbreviated with the unit followed by a superscript 2, such as cm^2 or in^2. These units should be read as "square" followed by the name of the unit, and not as unit "squared." For example, "cm^2" is read as "square centimeters" and not as "centimeters squared". "Four square centimeters" is an area of 4 squares each 1 centimeter on the side, whereas "four centimeters squared" could be taken to mean a square 4 centimeters on the side.

Area of Rectilinear Figures

Students will learn to find the area of a rectangle by multiplying the length and the width together. Then they will find the area of composite figures made up of rectangles. These are figures with all right angles, which this guide will call "rectilinear" figures.

We can find the area of these figures either by splitting it into smaller rectangles and adding their areas, or by subtracting a "cut-out" or missing part from a larger rectangle. Being able to find the area using the second method will be useful in later levels for problems involving paths around a figure, which they will see in later levels. For example, the area of the shaded region in each of the figures below is the same, and can be found by subtracting the area of a smaller rectangle from a larger rectangle.

Perimeter

As early as Dimensions Math® 1A, students have found the distance around figures with straight sides. Here, they will learn that the distance around figures is called the perimeter. The term "perimeter" refers to both the boundary of a two-dimensional closed surface and the length of that boundary. They will also learn two ways to calculate the perimeter of rectangles, given the length and width. This can be used as an introduction to the distributive property which students will learn later. They can either multiply the length and width each by 2 and then add the products, or add the length and width and then multiply the sum by 2.

Students will learn that rectilinear figures with the same area can have different perimeters, and figures with the same perimeter can have different areas.

Activity

- After Lesson 1
  Materials: Graph paper (**Centimeter Graph Paper** printout), square tiles or cubes
  Purpose: Create shapes with the same area.
  Procedure: Have your students make as many shapes as possible by joining 5 squares edge to edge, and record them on the graph paper. There are 12 possible shapes, called pentominoes:

Your student can then cut them out, and see if they can fit them together to form a 3 by 10 rectangle, a 5 by 6 rectangle, and a 4 by 5 rectangle. There are several solutions for each. For more challenge, they could try to form a 6 by 10, 5 by 12, 4 by 15, or 3 by 20 rectangle. If they are interested, search online to find a variety of puzzles involving pentominoes

Games

- After Lesson 1
  Materials: **Pentominoes** printout (cut out the 12 pentomino shapes)
  Purpose: Spatial thinking.
  Goal: Be the last player to place a tile on the board.
  Procedure: Players take turns placing the pentominoes on the 16 by 16 board so that they do not overlap with existing tiles and no tile is used more than once.

- After Lesson 3 or 4
  Materials: Graph paper (**Graph Paper** printout or **Centimeter Graph Paper** printout), two dice, crayons
  Purpose: Draw rectangles or figures of a given area.
  Goal: Color the most area.
  Procedure: The more squares on the graph paper, the more turns possible. Players should each have a crayon or marker of a different color. Players take turns rolling the dice and drawing a rectangle with the dimensions given by the numbers rolled. For example, if they roll a 3 and a 4, they draw a 3 by 4 rectangle. The first player can draw their rectangle anywhere on the graph paper. The next player's rectangle has to touch the first player's rectangle on at least one side for at least one unit. When no more rectangles can be drawn, players add up their total area.
  Variation: Players can draw any rectilinear shape with the area given by the dice.

Chapter Opener (p. 155)

The purpose of this Chapter Opener is to get students to think about area and how it could be measured.

You can simply have your student look at the Chapter Opener and discuss it. Ask whether Alex's idea is a good one. It is not, since the children's sizes and how far apart they sit varies. In this case, Mei's suggestion works well, since one blanket is shorter in both length and width. It is therefore easy to compare them directly.

You can expand on the Chapter Opener by with an activity where it is not as easy to see which object has more "room." You could use towels or small blankets where where one is shorter but wider than the other. You could also use different hallways in the house, if you have two that are fairly similar in floor area. Have your student think of ways they could compare their sizes. You can ask them if they can think about the difficulties with determining the number of children that can sit on the blankets in the Chapter Opener and how they could fix those issues. They might think if "tiling" the space with something smaller that can be fit right next to each other, such as sheets of paper.

You can then continue to Lesson 1, where students compare a square and a rectangle under very controlled circumstances. The rectangle is longer than the square in one dimension but shorter in the other dimension by the same amount.

Lesson 1 Area (pp. 156 – 159)

Think (p. 156)

Use several copies of the **Lesson 13-1** printout and cut out the squares and rectangles.
Ask your student to find out which of the two shapes is larger. They may be able to just see that the purple square is larger, but they need to prove it. Let them use any method they want, including cutting up the shapes.

Learn (pp. 156–157)

Use two copies of the shapes on **Lesson 13-1** and cut out the squares and rectangles. Also use square one-inch tiles, or cut out squares using the **Inch Graph Paper** printout. Have your student do both of the methods for comparing the areas shown here (unless they already came up with one of the methods for Think). Both work easily in this case because the area of each figure is a whole number of square inches. When the two strips are cut out they are the same width.

Point out that length is a measurement in one direction along a straight line, while area is a measurement in two directions at right angles to each other. We measure area as the number of square units that cover the surface, with no gaps or overlaps.

Do (pp. 158–159)

❸ Students are introduced to the idea that the figure they are measuring does not have to be composed of whole squares. They can imagine the half squares being rearranged, count 1 whole for every two half squares, or count the total half squares and divide by 2.

Answers

25
24
The **square** has a greater area than the **rectangle**.

❶ (a) X: 9 square units
Y: 8 square units
Z: 6 square units
(b) X
(c) Z

❷ Each figure has the same area of 5 square units.

❸ 6 square units

❹ (a) K: 12 square units
L: 8 square units
M: 14 square units
N: 8 square units
O: 6 square units
P: 10 square units
Q: 9 square units
(b) M
(c) O
(d) L and N

Lesson 2 Units of Area (pp. 160 – 162)

Think (p. 160)

Have your student find the area of each figure and then answer the questions (without looking at the bottom of the page). If necessary, help them see that the triangle that cuts two squares in half has an area of 1 square centimeter. One way to see this is to imagine the part in one square flipped and rearranged to fit the part in the other square.

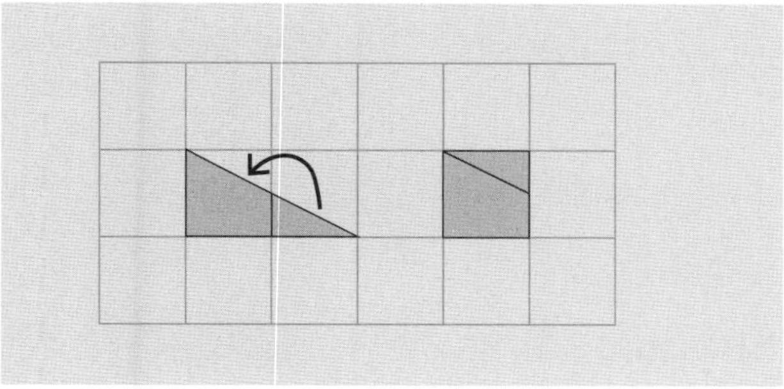

Another way is to simply see that two squares together are cut in half. Half of two squares is one square.

Learn (p. 160)

Here, students learn to write the abbreviation for square centimeters. Read cm^2 only as square centimeters, not centimeters squared.

This also shows a way of rearranging the squares to find the area for Figure D. Two halves of two squares is two squares.

Answers

B

C

A and D

❷ E: 6 cm^2 F: 2 cm^2 G: 5 cm^2
H: 4 cm^2 I: 6 cm^2 J: 6 cm^2
K: 5 cm^2 L: 5 cm^2 M: 7 cm^2
N: 9 cm^2 O: 7 cm^2

❸ 6 in^2

❹ 1 ft^2

❺ 1 m^2

Do (pp. 161–162)

❸ Students should realize that square units of any of the length units can be used as a unit to measure area.

❹ If you do not have four rulers, use strips of paper each 1 foot long. The floor area of rooms or walls are often measured in square feet. A typical car parking stall is about 200 ft^2.

❺ Since you are unlikely to have four meter sticks, you can mark out the area in a corner of the room, using two walls as two of the sides. (If you don't have a meter stick, use a ruler or tape measure to mark sides of 100 cm.) In most countries, square meters are used for measuring rooms, houses, blocks of land, and so on. A typical car parking space is about 18 m^2.

Lesson 3 Area of Rectangles (pp. 163 – 165)

Think (p. 163)

Use one-inch square tiles, or cut square inches from the **Inch Graph Paper** printout. Your student should find that the squares fit side by side with no overlap on the picture to make a 6 by 4 array, and might realize that they can find the total number using multiplication: either 6 × 4 or 4 × 6.

Answers

24
24

24
24

❶ (a) 12 by 1, 6 by 2, or 4 by 3
(b) 12 square units

❸ A: 36 cm^2 B: 15 in^2
C: 96 cm^2 D: 15 in^2
E: 16 ft^2 F: 180 m^2

Learn (p. 164)

To find the area of a rectangle, we find the product of the length and the width. The "formula" for area of a rectangle is often given as Area = Length × Width. Your student should have no trouble knowing that it does not matter which measurement (length or width) is considered as the number of groups; the answer will be the same.

Do (p. 165)

❸ Students should pay attention to the units. (They should understand that the scale is different for each figure. The size of E is not really the same as the size of A, for example.)

Extension

You can have your student measure and find the area of some square rooms in the house in square feet. Use a measuring tape to measure the sides. They will have to round the lengths to a whole number of feet.

Enrichment

You may want to discuss some other units of measurement for area. For example:

In the metric system:

- Square kilometer: a square with 1,000 meters on each side
- Are: a square with 10 meters on each side
- Hectare: a square with 100 meters on each side

In the U.S. customary system:

- Square yard: a square with 3 ft on each side
- Acre: 4,840 square yards
- Square mile: 640 acres

Lesson 4 Area of Composite Figures (pp. 166 – 169)

Think (p. 166)

Ask your student to come up with a method for finding the area that does not involve simply counting the squares but instead uses what they learned about calculating the area of a rectangle.

Answers

16	16
16	16
16	16

1. A: 30 cm^2 B: 16 cm^2
   C: 29 cm^2 D: 26 cm^2
2. (a) 22 in^2
   (b) 48 m^2
3. 9 in × 12 in = 108 in^2
   9 in × 5 in = 45 in^2
   108 in^2 + 45 in^2 = 153 in^2

   12 in + 5 in = 17 in
   17 in × 9 in = 153 in^2
4. The figure can be split into two rectangles with the same height. This makes it possible to cut and move parts, or double and flip the figure to get a rectangle.

Learn (p. 167)

Discuss the three methods that can be used to find the area of the figure. Students may be less likely to have used the third method in Think. Make sure your student understands it, since using it can make finding the area of some composite figures easier, and thinking in terms of subtracting a "missing part" to find the area of other figures will be useful in later levels.

Do (pp. 168–169)

1. Your student should not count squares. The grid is provided only so that it is easy to find the length of each side. Ask your student to write the equations they use to find the areas, and to show what rectangles they used. Because there are a variety of possible methods, only the answers are given here.

2. Students will need to find some unmarked lengths, whichever method they use, which they can find using subtraction. For example, in (a), they can subtract the length of the shorter side from the longer side opposite it to get the unmarked length.

3. Students should not have any difficulty with this problem. It is only here as a required informal introduction to the distributive property, which they have had plenty of informal experience with already. We can multiply to find the area of each rectangle separately then and add the areas together, or we can add find the total length of each side and then multiply to find the area.

4. This shows some alternate methods for the problem in Think. These only work in special circumstances.

Lesson 5 Practice A (pp. 170 – 171)

Enrichment

All the figures in this chapter are either rectilinear or composed of squares or parts of squares that can easily be combined into a whole. Area is measured in square units even if that area is not easily tiled with squares or half squares, or the edges are not straight lines.

Give your student the **Area of Figures** printout. The grid is made of 1-cm squares. Ask your student to estimate the area of the small figure in the upper right. They should imagine part of it cut out and rearranged and see that it would then cover about one square. Its area is about 1 cm^2. Then see if they can find the approximate area of the beech leaf-shaped figure to the right. They should count whole squares, and then think of ways combine the rest to make whole squares. They can then find the approximate area of the circle, and for more challenge, the maple leaf figure.

The beech leaf is about 18 cm^2, the circle is about 50 cm^2, and the maple leaf is about 47 cm^2. Any answer within perhaps 3 cm of these is acceptable.

If your student is still interested, you can give them the **Centimeter Graph Paper** printout and they can trace something else, such as their hand or foot, and find the approximate area of those tracings. They might also compare the size of their foot tracing to their hand tracing.

Answers

1 (a) R: 12 square units
S: 8 square units
T: 11 square units
U: 5 square units
V: 12 square units
W: 8 square units
X: 8 square units
Y: 11 square units
Z: 15 square units

(b) Z

(c) U

(d) S, W, and X
T and Y
R and V

2 (a) 160 cm^2
(b) 72 in^2
(c) 96 m^2

3 (a) 81 cm^2
(b) 49 cm^2
(c) 4 in^2

4 (a) 57 cm^2
(b) 125 cm^2

5 **334 ft^2**

Methods can vary.

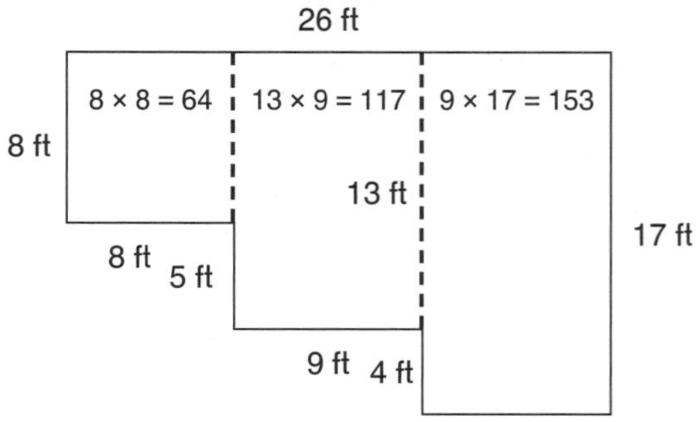

64 + 117 + 153 = 334

Lesson 6 Perimeter (pp. 172 – 174)

Think (p. 172)

Have your student read the question and find the answer. They will have to subtract to find the length of two unmarked sides, similar to what they had to do to find some unmarked sides when finding area in Lesson 4 and Practice 5. They should assume that the shape is formed from rectangles.

Answers

2

2

4 + 6 + 6 + 8 + **2** + **2** = **28**

28

28

1. Answers can vary.

2. A: 24 cm B: 18 cm
   C: 24 cm D: 12 cm
   E: 12 cm F: 24 cm

3. (a) 22 cm (b) 26 cm
   (c) 17 ft (d) 40 m

4. Methods can vary.

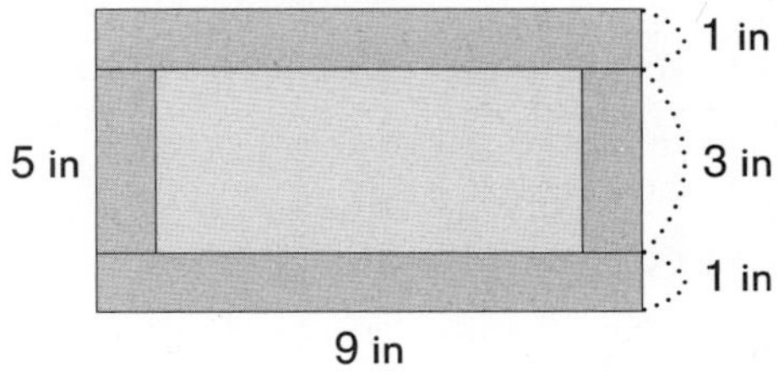

9 in + 9 in + 3 in + 3 in = 24 in

24 in

Learn (p. 172)

Students learn that the distance around a figure is called the "perimeter." You can tell your student that the prefix peri- means "around" and the suffix -meter means "measure." Another way to help them remember the meaning of the word is to point out the "rim" in peRIMeter. This is a measure of length, so the units of measure is the same as those used for length.

Do (pp. 173–174)

1. When forming the shapes, the edges of the square tiles should line up with each other. Ask your student to form at least 3 different shapes. Ask them for the area of each shape as well. They should realize that figures with the same area do not necessarily have the same perimeter.

2. Students can find the perimeter by either counting each length of 1 cm all the way around the figure, or by counting to find some of the side lengths and then mentally calculating the perimeter. For example, for E, they could count 3 for the sides of one of the arms, then multiply that by 4. For F, if they did Lesson 7 in Chapter 12, you could ask them to find the the unknown length using a compass and the background grid.

3. Students will have to find some unmarked lengths for (a) and (b). Additional strategies for finding the perimeter of rectilinear figures will be given in Dimensions Math® 4B.

4. Students need to take into account that there will be no overlap of the ribbon.

Lesson 7 Perimeter of Rectangles (pp. 175–176)

Think (p. 175)

If your student does not have an idea of how to use multiplication to calculate the perimeter, remind them that opposite sides on a rectangle are the same, and all four sides of a square are the same.

Learn (p. 175)

Discuss the two methods for finding the perimeter of the rectangle. The first method is to multiply each side by 2, then add the products together. The second method is to add the length of the sides, then multiply the sum by 2. There are fewer calculations with the second method. Using the first method can sometimes lead to easier calculations that can be done mentally.

Both methods can be used for squares, but it makes more sense to simply multiply one side by 4, as shown here.

Do (p. 176)

Students can use either method for the shapes that are not squares. You can ask them to write equations if you want. They should be careful not to confuse area and perimeter, pay attention to the units, and use the correct abbreviation for either the units of length or units of area.

Answers

28
28
28
28
24
24

1 (a) Perimeter: 52 cm
Area: 133 cm^2
(b) Perimeter: 42 ft
Area: 90 ft^2
(c) Perimeter: 36 in
Area: 80 in^2
(d) Perimeter: 44 m
Area: 117 m^2

2 (a) Perimeter: 40 m
Area: 100 m^2
(b) Perimeter: 32 ft
Area: 64 ft^2

3 **170 m**
56 m + 29 m = 85 m
2 × 85 m = 170 m

Enrichment

Ask your student if the perimeter of a rectangle (with sides of a whole number of units) can be an odd number. It cannot since there are always an even number of equal sides. Ask them under what circumstances the area of a rectangle would be odd. It would be odd if the length and width were both an odd number.

Lesson 8 Area and Perimeter (pp. 177–179)

Think (p. 177)

Give your student at least 12 toothpicks, or any other type of stick where they are all the same length. If you have enough, give them at least 36 toothpicks so they do not have to reuse them to create more rectangles. They will find that they can make 3 different rectangles. (A rectangle with the same dimensions but different orientation is not a different rectangle in this case.) They should know already that the perimeter of each is 12 units. They will find that the area of each is different.

Learn (p. 177)

This reiterates what students found in Think. Shapes can have the same perimeter but different areas. Have your student answer Mei's question and Dion's question. For rectangles with the same perimeter, the shape with the shortest width has the smallest area, and the shape with width and length the closest to each other will have the largest area.

Do (pp. 178–179)

❶ Students were asked to do something similar with tiles in ❶ of Lesson 6, and should already know that figures with the same area can have different perimeters. For rectangles with the same area, the one with the shortest width has the longest perimeter, and the one with width and length closest to each other has the shortest perimeter.

Answers

5
8
9

❶ Perimeter

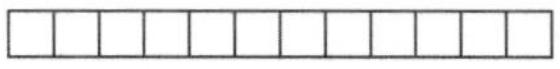
26 cm

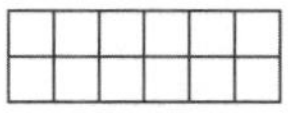
16 cm

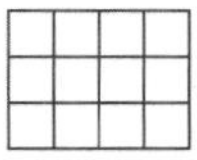
14 cm

(a) 26 cm
(b) 14 cm

❷

	Perimeter	Area
J	14 cm	10 cm²
K	18 cm	10 cm²
L	14 cm	9 cm²
M	14 cm	9 cm²
N	18 cm	8 cm²
O	16 cm	10 cm²

(a) J, K, O
(b) K and N
J and L
J and M
(c) L, M

❸ A: Perimeter: 34 m
Area: 60 m²
B: Perimeter: 32 m
Area: 63 m²
Garden B has a greater area and shorter perimeter.

❹ Students may simply state that in (a) the area decreases but the perimeter stays the same, whereas in (b) the area decreases but the perimeter increases, which is an adequate conclusion at this level. More capable students may see from this problem a "short-cut" method of finding the perimeter when a piece is "cut out" of a corner, or already know it if they did Challenge in Workbook Exercise 6.

Answers (continued)

❹ (a)

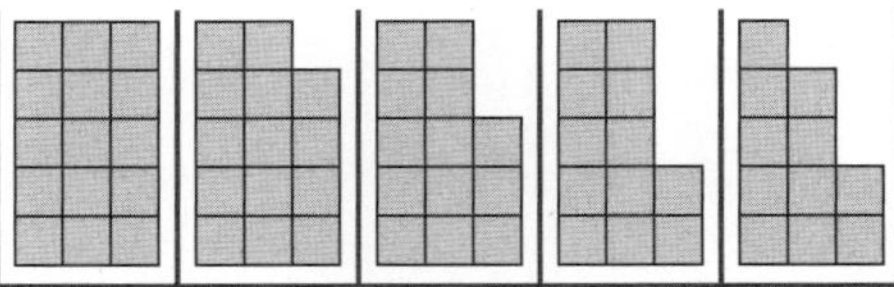

Area (units^2)	15	14	13	12	11
Perimeter (units)	16	16	16	16	16

(b)

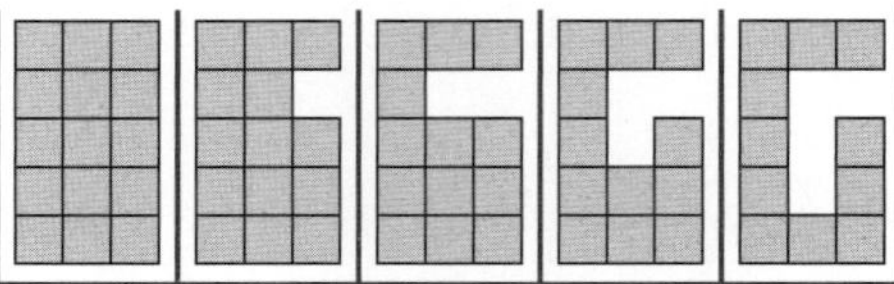

Area (units^2)	15	14	13	12	11
Perimeter (units)	16	18	20	22	24

Removing a square from a corner does not change the perimeter. Removing a square from a side adds 2 units to the perimeter

Practice B (pp. 180–182)

3 Methods can vary. Here is a possible method for each.

(a)

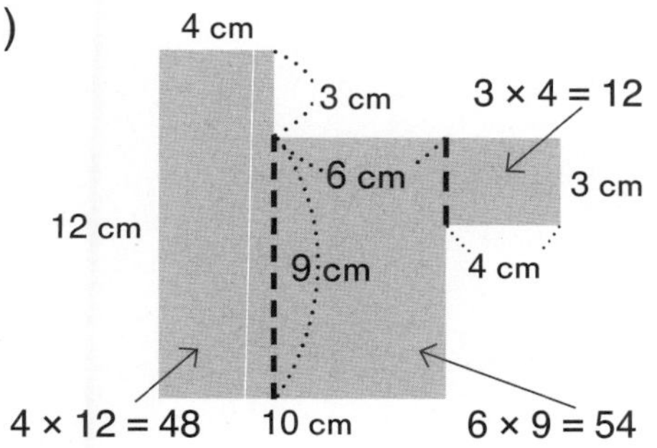

Area: 48 + 12 + 54 = 114; 114 cm^2

Perimeter:

4 + 3 + 6 + 4 + 3 + 4 + 6 + 10 + 12 = 52

52 cm

(b)

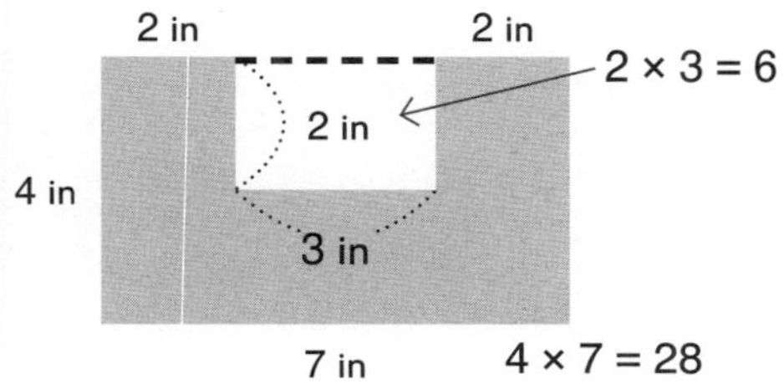

Area: 28 − 6 = 22; 22 in^2

Perimeter:

2 + 2 + 3 + 2 + 2 + 4 + 7 + 4 = 26: 26 in

(c)

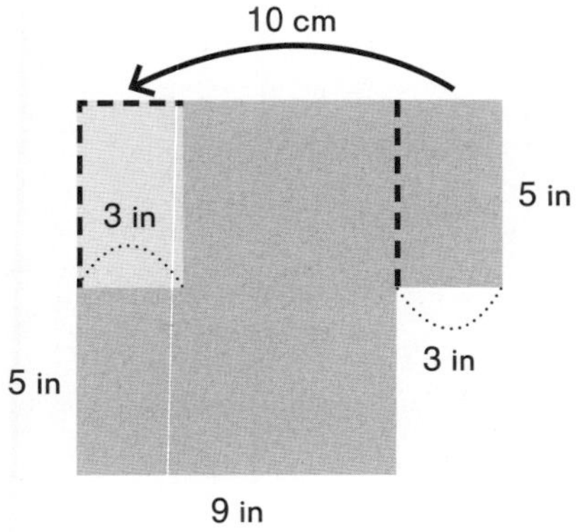

Area: 10 × 9 = 90; 90 in^2

Perimeter:

9 + 9 + 5 + 5 + 5 + 5 + 3 + 3 = 44; 44 in

Answers

1 (a) 25 m (b) 72 in
(c) 96 in (d) 126 cm

2 (a) Area: 126 cm^2 Perimeter: 54 cm
(b) Area: 88 m^2 Perimeter: 38 m
(c) Area: 81 ft^2 Perimeter: 36 ft

3 (a) Area: 114 cm^2 Perimeter: 52 cm
(b) Area: 22 in^2 Perimeter: 26 in
(c) Area: 90 in^2 Perimeter: 44 in

4 **1,040 ft**

360 + 160 = 520

520 × 2 = 1,040

5

	Perimeter	Area
P	16 cm	10 cm^2
Q	16 cm	9 cm^2
R	18 cm	10 cm^2
S	20 cm	13 cm^2
T	14 cm	8 cm^2

(a) T
(b) S
(c) S
(d) T
(e) P and Q
(f) P and R

Chapter 13 Workbook Answers

Exercise 1 pp. 143–145

1. (a) J: 12 K: 9
   L: 10 M: 9
   N: 7 O: 8
   (b) J
   (c) N
   (d) K and M

2. Drawings can vary. Examples:

   (a)
   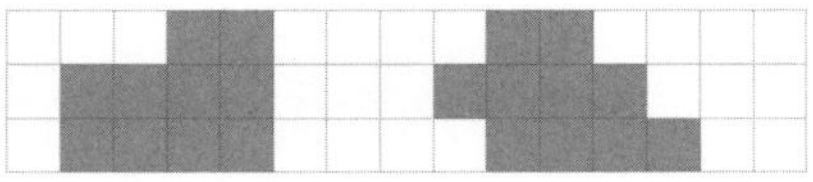

   (b)
   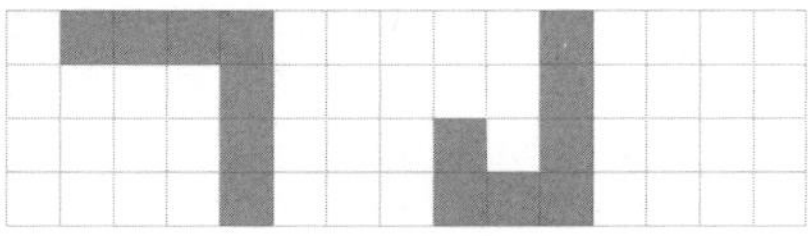

   (c)
   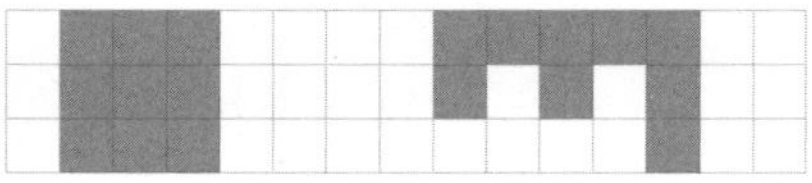

3. Drawings can vary. Example:

   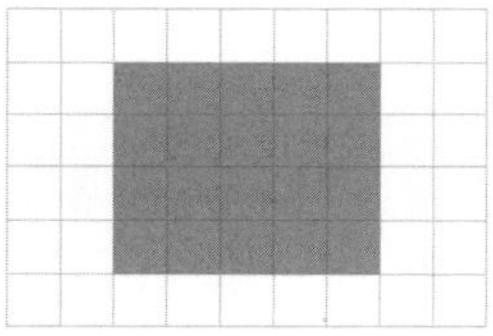

4. Drawings can vary. Example:

   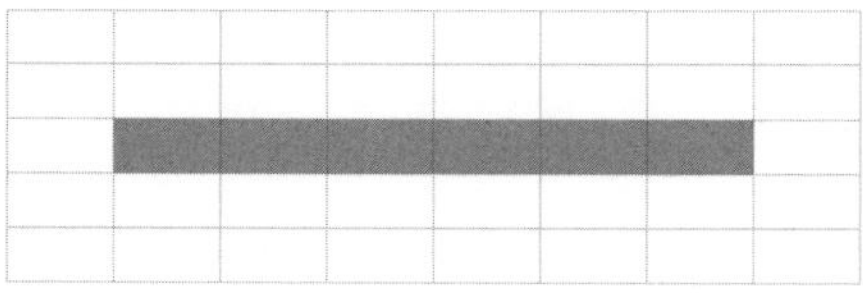

   Students should understand that they can compare the area of objects even if they cannot find square units, as long as they can use units that are the same area.

5. Drawings can vary. Example:

   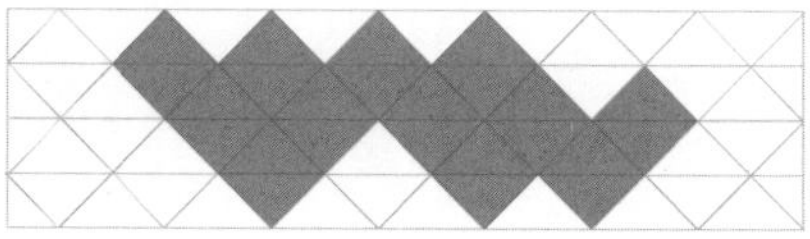

6. Answers can vary by several square units.
   15 20

Exercise 2 pp. 146–149

1. (a) P: 8 Q: 7
   R: 8 S: 8
   T: 18 U: 6
   (b) T
   (c) U
   (d) P, R, S

2. Drawings can vary. Examples:

   (a) 18 cm²
   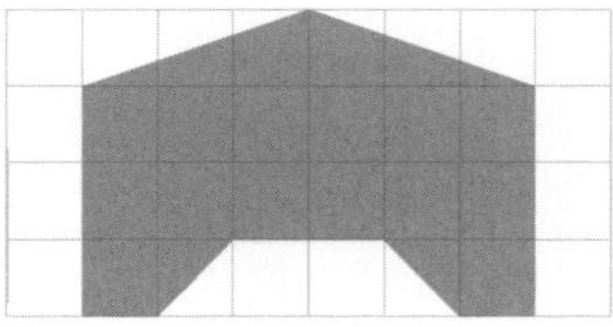

   (b) 10 cm²
   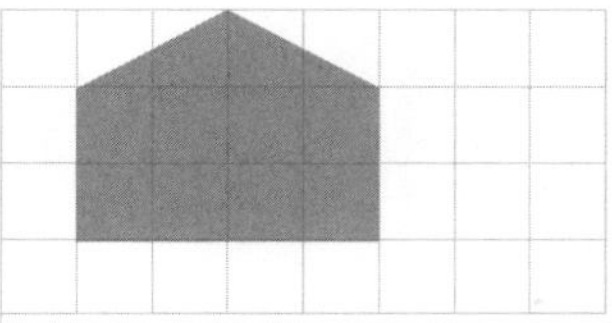

   (c) 10 cm²
   (13 cm²)
   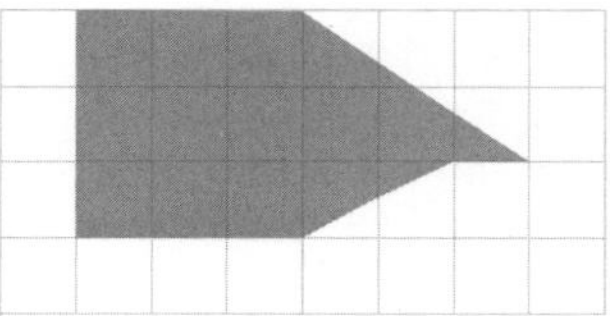

   (d) 4 cm²
   (10 cm²)
   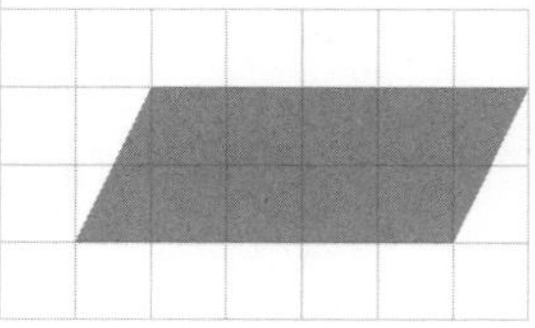

   (e) 14 cm²
   (12 cm²)
   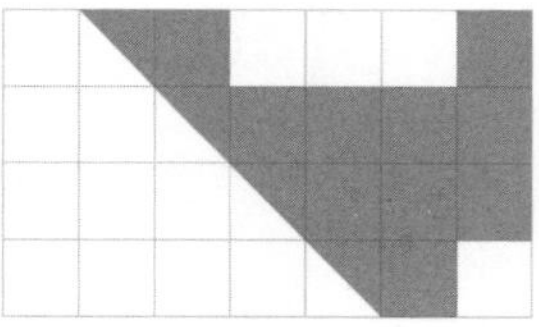

   (f) 22 cm²
   (17 cm²)
   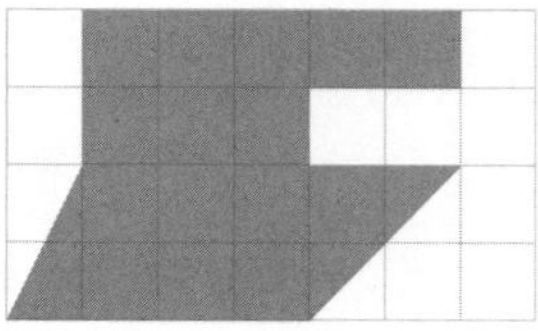

Chapter 13 Workbook Answers

3. 5 in²

4. (a) ft²
   (b) in²
   (c) m²

5. Methods can vary.
   (a) 2 cm²

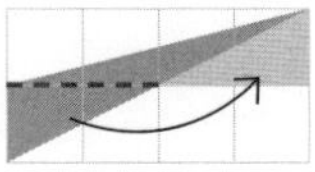

   (b) 4 cm²

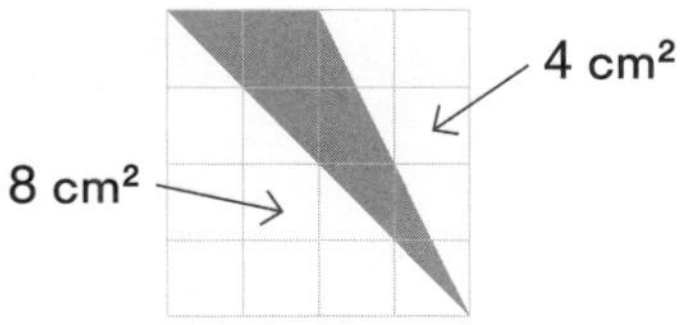

Total: 16 cm²

16 − 8 − 4 = 4

Exercise 3 pp. 150–152

1. (a) 3 × 4 = 12
   4 × 3 = 12
   12
   (b) 5 × 6 = 30 or 6 × 5 = 30
   30
   (c) 16
   (d) 12

2.

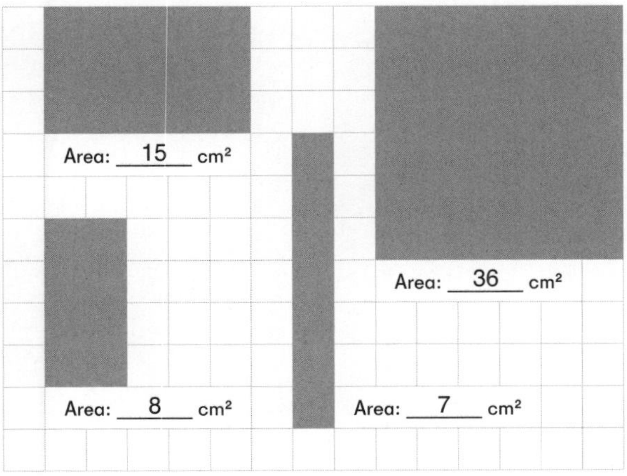

3. (a) 9 cm² (b) 28 cm²

4. (a) 135 m² (b) 84 in²

5. (a) 1 cm and 24 cm
   2 cm and 12 cm
   3 cm and 8 cm
   4 cm and 6 cm
   (b) 1 cm and 27 cm
   3 cm and 9 cm

6. **60 cm²**
   5 × 3 = 15 (squares)
   2 cm × 2 cm = 4 cm²
   15 × 4 cm² = 60 cm²
   or:
   5 × 2 cm = 10 cm
   3 × 2 cm = 6 cm
   10 cm × 6 cm = 60 cm²

7. **60 cm²**
   2 cm × 3 cm = 6 cm²
   10 × 6 cm² = 60 cm²
   or:
   3 + 3 + 2 + 2 + 2 = 12 (length)
   2 + 3 = 5 (width)
   12 cm × 5 cm = 60 cm²

Exercise 4 pp. 153–156

1. (a) **97**
   8 cm × 9 cm = 72 cm²
   5 cm × 5 cm = 25 cm²
   72 cm² + 25 cm² = 97 cm²
   (b) **47**
   8 cm × 9 cm = 72 cm²
   5 cm × 5 cm = 25 cm²
   72 cm² − 25 cm² = 47 cm²
   (c) **120**
   8 cm × 5 cm = 40 cm²
   3 × 40 cm² = 120 cm²

Chapter 13 Workbook Answers

2 Methods can vary. Measurements are shown here.

(a)

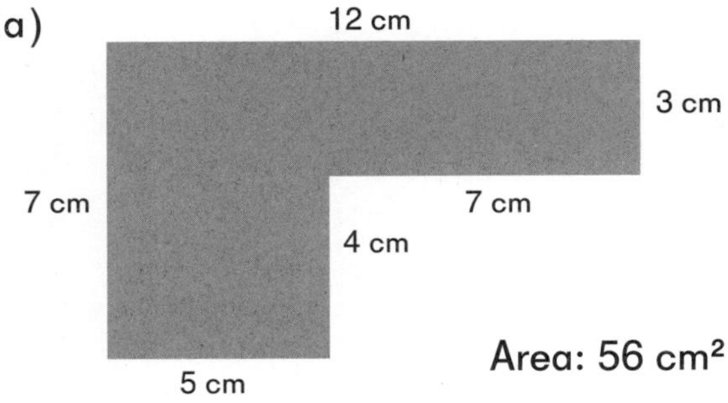

Area: 56 cm^2

(b)

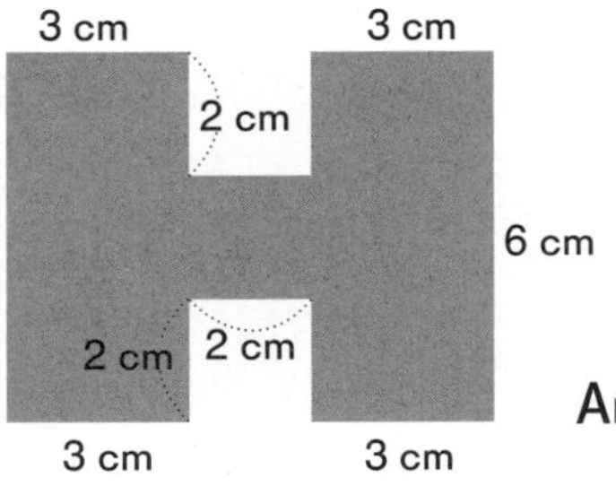

Area: 40 cm^2

(c)

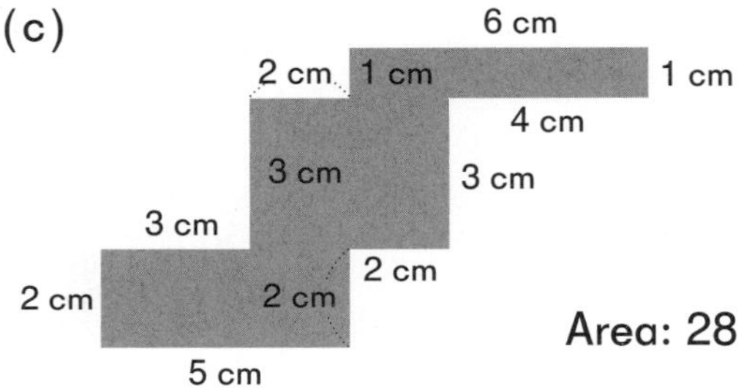

Area: 28 cm^2

3 (a) 8 × 5 = 40
8 × 8 = **64**
40 + **64** = **104**

(b) 8 + 5 = **13**
8 × **13** = **104**
104

4 Methods can vary. Examples:

(a) **42 square units**
8 units × 9 units = 72 $units^2$
6 units × 5 units = 30 $units^2$
72 $units^2$ – 30 $units^2$ = 42 $units^2$

(b) **48 square units**
8 units × 8 units = 64 $units^2$
2 units × 2 units = 4 $units^2$
4 × 4 $units^2$ = 16 $units^2$
64 $units^2$ – 16 $units^2$ = 48 $units^2$

5 **113 square units**
Method can vary. Example:
Total length: 15 + 5 = 20
Unlabeled width of smallest cut-out:
20 – 9 – 2 – 3 – 3 = 3
Area of a large rectangle:
20 × 8 = 160
Areas of cut-out rectangles:
4 × 5 = 20
5 × 3 = 15
4 × 3 = 12
Area of figure:
160 – 20 – 15 – 12 = 113

6 (a) **31 square units**

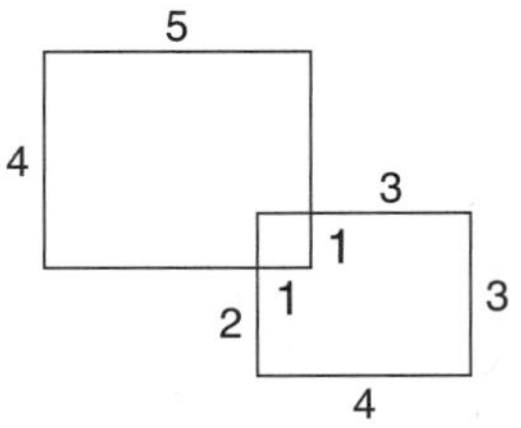

Add the areas of the two overlapping rectangles and subtract the area of the overlap.
5 × 4 = 20
4 × 3 = 12
20 + 12 – 1 = 31

(b) **35 square units**

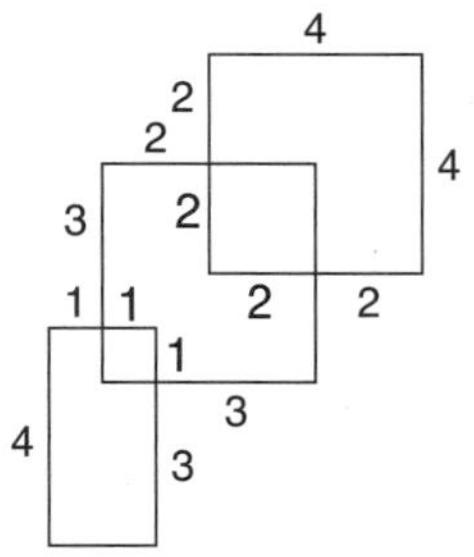

16 + 16 + 8 – 4 – 1 = 35

Chapter 13 Workbook Answers

Exercise 5 pp. 157–160

1. Drawing can vary. Example:

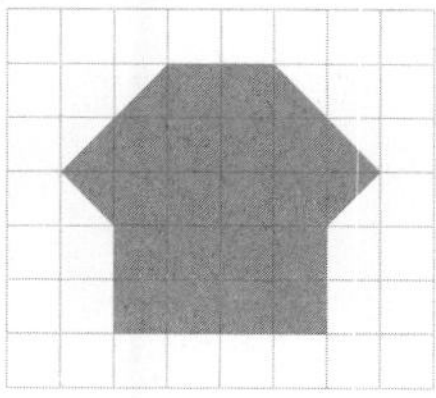

2. Drawings can vary. Examples:

(a)

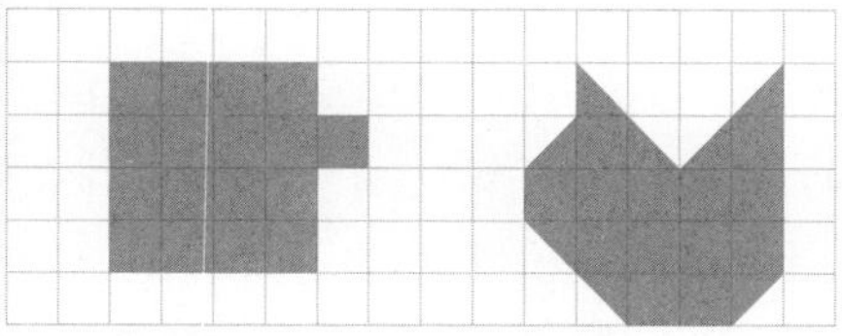

(b)

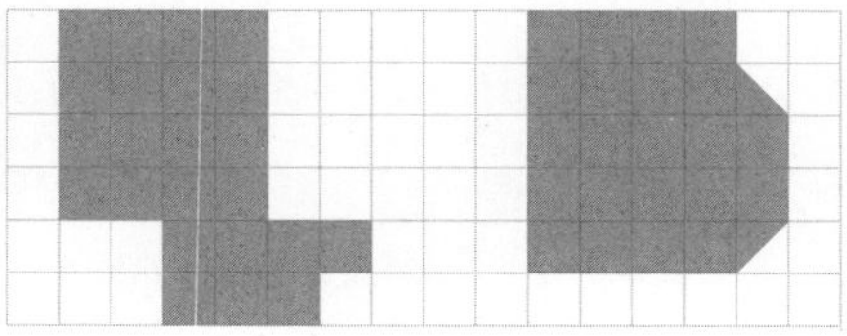

3. **31 cm^2**

Drawing can vary. Example:

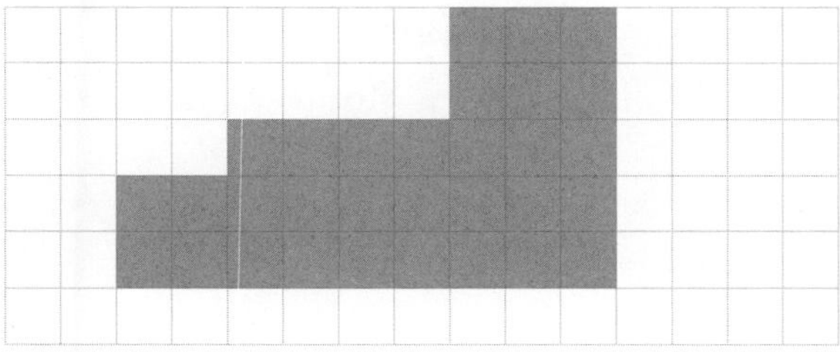

4. Possible rectangles:
1 cm by 16 cm
2 cm by 8 cm
4 cm by 4 cm

5. **256 cm^2**
$32 \text{ cm} \times 8 \text{ cm} = 256 \text{ cm}^2$

6. **48 ft^2**
$3 \times 4 \text{ ft} = 12 \text{ ft}$ (length)
$4 \text{ ft} \times 12 \text{ ft} = 48 \text{ ft}^2$

7. **486 cm^2**
$54 \text{ cm} \div 6 = 9 \text{ cm}$ (width)
$54 \text{ cm} \times 9 \text{ cm} = 486 \text{ cm}^2$

8. **27 cm^2**
$3 \text{ cm} \times 3 \text{ cm} = 9 \text{ cm}^2$
$36 \text{ cm}^2 - 9 \text{ cm}^2 = 27 \text{ cm}^2$

9. **$1,656**
Method for finding area can vary.
$9 \text{ ft} - 6 \text{ ft} = 3 \text{ ft}$ (one of the side lengths)
$27 \text{ ft} - 15 \text{ ft} = 12 \text{ ft}$ (another side length)
$27 \text{ ft} \times 9 \text{ ft} = 243 \text{ ft}^2$
$3 \text{ ft} \times 12 \text{ ft} = 36 \text{ ft}^2$
$243 \text{ ft}^2 - 36 \text{ ft}^2 = 207 \text{ ft}^2$
$207 \times \$8 = \$1,656$

10. **160 cm^2**
Area of each square: 100 cm^2
Area of overlap: 40 cm^2
$100 \text{ cm}^2 + 100 \text{ cm}^2 - 40 \text{ cm}^2 = 160 \text{ cm}^2$
or:
Length: $10 \text{ cm} + 10 \text{ cm} - 4 \text{ cm} = 16 \text{ cm}$
$16 \text{ cm} \times 10 \text{ cm} = 160 \text{ cm}^2$

11. **6 cm**
Students can build on the concepts from the previous problem.
Areas: 90 cm^2 and 108 cm^2
$108 \text{ cm}^2 + 90 \text{ cm}^2 = 198 \text{ cm}^2$
$198 \text{ cm}^2 - 144 \text{ cm}^2 = 54 \text{ cm}^2$ (overlap)
$54 \text{ cm}^2 \div 9 \text{ cm} = 6 \text{ cm}$
or:
$144 \text{ cm}^2 \div 9 \text{ cm} = 16 \text{ cm}$
$10 \text{ cm} + 12 \text{ cm} = 22 \text{ cm}$
$22 \text{ cm} - 16 \text{ cm} = 6 \text{ cm}$

12 **21 tiles**

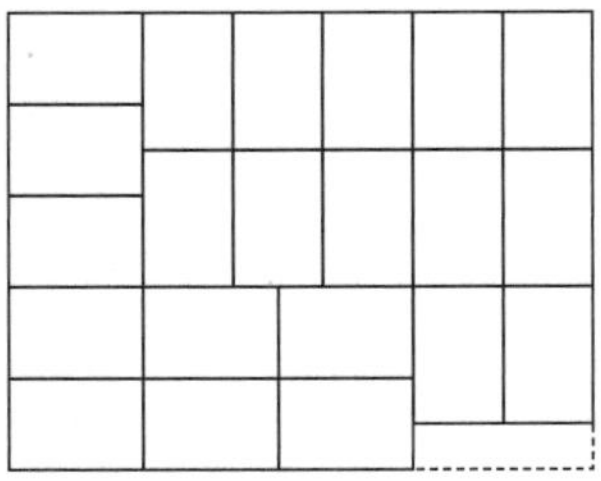

Students can try different ways of arranging the tiles by drawing on graph paper, or cutting out tiles and arranging them. The entire cardboard cannot be covered. Other arrangements are possible.

Exercise 6 pp. 161–163

1 15

15

2 (a)

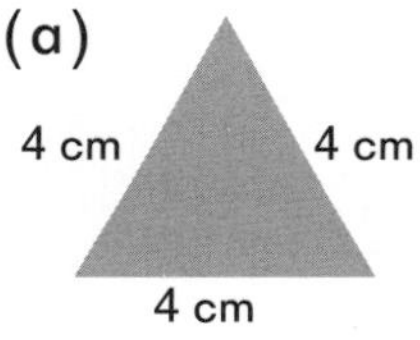

Perimeter: 12 cm

(b)

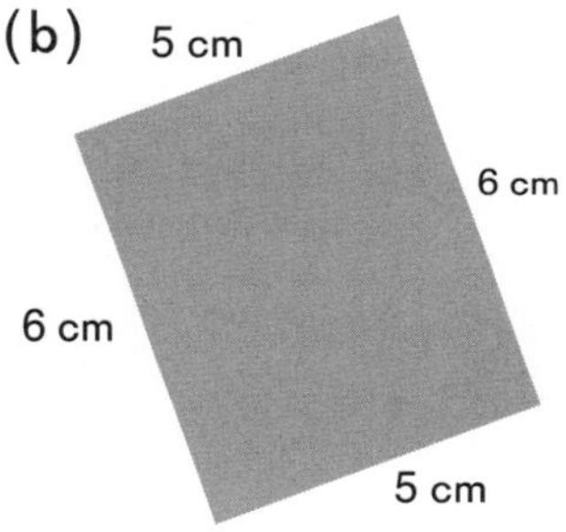

Perimeter: 22 cm

(c)

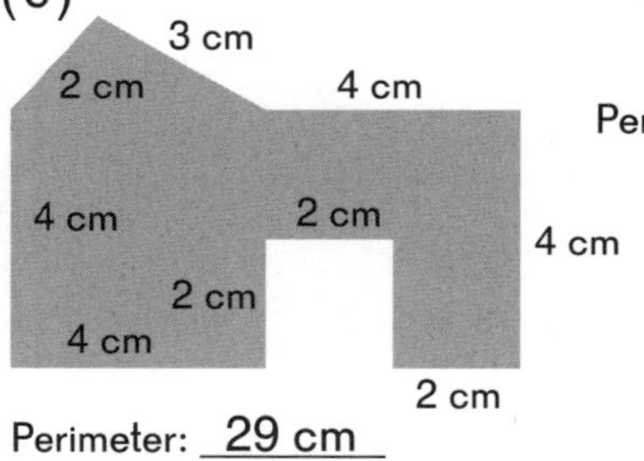

Perimeter: 29 cm

3 (a) 18 units (b) 25 units

(c) 74 units

(This is the same figure as for **5** of Exercise 4.)

4 **72 cm**

6×12 cm = 72 cm

5 **112 cm**

84 cm ÷ 3 = 28 cm

4×28 cm = 112 cm

6 If necessary, suggest to your student that they think about making a larger rectangle for both. The sides can be "pushed" out to form a rectangle. They will formally learn this strategy in Dimensions Math® 4B, but if your student is capable of understanding it now, it will simplify calculations for perimeter considerably. If the shape could be formed by cutting out a rectangle from the corner of a larger rectangle, we can imagine some of the sides pushed out to form the larger rectangle. This does not change the perimeter, and we can simply find the perimeter as if the figure were a rectangle.

(a)

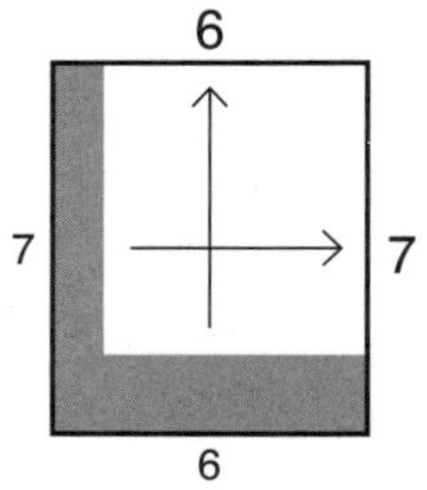

Perimeter: 26 units

(b)

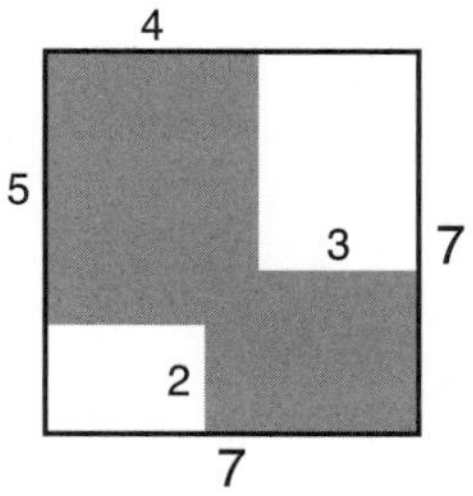

Perimeter: 28 units

Chapter 13 Workbook Answers

Exercise 7 pp. 164–166

1. (a) 28
   (b) 5 × 2 = **10**
   18 + **10** = **28**
   28

2. 4 × **7** = **28**
   28

3. (a) 16 units (b) 14 units

4. (a) 24 units (b) 16 units

5. **46 m**
   15 m + 8 m = 23 m
   2 × 23 m = 46 m

6. **72 cm**
   4 × 18 cm = 72 cm

7. **10 cm**
   40 cm ÷ 4 = 10 cm

8. **7 cm**
   Sum of the length and the width:
   30 cm ÷ 2 = 15 cm
   Length of the other side.
   15 cm − 8 cm = 7 cm

9. **16 cm**
   Length of one side of the larger square:
   32 cm ÷ 4 = 8 cm
   Length of one side of smaller squares:
   8 cm ÷ 2 = 4 cm
   Perimeter of small square:
   4 cm × 4 = 16 cm

Exercise 8 pp. 167–169

1.

	Perimeter	Area
K	30 units	26 units^2
L	24 units	23 units^2
M	32 units	28 units^2
N	26 units	30 units^2
O	26 units	30 units^2
P	24 units	26 units^2

   (a) K and P
   (b) L and P
   (c) N and O

2. Drawings will vary. Possible areas:
   7 square units
   12 square units
   15 square units
   16 square units

3. (a)
   (b)
   (c)

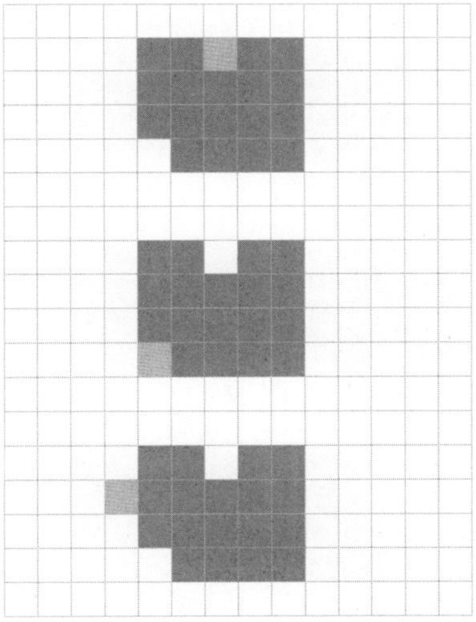

Answers may vary for (c): shade any square around the perimeter except those shaded in (a) and (b).

Chapter 13 Workbook Answers

4 Drawings can vary. Examples:

(a)

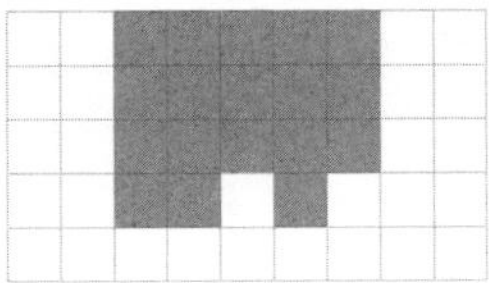

(b)

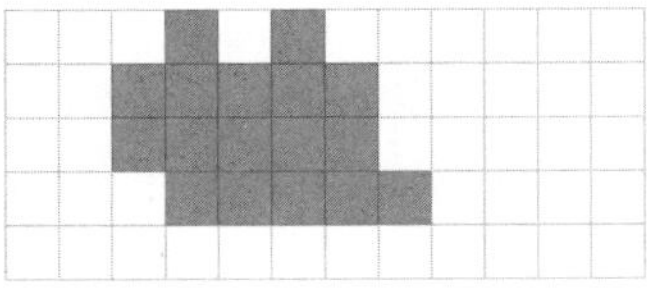

5

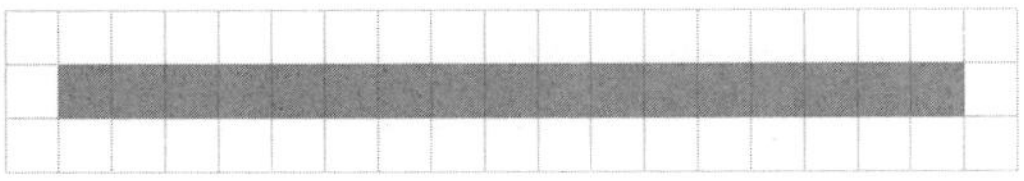

Exercise 9 pp. 170–172

1

	Area	Perimeter
A	32 units²	24 units
B	36 units²	24 units
C	120 units²	56 units
D	163 units²	68 units
E	140 units²	66units

2 **Area: 144 cm²**

Perimeter: 50 cm

16 cm × 9 cm = 144 cm²

16 cm + 9 cm = 25 cm

2 × 25 cm = 50 cm

3 **15 units**

Radius: 3 units

5 × 3 units = 15 units

4 Drawings can vary. Example:

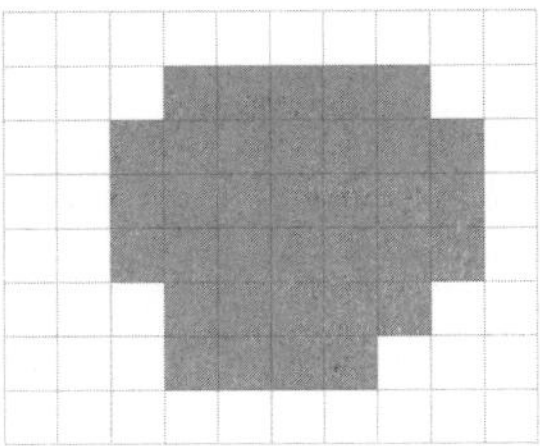

5 **36 cm²**

Length of one side of the smaller square:

12 cm ÷ 4 = 3 cm

Length of one side of larger square:

3 cm + 3 cm = 6 cm

Area of larger square:

6 cm × 6 cm = 36 cm²

6 **48 cm**

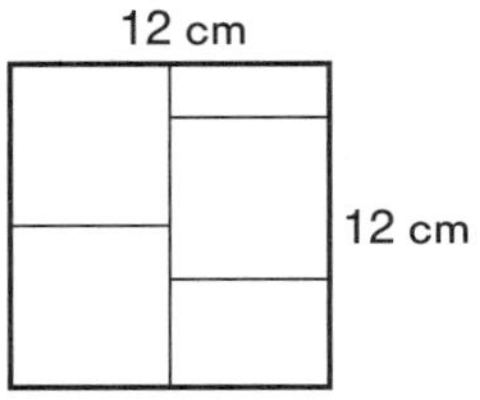

12 cm × 4 = 48 cm

7 **Perimeter: 34 cm**

Area: 52 cm²

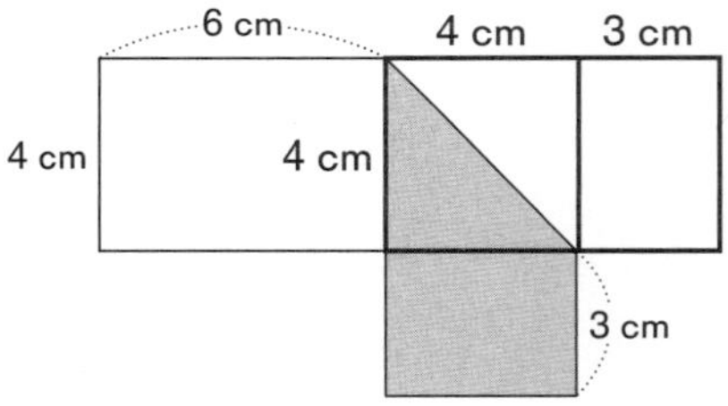

13 cm + 4 cm = 17 cm

2 × 17 cm = 34 cm

13 cm × 4 cm = 52 cm²

Chapter 14 Time

	Lesson	Page	Objectives
	Chapter Opener	153	
1	Units of Time	154	Understand the second as a unit of time. Review telling time on an analog clock. Review the meaning of a.m. and p.m. Convert between minutes or seconds and compound units of hours and minutes or minutes and seconds.
2	Calculating Time — Part 1	156	Calculate elapsed time within a.m. or p.m. Calculate end time given start time and elapsed time, within a.m. or p.m. Add time using mental math strategies for "making 60."
3	Practice A	158	
4	Calculating Time — Part 2	159	Calculate elapsed time or end time when time changes from a.m. to p.m. or p.m. to a.m.
5	Calculating Time — Part 3	161	Subtract periods of time within a.m. or p.m.
6	Calculating Time — Part 4	162	Subtract periods of time when the time crosses noon or midnight.
7	Practice B	164	

Materials

Materials

- Analog demonstration clock with geared hands
- Stopwatch or timer

Mental Math Sheets

(singaporemath.com/higprintouts)

Mental Math		After Lesson
24	Subtract minutes from 1 hour	1
25	Add time in compound units	2
26	Convert between 12-hour clock and 24-hour clock	3 (enrichment)
27	Subtract time in compound units	5
28	Add and subtract time in compound units	5

Notes

Telling Time

In Dimensions Math® 2B, students learned to tell time to the one-minute mark on an analog clock (clock face), and to read and write the digital representation of time. They learned to use a.m. and p.m. They also found the end time, start time, or elapsed time given the other two values either in minutes only or in hours only. They always had a clock face they could look at.

In this chapter, students will continue to do calculations involving time, but the elapsed time will now be in both hours and minutes, and they will no longer see a clock face all the time. They will add and subtract periods of time, even when the time crosses a.m. or p.m. To be able to thoroughly calculate time, they do need to be able to tell time on an analog clock, which makes it easer for them to understand time calculations involving a sexigesimal system (base 60) and well as a 12-hour system.

By convention, 12 a.m. denotes midnight and 12 p.m. denotes noon, and this is what will be shown on digital clocks. Because of the potential for confusion, this curriculum uses 12 noon and 12 midnight.

Abbreviations for hours, minutes, and seconds are not standardized. This curriculum uses h for hours, min for minutes, and s for seconds.

Compound Units

Time given in hours and minutes is similar to other measurements in compound units. Students will first convert from hours and minutes to minutes only by multiplying the number of hours by 60 mentally and then adding on the minutes. For example: 3 h 40 min = 180 min + 40 min = 220 min. They will then convert from minutes to hours and minutes. One way to do this is to divide the minutes by 60: the quotient is the number of hours and the remainder the number of minutes. Since students have not yet formally learned to divide by a two-digit number, the total hours will not be more than 5, and students will need to recall that 1 h = 60 min, 2 h = 120 min, 3 h = 180 min, 4 h = 240 min, and 5 h = 300 min from having first converted hours to minutes. For example, 205 min is greater than 180 min (3 h) and less than 240 min (4 h); 205 – 180 = 25, so 205 min = 3 h 25 min.

Adding and Subtracting Time

Students will learn strategies for finding the end time or elapsed time, which involves adding time in compound units, and for finding start times, which involves subtracting time in compound units. These strategies are similar to strategies they have learned previously for adding and subtracting whole numbers, money, and metric measurements in compound units, except that the base is now 60, rather than 10 or 100. They will therefore "make 60" or "subtract from 60". Most of the minutes will be multiples of 5, so your student should be able to easily make 60 or subtract from 60 mentally.

12-Hour Clock

This curriculum is written for U.S. students and so assumes that students live in a country that still commonly uses a "12-hour clock." Many countries now use a "24-hour clock," which uses 00:00 (midnight) to 23:59. In the U.S., this may be called "military time." Military usage does not include the colon separating hours and minutes, and leading 0s are written. Some countries use a period to separate hours and minutes. Thus, 8:00 a.m. might be written 08:00, 0800, or 08.00, and might be read as "oh eight hundred." If you are currently living in a country that uses a 24-hour clock, you will need to adjust the lessons accordingly or expand on them and teach your student to convert between times in the 24-hour clock and 12-hour clock (by adding or subtracting 12 for times between noon or midnight). If you do teach the 24-hour clock, you can ask your student to give afternoon times both ways.

Chapter Opener (p. 183)

Your student should be able to read time at least to the 5-minute mark before starting this chapter. Students did learn to tell time to the one-minute mark in Dimensions Math® 2B. This is not specifically reviewed in this chapter, and many of the times are to the 5-minute mark to facilitate calculations. If your student cannot tell time to the one-minute mark with an analog clock, spend a little time now helping them to tell time for any time on the clock. Use a demonstration clock and set a time to a five-minute mark, such as 4:40. Ask your student for the time. Move the hand a few minutes, such as to 4:42, and ask them to tell you the new time. They should realize that they can simply count count on from 4:40. Set some other times and have your student tell you the time. Ask them to show you some times, such as 6:22.

To answer the questions in Chapter Opener, your student can either use the pictures of the clock faces, or you can give them an analog clock with geared hands and let them move the hands. The first three questions and the last one of the Chapter Opener reviews concepts from Dimensions Math® 2B.

Alex: The time is 8:30.

Emma: The current time is 9:30. In 1 hour it will be 10:30. Math class is over at 10:30.

Dion: The current time is 10:10. 10:30 is 20 minutes later. There are 20 minutes left to play the math game.

Sofia: Sofia's question introduces finding elapsed time that is in hours as well as minutes. The current time is 10:50. It is 10 minutes to 11:00, and an hour to 12:00. Or, it is 1 hour to 11:50, and then another 10 minutes until noon. So it is 1 hour and 10 minutes until lunch.

Mei: The current time is 2:15. 3:00 is 45 minutes later. They have 45 minutes to work on the art project.

Lesson 1 Units of Time (pp. 184–189)

This lesson is long and could take more than a day.

Think (p. 184)

These activities help students get a feel for how long a minute is. Passage of time is less easy to estimate than a measurement such as length, because we are not measuring an object we can see and handle, and because of the subjective nature of time. Time seems to pass more slowly under some circumstances than others. A minute seems like a longer time when it is being timed, versus when we are not paying attention to time.

Have your student do some activities for 1 minute as you time it. Then have them estimate how long a minute is by doing one of these activities again while you time them and stopping when they think a minute has passed. They can compare their estimate with the actual amount of time. Your student probably knows what seconds are but, if not, you can simply say the approximate time, such as, "Not quite a minute" or, "Almost two minutes."

Have you student give or estimate how long some familiar activities take in minutes or hours, such as brushing their teeth for 3 minutes or driving somewhere that takes 3 hours.

Discuss other measurements of time such as hours, days, weeks, months, and years.

Answers

24

2 (a) 60 minutes
(b) 12 hours
(c) 2 times
(d) 24 times
(e) 60 times

3 (a) minutes (b) minutes
(c) hours (d) seconds

4 90 min

5 (a) 120 min
(b) 125 min
(c) 180 min
(d) 195 min

6 110 s

7 (a) 120 s
(b) 175 s
(c) 240 s
(d) 272 s

8 2 h 10 min

9 (a) 1 h 15 min (b) 1 h 40 min
(c) 2 h 35 min (d) 3 h 24 min

10 (a) 2 min 10 s (b) 1 min 50 s
(c) 1 min 25 s (d) 1 min 16 s

11 52 hours

12 168 hours $7 \times 24 \text{ h} = 168 \text{ h}$

13 (a) p.m. (b) a.m.
(c) a.m. (d) p.m.
(e) p.m. (f) a.m.

14 21 days

Learn (p. 185)

If your student is not familiar with seconds, make sure they realize it as a short unit of time, and tell them that there are 60 seconds in a minute. Let them watch the seconds pass on either an analog clock with a second hand or on a digital clock or timer that shows seconds. We can estimate seconds by counting steadily, saying a word after the number that takes about a second to say, such as "one thousand," "potato," "hippopotamus," etc. You can have your student count seconds this way, perhaps to 15 seconds, and use a timer to see how close they come to the actual number of seconds.

Discuss Sofia's question. If there are three hands on a clock, one is for seconds.

Review the use of a.m. and p.m. Since the clock only shows 12 hours, we use a.m. for times between midnight and noon, and p.m. for times between noon and midnight. If your student is interested in words, tell them that a.m. is an abbreviation of the Latin phrase "ante meridiem," which means "before midday," and p.m. is an abbreviation for "post meridiem," which means "after midday."

Do (pp. 186–189)

1. Point out the abbreviation for seconds, minutes, and hours.

2. This is review. Discuss the answers as needed.

4. Dion is showing with a type of number bond that we can find the total minutes in 1 h 30 min by adding the number of minutes in 1 hour (60 min) and 30 min.

5. We can find the total number of minutes by multiplying 60 by the number of hours, and then adding any minutes. Ask your student to also find the number of minutes in 4 h and 5 h.

6. We use the same calculations to convert minutes and seconds to seconds only.

8. Emma is showing that we can find the number of hours by thinking of the number of minutes in hours. 130 min is more than 60 min (1 h) and 120 min (2 h) but less than 180 min (3 h). So she knows the number of hours is 2. Then she mentally subtracts 130 from the number of minutes in 2 h (120) to find the number of minutes. Notice that this is in a thought bubble. Students can do this type of calculation mentally; they do not have to write their steps.

9. If necessary, you can have students make a list or table of the number of minutes in 1 h, 2 h, 3 h, 4 h, and 5 h to refer to.

10. We use the same calculations to convert seconds to minutes and seconds.

11. To find the number of hours in a given number of days, multiply the number of days by 24 and then add the hours.

14. Discuss Sofia's question. Share any methods you might have to remember the number of days in each month (such as using a rhyme or the knuckles of your hands).

Lesson 2 Calculating Time — Part 1 (pp. 190–193)

Think (p. 190)

Have your student try to find the answers without a demonstration clock.

Learn (p. 191)

The strategy shown using the clocks is "make the next hour," similar to making a ten, except that we "make 60" instead. Make sure your student understands the methods shown here.

(a) We are finding an end time given a start time and an elapsed time. 8:50 is 10 minutes to 9:00 (50 and 10 make 60), so we can split the 50 min into 10 and 40. Add 10 min to get to 9:00, and then 40 min to get to 9:40. Imagining a clock face helps with calculations. You may want to tell your student that we can also think in terms of adding time in compound units. 8:50 a.m. is 8 hours after midnight and we are simply adding another 50 minutes: 8 h 50 min + 50 min. We can solve this by "making the next hour" or thinking how many minutes there are until the next hour and how many minutes that leaves after subtracting it from the 50 minutes.

(b) We are finding the elapsed time given the start time and end time. We can think of how many minutes it takes to get from 9:40 to 10:00 (40 and 20 make 60), then the number of minutes to get from 10:00 to 10:15, and add those two times.

(c) 12:00 is more than an hour after 10:15. We can first count up by hours to a time in the hour before 12:00 (11:15, 1 h) and then add the 45 minutes remaining (15 and 45 make 60). We could also think that there are 45 minutes until 11:00, and then another hour until 12:00.

Answers

(a) 9:40
9:40

(b) 35 min
35 min

(c) 1 h 45 min
1 hour and 45 minutes

1 (a) 35 min
(b) 50 min
(c) 4 h
(d) 4 h 15 min

2 (a) 6:53 a.m.
(b) 7:00 a.m.
(c) 7:20 a.m.
(d) 9:45 a.m.
(e) 10:18 a.m.

3 2 h 30 min 15 min
2 h 45 min

4 1 h 5 min

5 11:15 a.m.

6 3 h 45 min 4 h 5 min
4 h 5 min

Do (pp. 192–193)

1. (a) Students can use the supplied clock face, if needed, to see that there are 35 minutes to 4:00 p.m.

   (b) Students should realize they just need to add another 15 minutes to the answer for (a).

   (d) Students can use the answer to (c); 15 min pass between 25 after the hour and 40 after the hour.

2. (a) Students need to recognize when adding the minutes will not make the next hour, so they do not have to try to "make 60."

   (c) From (b), it is 15 minutes from 6:45 to 7:00. 35 minutes from 6:45 is another 20 minutes more (35 is 15 and 20.

   (e) From (d), it is 3 hours to 9:45. Then It is 15 minutes to the next hour, and another 18 minutes to have a total of 33 minutes (33 is 15 and 18).

3. This problem shows how we can think in terms of a "time line" to find the elapsed time. We can first add on 2 h to get from 7:30 to 9:30, then 30 min to get to 10:00, then 15 min to get to 10:15. Students can draw a rough time line for problems if they need to, or they can use it as a mental visualization tool. They can find each elapsed time mentally and add on, or write down each first (2 h, 30 min, 15 min) and then add. There is more than one method of solution. For example, it is 30 minutes to 8:00, 2 hours until 10, and 15 minutes until 10:15.

4. Students need to give the total time in compound units of hours and minutes when it is more than 1 hour. Two methods are provided for adding the minutes. Dion thinks of how to "make 60" with 50 and splits 15 into 10 and 5, so the answer is 1 h 5 min. Emma adds the minutes to get 65 min and then converts to compound units. Your student can use this method if they struggle with Dion's method, but if they could do the previous three problems they should have no trouble thinking in terms of "making 60."

5. To find the end time, we can add 2 h 45 min to the start time. We can think of the start time as 8 h 30 min and add in compound units, using strategies similar to adding compound units in Chapter 8. The strategy shown here is to first add the hours, then the minutes. To add the minutes, Sofia is using a "make 60" strategy. Students could instead add 30 minutes and 45 minutes to get 75 minutes and then convert that to 1 h 15 min.

6. Here, we are finding a total time when the times are given in compound units, and can use the strategy of "making 60" to mentally add the 20 minutes.

Lesson 3 Practice A (pp. 194–195)

Enrichment

This curriculum uses a "12-hour clock." Tell your student that most countries, as well as the military, use a "24-hour clock" in which the time from midnight to midnight is divided into 24 hours rather than two 12 hour segments. 1:15 p.m. is 13:15. Midnight is 00:00. 7:15 a.m. is recorded as 07:15 and might be read as "oh seven fifteen." The minutes for time on the hour are sometimes read as "hundred" even though there are not 100 minutes in an hour. For example, 09:00 is "oh nine hundred." Digital clocks can usually be set to show the time either way.

Have your student convert some written times from the "12-hour clock" to the "24-hour clock." For p.m. times, we add 12 to the hours:

12:30 a.m. ⟶ 00:30
1:00 p.m. ⟶ 13:00
9:40 p.m. ⟶ 21:40
11:20 p.m. ⟶ 23:20

Then have them do the reverse:

00:45 ⟶ 12:45 a.m.
07:15 ⟶ 7:15 a.m.
12:45 ⟶ 12:45 p.m.
14:00 ⟶ 2:00 p.m.
20:30 ⟶ 8:30 p.m.

You can use **Mental Math Sheet** 26 for more practice.

Answers

❶ (b) Multiply the answer from (a) by 6.

❷ (a) 105 s (b) 1 min 45 s
(c) 135 min (d) 2 h 5 min
(e) 72 h (f) 49 days

❸ (a) 2 h 45 min
(b) 7:15 p.m.
(c) 7 h 15 min

❹ (a) 50 s (b) 15 s
(c) 25 min (d) 20 min
(e) 40 min (f) 54 min

❺ (a) 4 h 40 min (b) 4 h
(c) 4 h 15 min (d) 5 h 15 min
(e) 8 h 25 min (f) 6 h 15 min
(g) 5 h 55 min (h) 8 h 10 min

❻ **2:53 p.m.**

$12{:}25 \xrightarrow{2\text{ h}} 2{:}25 \xrightarrow{28\text{ min}} \mathbf{2{:}53}$

❼ **1 h 30 min**

30 min + 35 min + 25 min = 90 min
90 min = 1 h 30 min

❽ **1 h 35 min**

$10{:}25 \xrightarrow{1\text{ h}} 11{:}25 \xrightarrow{35\text{ min}} 12{:}00$

❾ 2 h 27 min

$2{:}20 \xrightarrow{2\text{ h}} 4{:}20 \xrightarrow{27\text{ min}} 4{:}47$

Lesson 4 Calculating Time — Part 2 (pp. 196–199)

Think (p. 196)

Your student can use a demonstration clock to find the answers if needed. They will find that the time changes from a.m. to p.m. For (a), students learned in Dimensions Math® 2B how to find the end time even when just adding on minutes.

Learn (p. 197)

The strategy shown for (a) is similar to that in Lesson 2, except here a.m. goes to p.m. the next hour after 12. For (b), two methods are shown. Discuss both of them.

We can count the hours from 8:50 to 1:50 (9:50, 10:50, 11:50, 12:50, 1:50; it is fine to use fingers to keep track of the hours). Or, we can also think 12 minus 8 is 4 hours to 12:50, then another hour to 1:50. Then we know it is another 35 minutes to 2:25 (as learned in Lesson 2).

Or, we can find how long it will be from 8:50 to 12:00, then from 12:00 to 2:25, and then add the two elapsed times together. This will likely be a less common method in everyday life since we have to keep track of the both elapsed times before adding them together.

Other methods are possible, such as determining that it is 10 minutes to get to 9:00, 5 hours to get to 2:00, another 25 minutes to get to 2:25, for a total of 5 hours and 35 minutes.

Answers

(a) 12:15
12:15

(b) 5 h 35 min
5 h 35 min

(c) 5 hours and 35 minutes

1. 1:15 p.m.

2. (a) 11:00 p.m.
(b) 11:55 p.m.
(c) 2:25 a.m.
(d) 3:13 a.m.

3. (a) 3 h 15 min
(b) 3 h 30 min
(c) 6 h 45 min

4. 5:09 p.m.

5. 7 h 35 min
3 h 45 min 3 h 50 min
7 hours and 35 minutes

6. **6:05 a.m.**

9:35 p.m. $\xrightarrow{\text{8 h}}$ 5:35 a.m.
$\xrightarrow{\text{25 min}}$ 6:00 a.m. $\xrightarrow{\text{5 min}}$ 6:05 a.m.

7. **1:47 p.m.**

11:20 a.m. $\xrightarrow{\text{2 h}}$ 1:20 p.m.
$\xrightarrow{\text{27 min}}$ 1:47 p.m.

8. **3 h 45 min**

9:20 p.m. $\xrightarrow{\text{3 h}}$ 12:20 p.m.
$\xrightarrow{\text{40 min}}$ 1:00 a.m. $\xrightarrow{\text{5 min}}$ 1:05 a.m.
3 h + 40 min + 5 min = 3 h 45 min

Do (pp. 198–199)

Students should write a.m. or p.m. after each time.

1. This reminds student that the next hour after 12:45 p.m. is 1:00 p.m. and does not change to a.m., even though the hour goes from 12 to 1. It would change when the hour goes from 11 to 12. This can be confusing for some students.

2. Students are finding the end time in each of these. For (c), they could count on, keeping track of how many hours they count (11:25, 12:25, 1:25, 2:25) and know that p.m. changes to a.m. For (d), they can use the answer to (c) and find the time 48 minutes after 2:25 p.m. They could split 48 into 35 and 13, since it is another 35 minutes to get from 2:25 to 3:00.

3. This problem uses the second method from Learn to find the total elapsed time. Students know how to find each of the two time intervals from Lesson 2. For (c), they add the two time intervals.

4. Students can use any method. 4 hours after 8:45 is 12:45, another 4 hours is 4:45, another 15 minutes is 5:00, 15 to 24 is 9, so it will be 5:09 p.m. They can draw a rough time line, if that helps.

5. Mei uses the first method in Learn and Emma uses the second method. Their methods are in thought bubbles. Students should eventually be able to solve problems like this mentally.

6. 7. 8. The solutions in the guide show one possible method for each. Your student's thought processes might vary. You may want to occasionally require that they show their methods. They could write an "arrow diagram" similar to the ones in this guide or draw a rough timeline, marking the times and the intervals.

Lesson 5 Calculating Time — Part 3 (pp. 200–203)

Think (p. 200)

Have your student find the answer any way they want, including "counting on" from 55 minutes to 2 hours 20 minutes, similar to what they have been doing in previous lessons.

Learn (pp. 200–201)

Discuss these three methods, even if your student used a different method altogether for Think. Number bonds and arrow diagrams are used to explain the process.

We can subtract 55 minutes by subtracting from one of the hours, then add that difference (5 min) and a time that is one hour less (1 h 20 min).

55 min is close to an hour. We can subtract an hour, and then add back in the difference.

We can split 55 into 20 and 35 so that we can first subtract 20 to get a whole number of hours, and then subtract 35 from one of those hours.

Do (pp. 202–203)

1. None of these problems cross a.m. or p.m., so students can solve these as if subtracting from 6 h 15 min.

4. This shows that we can think of a time as compound units: 7:25 is 7 h 25 min. Since 3 h 40 min is less than 7 h 25 min, they do not have to be concerned that the time will go from p.m. to a.m.

Answers

1 h 25 min
1 h 25 min
1 h 25 min
1 hour and 25 minutes

1. (a) 6:09 p.m.
   (b) 6:00 p.m.
   (c) 5:40 p.m.
   (d) 3:15 p.m.
   (e) 2:45 p.m.

2. (a) 35 min
   (b) 2 h 35 min
   (c) 2 h 45 min
   (d) 3 h 24 min

3. (a) 40 min 1 h 40 min 1 h 50 min
   (b) 15 min 5 h 15 min 6 h 5 min
   (c) 57 min 2 h 57 min 3 h 47 min

4. 4:25 3:45
   7 3:45

5. (a) 4 h 30 min
   (b) 3 h 15 min
   (c) 2 h 30 min

6. (a) 20 min (b) 1 h 20 min
   (c) 4 h 40 min (d) 3 h 48 min

7. **2:35 p.m.**

   4:25 $\xrightarrow{-1\text{ h}}$ 3:25

   $\xrightarrow{-25\text{ min}}$ 3:00 $\xrightarrow{-25\text{ min}}$ 2:35

Lesson 6 Calculating Time — Part 4 (pp. 204–206)

Think (p. 204)

Your student should try to find the answer without a demonstration clock. If they struggle, you can encourage them to draw a time line to help them find the answer. They can start by marking 12 midnight, each hour after 12 midnight to at least 6:00 a.m., and label 6:15 a.m. They can then mark some hours before 12:00 midnight as count the hours back.

Learn (p. 204)

In Method A, after we "hop" back 6 h and 15 min to midnight we need to hop another 2 h and 15 min back to have hopped a total of 8 h 30 min.

Use this timeline to explain to your student that one way to find the answer is to use the mental math strategies for subtracting time they learned in the previous lesson. 6:15 a.m. is 6 h 15 min after midnight. The elapsed time is greater than this. We can subtract the end time of 6 h 15 min from the elapsed time to find out how much greater and then subtract that from 12 hours:

8 h 30 min − 6 h 15 min = 2 h 15 min

12 h − 2 h 15 min = 9 h 45 min

The answer to the second subtraction is the amount of time after 12:00 noon of the previous day, so the answer is 9:45 p.m.

Answers

9:45 p.m.
9:45 p.m.
9:45 p.m.

1 (a) 12:30 p.m.
(b) 12:00 p.m. (12:00 noon)
(c) 11:30 a.m.
(d) 9:05 a.m.
(e) 8:20 a.m.

2 (a) 12:00 p.m.
(b) 11:30 a.m.
(c) 11:15 a.m.
(d) 5:30 a.m.
(e) 7:30 a.m.
(f) 6:45 a.m.

3 3 h 30 min
(a) 3 hours and 30 minutes
(b) 9:40 a.m.
(c) 9:40 a.m.

4 (a) 11:40 p.m.
(b) 9:40 p.m.
(c) 10:40 p.m.
(d) 10:30 a.m.
(e) 9:40 a.m.

5 11:00 a.m.

In Method B, we simply find 8 hours before 6:15 (students can use fingers and count the hours backward) and then find the time another 30 minutes before 10:15 mentally.

<u>Do</u> (pp. 205–206)

1. (a) 35 is 5 and 30, so find 30 minutes before 1:00. Even though 1 goes back to 12, p.m. does not go to a.m.
   (b) The earlier time is still p.m. Students can also answer 12:00 noon, though.
   (c) The earlier time is now a.m.
   (e) From (d), 4 h earlier is 9:05. Another 45 min is 40 min earlier than 9:00.

2. (b) The time changes from p.m. to a.m.
   (c) Find 15 min earlier than 11:30, the answer to (b).
   (d) Any time that is 12 hours earlier or later is the same time, but a.m. changes to p.m. or vice-versa.
   (e) Students might realize that they can simply add 2 hours to the answer to (d).
   (f) Find 45 min earlier than 7:30, the answer to (e).

3. This problem uses Method 1 in <u>Learn</u> to find the answer to (c). If (c) were given alone, students could solve it subtracting twice:
   5 h 50 min − 3 h 30 min = 2 h 20 min
   12 h − 2 h 20 min = 9 h 40 min

4. (b) Subtract 2 hours from the answer to (a).
   (c) 1 a.m. is 1 hour later than midnight, so add 1 hour to the answer to (b).
   (e) Subtract 50 minutes from the answer to (d).

5. This problem should be easy, but is a common type of situation in which we need to determine an earlier time from a later time when the elapsed time is given in several time intervals.

Lesson 7 Practice B (pp. 207–208)

❷ Students should realize that if a clock is fast, the actual time is earlier, and if a clock is slow, the actual time is later than the time shown on the clock face.

Methods can vary for the problems on page 208. Students can draw a time line, use an arrow diagram, write expressions, or a combination. They might also count on or back hours and then determine the minutes mentally. They should include a.m. or p.m. for all of their answers. If you want them to practice showing their work, or if they get an incorrect answer and did not show any work, ask them to justify some of their answers using one of the written methods.

Enrichment

- You may want to have your student research UTC (Coordinated Universal Time) and what methods are used to keep track of the official time.
- You may want to help your student understand international time zones, which does involve an understanding of the rotation of the earth. If you live on the west coast of the United States, for example, the time for a friend or relative on the east coast is 3 hours later (depending on which state and whether daylight savings time is observed in both states). The time in New Zealand might be a day later than the time in the United States.

Answers

❶ (a) 20 min (b) 5 h
(c) 25 min (d) 4 h 25 min
(e) 1 h 25 min (f) 8 h 48 min

❷ (a) 10:09 (b) 3:03

❸ (a) 4 h 15 min (b) 4 h 25 min
(c) 2 h 25 min (d) 3 h 10 min
(e) 11 h 40 min (f) 12 h 20 min
(g) 11 h 50 min (h) 5 h 50 min
(i) 1 h 20 min (j) 25 min

❹ **9:55 a.m.**
3 h 50 min – 1 h 45 min = 2 h 5 min
12 h – 2 h 5 min = 9 h 55 min

❺ **9:30 a.m.**
10 h 15 min – 45 min = 9 h 30 min

❻ **2:53 p.m.**
12:25 p.m. to 1:25 p.m. is 1 hour
1 h 25 min + 1 h 28 min = 2 h 53 min

❼ **6 h 55 min**
12 h – 9 h 50 min = 2 h 10 min
2 h 10 min + 4 h 45 min = 6 h 55 min

❽ (a) **4 h 30 min**
2 h 35 min + 1 h 55 min
= 4 h 30 min
(b) **40 min**
2 h 35 min – 1 h 55 min = 40 min

❾ **10:45 a.m.**
2 h 30 min – 1 h 15 min = 1 h 15 min
12 h – 1 h 15 min = 10 h 45 min

Chapter 14 Workbook Answers

Exercise 1 pp. 173–176

1. (a) s
   (b) min
   (c) h
   (d) s
   (e) min
   (f) h

2. (a) a.m.
   (b) p.m.
   (c) a.m.
   (d) p.m.
   (e) a.m. p.m.

3. (a)
   180 min
   195 min
   (b) 1 h
   2 h
   2 h 10 min

4. (a)
   120 s
   165 s
   (b) 1 min
   3 min
   3 min 20 s

5. (a) 24 h
   120 h
   (b) 7 days
   105 days

6. 60 360
   120 420
   180 480
   240 540
   300 600

7.

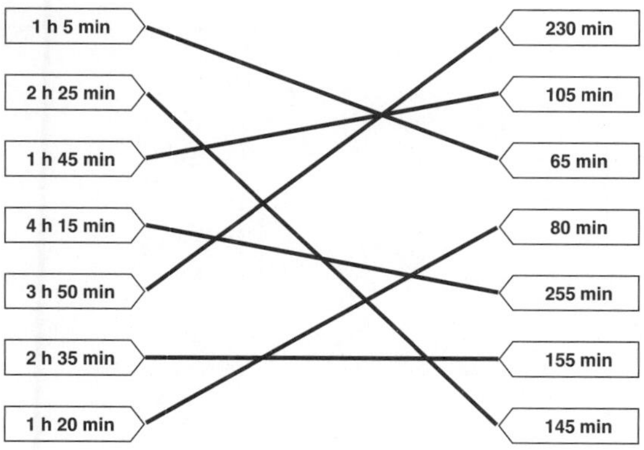

8. (a) 305 s
   (b) 92 s
   (c) 2 min 20 s
   (d) 5 min 35 s

9. (a) 9 days
   (b) 2 weeks 2 days

10. **25 days**
    3 × 7 days = 21days
    21 days + 4 days = 25 days

11. **Valentina, 5 min longer**
    85 min = 1 h 25 min or
    1 h 20 min = 80 min
    85 − 80 = 5

12. **Caden, 25 min faster**
    4 × 60 min = 240 min
    240 min + 13 min = 253 min
    4 h 13 min = 253 min
    253 − 228 = 25

13. **52 weeks 2 days**
    366 ÷ 7 is 52 with a remainder of 2

14. **29 days**
    The first Wednesday until 4th Tuesday:
    4 weeks. Wednesday is another 1 day

Exercise 2 pp. 177–179

1. (a) 4:25 p.m. —35 min→ 5:00 p.m. —10 min→ 5:10 p.m.
   5:10 p.m.
   (b) 1:25 a.m. —3 h→ 4:25 a.m. —45 min→ 5:10 a.m.
   5:10 a.m.
   (c) 5 h 10 min

Chapter 14 Workbook Answers

2 4 h → 15 min → 20 min →

4 hours and 35 minutes

3 (a) 2 h 25 min
(b) 2 h 45 min
(c) 5 h 45 min

4 (a) 8:10 p.m.
(b) 9:00 p.m.
(c) 9:05 p.m.

5 (a) 45 (b) 40
(c) 25 (d) 4
(e) 13 (f) 51

6 (a) 1 h 5 min
(b) 1 h 8 min
(c) 1 h 4 min
(d) 1 h 14 min

For the word problems, students can draw a rough time line if it is helpful. Possible time lines are shown for some problems.

7 **10:18 p.m.**

43 min − 25 min =

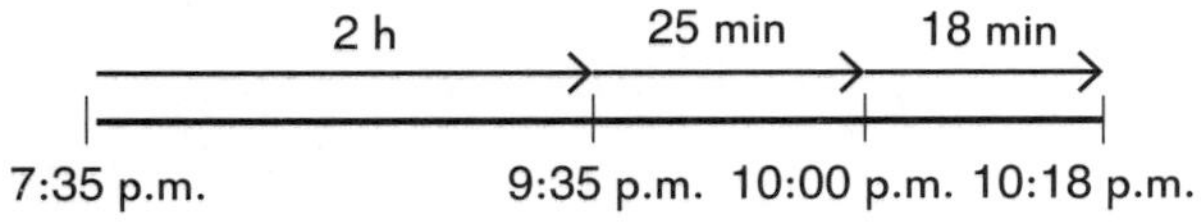

8 **1 h 50 min**

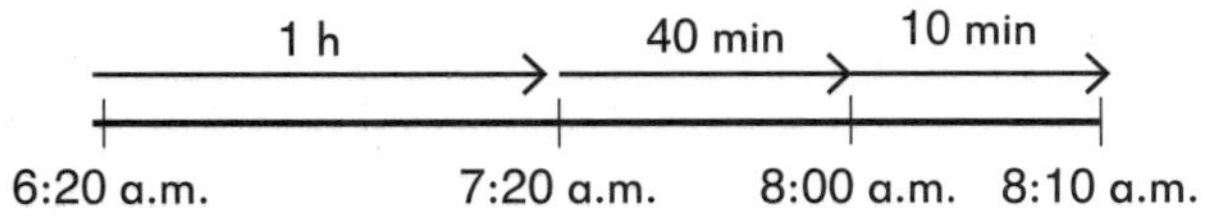

9 **2 h 10 min**
1 h 20 min + 50 min = 2 h 10 min

10 **7:15 p.m.**
165 min = 2 h 45 min
2 h 45 min after 4:30 p.m. is 7:15 p.m.

Exercise 3 pp. 180–182

1 2 min 15 s, 165s, 3 min 5 s, 190 s

2 (a) 8 h 30 min
(b) 8 h 33 min
(c) 17 h 42 min
(d) 7 h 20 min

3 (a) **1 h 25 min**

2:35 p.m. —1 h→ 3:35 p.m.
—25 min→ 4:00 p.m.

(b) **2 h 49 min**

8:50 a.m. —2 h→ 10:50 a.m.
—10 min→ 11:00 a.m. —39 min→ 11:39 a.m.

(c) **2 h 18 min**

1:22 p.m. —2 h→ 3:22 p.m.
—18 min→ 3:40 p.m.

4 **Sunday**
Today is Wednesday, 1 week from today is Wednesday, 4 more days is Sunday.

5 **8 weeks 6 days**
62 ÷ 7 is 8 with a remainder of 6

6 **1 h 45 min**

4:35 p.m. —1 h→ 5:35 p.m.
—25 min→ 6:00 p.m. —20 min→ 6:20 p.m.

7 **7:54 a.m.**

6:12 a.m. —1 h→ 7:12 a.m.
—42 min→ 7:54 a.m.

Chapter 14 Workbook Answers

❽ **11:43 a.m.**

8 h 50 min + 2 h 20 min = 11 h 10 min

11 h 10 min + 33 min = 11 h 43 min

❾ **7:30 p.m.**

15 min + 2 h 20 min = 2 h 35 min

2 h 35 min + 25 min = 3 h

3 h after 4:30 p.m. is 7:30 p.m.

❿ **8 buses**

9:10, 9:25, 9:40, 9:55, 10:10, 10:25, 10:40, 10:55

Exercise 4 pp. 183–186

❶ (a) 12:50 p.m.
(b) 1:25 p.m.
(c) 3:25 p.m.

❷ (a) 3 hours and 15 minutes
(b) 6 hours and 30 minutes
(c) 9 hours and 45 minutes

❸ 5:50 p.m. 6:15 p.m.
6:15 p.m.

❹ (a) 1 h 20 min
(b) 3 h
(c) 3 h 35 min
(d) 3 h 38 min
(e) 3 h 33 min
(f) 3 h 36 min

❺ (a) 4:15 a.m.
(b) 4:20 a.m.
(c) 4:22 a.m.
(d) 4:24 a.m.
(e) 4:26 a.m.

Methods can vary.

❻ (a) **16 h 15 min**

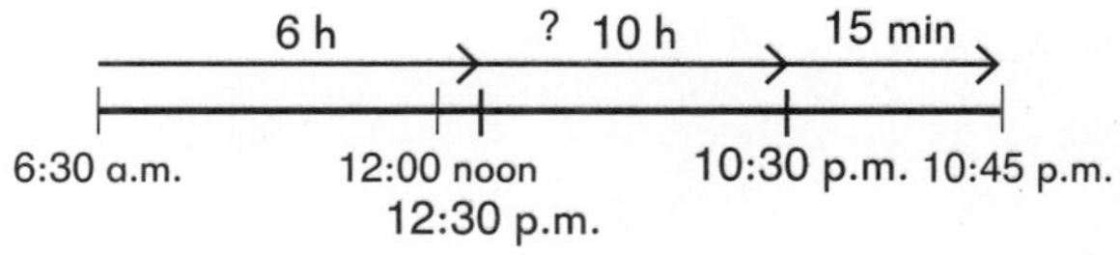

(b) **7 h 45 min**

10:45 p.m. $\xrightarrow{2\text{ h}}$ 12:45 a.m.

$\xrightarrow{5\text{ h}}$ 5:45 a.m. $\xrightarrow{45\text{ min}}$ 6:15 a.m.

❼ **5:20 p.m.**

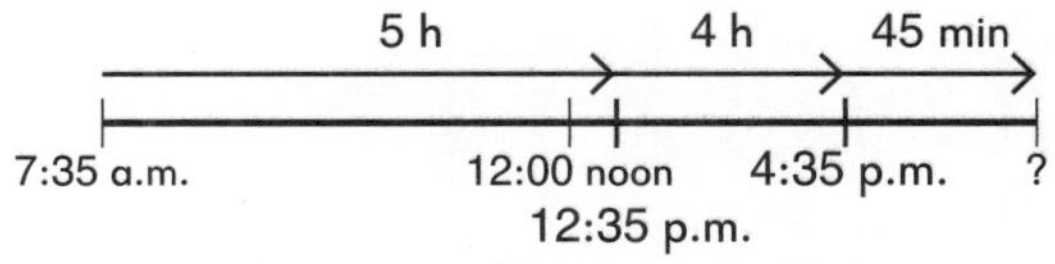

4 h 35 min + 45 min = 5 h 20 min

❽ **5:38 a.m.**

8 hours after 8:50 p.m. is 4:50 a.m.

4 h 50 min + 10 min = 5 h

5 h + 25 min + 13 min = 5 h 38 min

❾ **3:35 p.m.**

25 min + 30 min + 15 min + 25 min = 1 h 35 min

1 h + 2 h + 1 h 35 min = 4 h 35 min

4 h 35 min after 11 a.m. is 3:35 p.m.

❿ **32 h 30 min**

9:45 p.m. Friday to 6:15 a.m. Saturday is 8 h 30 min. It is 24 h to the same time Sunday.

8 h 30 min + 24 h = 32 h 30 min

⓫ **17 buses**

9:10, 9:35, 10:00, 10:25, 10:50, 11:15, 11:40, 12:05, 12:30, 12:55, 1:20, 1:45, 2:10, 2:35, 3:00, 3:25, 3:50

Chapter 14 Workbook Answers

Exercise 5 pp. 187–190

1. (a) 15 min
   (b) 25 min
   (c) 2 h 25 min
   (d) 2:25 a.m.

2. (a) 50 min
   (b) 3 h 50 min
   (c) 2 h 50 min
   (d) 2:50 p.m.

3. (a) 6 min
   (b) 2 h 26 min
   (c) 2 h 26 min
   (d) 2:26 p.m.

4. (a) 4:00 p.m.
   (b) 3:50 p.m.
   (c) 2:50 p.m.
   (d) 2:47 p.m.

5. (a) 4 h 28 min
   (b) 4 h 38 min

6. (a) 3 h 31 min
   (b) 3 h 42 min
   (c) 1 h 35 min

7. (a) 1:40 p.m.
   (b) 7:40 a.m.

Methods can vary.

8. **12:50 p.m.**

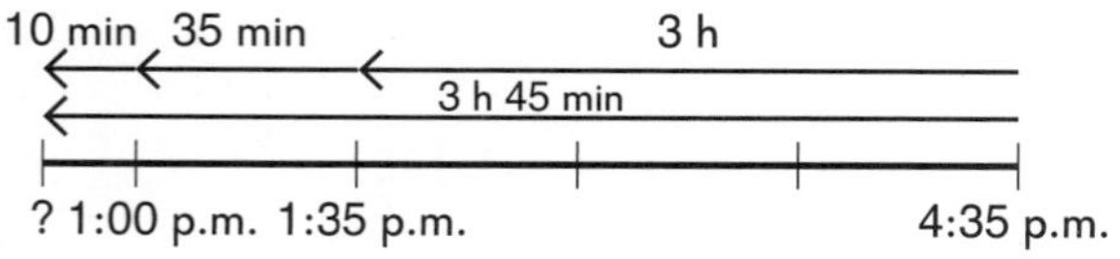

Or:

4 h 35 min − 3 h 45 min = 0 h 50 min
0 h is 12:00 noon, so 12:50 p.m.

9. **50 min longer**
   2 h 15 min − 1 h 25 min = 50 min

10. **3 h 20 min**
    35 min + 1 h 20 min = 1 h 55 min
    5 h 15 min − 1 h 55 min = 3 h 20 min

11. **5:50 p.m.**
    1 h 25 min + 15 min = 1 h 40 min
    7 h 30 min − 1 h 40 min = 5 h 50 min

12. **8:48 a.m.**
    24 × 3 min = 72 min = 1 h 12 min
    It loses 1 h 12 min.
    1 h 12 min before 10:00 a.m. is 8:48 a.m.

13. **18 buses**
    20 min intervals back from 9:10:
    8:50, 8:30, 8:10, 7:50, 7:30, 7:10, 6:50, 6:30, 6:10: 9 buses
    20 min intervals on from 9:10:
    9:30, 9:50, 10:10, 10:30, 10:50, 11:10, 11:30, 11:50; 8 buses
    9 buses + 8 buses + 1 bus (at 9:10) = 18 buses

Exercise 6 pp. 191–194

1. (a) 30 min 3 h 4 h 15 min
   7 hours and 45 minutes
   (b) 25 min 3 h 5 h
   8 hours and 25 minutes
   (c) 7:50 8:00 12:00
   7:50 a.m.
   (d) 3:55 4:35 12:35
   3:55 a.m.

2 (a) 12:25 p.m.
(b) 12:00 noon
(c) 11:00 a.m.
(d) 10:40 a.m.

3 (a) 12:15 a.m.
(b) 8:15 p.m.
(c) 8:00 p.m.
(d) 7:40 p.m.

4 (a) 11:10 a.m.
(b) 11:10 a.m.

Methods can vary.

5 **11:05 a.m.**

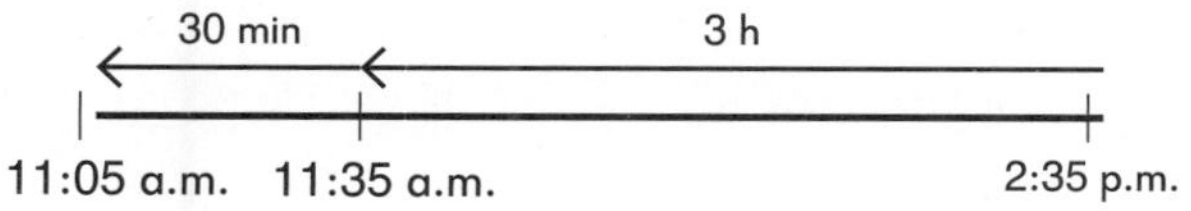

6 **7:15 a.m.**
15 h 15 min – 10 h 30 min = 4 h 45 min
12 h – 4 h 45 min = 7 h 15 min

7 **7:55 p.m.**
11 h 10 min – 7 h 5 min = 4 h 5 min
12 h – 4 h 5 min = 7 h 55 min

8 **3:38 a.m.**
According to the digital clock, the power was out for 2 h 37 min.
6 h 15 min – 2 h 37 min = 3 h 38 min

9 **9 buses**
25 min intervals back from 2:10 p.m.:
1:35 p.m., 1:00 p.m., 12:25 p.m., 11:50 p.m., 11:15 a.m.: 5 buses
2:10 p.m. on:
2:45 p.m., 3:20 p.m., 3:55 p.m.: 3 buses
5 buses + 3 buses + 1 bus (at 2:10) = 9 buses

Exercise 7 pp. 195–198

1 (a) 1 h 45 min
(b) 1 h 31 min
(c) 4 h 10 min
(d) 2 h 25 min
(e) 1 h 37 min

Methods can vary.

2 **5:30 a.m.**

8:45 p.m. $\xrightarrow{+4\text{ h}}$ 12:45 a.m. $\xrightarrow{+4\text{ h}}$ 4:45 a.m. $\xrightarrow{+45\text{ min}}$ 5:30 a.m.

3 **2 h 25 min more**
3 h 45 min – 1 h 20 min = 2 h 25 min

4 **90 min**

11:45 a.m. $\xrightarrow{+1\text{ h}}$ 12:45 p.m. $\xrightarrow{+30\text{ min}}$ 1:15 p.m.

5 **10:15 a.m.**

12:45 p.m. $\xrightarrow{-2\text{ h}}$ 10:45 a.m. $\xrightarrow{-30\text{ min}}$ 10:15 a.m.

6 **9 h 45 min**
11:00 a.m. to 2:45 p.m. is 3 h 45 min
5:30 p.m. to 11:30 p.m. is 6 h
3 h 45 min + 6 h = 9 h 45 min

7 **2:50 p.m.**
1 h 35 min + 45 min = 2 h 20 min
5 h 10 min – 2 h 20 min = 2 h 50 min

Chapter 14 Workbook Answers

8. **11:50 p.m.**
   600 min = 10 h
   200 min = 3 h 20 min
   10 h + 3 h 20 min = 12 h + 1 h 20 min
   12 hours after 10:30 a.m. is 10:30 p.m.
   10 h 30 min + 1 h 20 min = 11 h 50 min

9. (a) **Analog: 5:50 a.m.**
   Digital: 2:50 a.m.
   Analog:
   6 h 15 min – 25 min = 5 h 50 min
   Digital:
   At 3:00 a.m. the clock resets to 12 midnight. It comes back on after 25 min, so it loses 3 h 25 min.
   6 h 15 min – 3 h 25 min = 2 h 50 min

   (b) **2:20 a.m.**
   From (a), the difference in time between the two clocks is 3 hours, which is the time after midnight that the power went off. The digital clock showed a time 3 hours earlier than the analog clock because it reset to midnight, 3 hours earlier than when the power went out.
   Difference in time this night:
   5 h 5 min – 2 h 45 min = 2 h 20 min

10. Students can use a variety of approaches. One possible method:
    - Find the number of days in the years between the current year and the birth year, taking into account which years were leap years.
    - Find the number of days in the months in the birth year from the month after the birth month.
    - Find the number of days left in the month of the birth month.
    - Find the number of days in the months in the current year before the current month.
    - Add the day of the current month to the days found in all the previous steps.

Chapter 15 Money

	Lesson	Page	Objectives
	Chapter Opener	175	
1	Dollars and Cents	176	Review counting sets of coins and bills. Convert between cents and dollars to cents only, and from cents only to dollars and cents for amounts up to $100.
2	Making $10	177	Make $10 (1,000¢) using mental math strategies.
3	Adding Money	178	Add money amounts within $100.
4	Subtracting Money	179	Subtract money amounts within $100.
5	Word Problems	180	Solve word problems.
6	Practice	182	
	Review 4	183	
	Review 5	185	

Materials

Material

- Bills ($1, $5, $10, $20)
- Coins (100 pennies, 50 dimes, 50 nickels, and 20 quarters)

Optional

- Store cards (20 of them): pictures of objects on index cards, with a cost between $1.00 and $25.00 (you can use coupons with those amounts)

Mental Math Sheets

(singaporemath.com/higprintouts)

Mental Math		After Lesson
29	Make $10	2
30	Add money	3
31	Subtract money	4
32	Add and subtract money	4

Notes

In Dimensions Math® 1B, students learned to count money in sets of bills and coins, to express money amounts with a dot between dollars and cents, to convert between cents and dollars to cents only and vice versa, and to add and subtract money within $10 primarily using mental math strategies.

This chapter reviews these concepts and extends them to amounts of money within $100. Students can use mental math strategies for addition and subtraction, similar to those they used previously, such as when adding and subtracting meters and centimeters in compound units, which generally involve "making 100." They can use mental math particularly when the cents are in multiples of 5. Whenever it seems overwhelming to use mental math, they can instead add and subtract money using the standard algorithm, thinking of the money as being expressed in cents only.

Students will then solve word problems involving money. Some of these word problems will require drawing bar models to solve.

Students do not need to understand decimals in order to work with money in dollars and cents; expressing money using a dot between dollars and cents simply borrows from decimal notation, since a penny is one hundredth of a dollar. They can think of the dot as a symbol separating dollars and cents, and that writing $3.45 simpler than writing compound units such as 3 dollars 45 cents when money is involved. They do have to realize they can only do this with money, and will understand why when they learn about decimals. They will also have to remember that we always have two places for the cents, so we put a 0 after the dot if the amount of cents is less than 10.

This chapter is mostly a review of mental math strategies for addition and subtraction computation and solving word problems. It will not likely require a lot of instruction if your student did Dimensions Math® 2B and has mastered the material so far in Dimensions Math® 3. There are not many new concepts, since any mental math strategies are similar to those learned earlier with other calculations. There are quite a few computation problems. Assign only as many as you feel necessary.

Activity

- After Lesson 1
  Materials: Bills and coins (play money or index cards with $5, $10, $20, $100 on them can substitute for real bills), store cards
  Purpose: Count money and make change for a purchase.
  Procedure: One person is a cashier and has a collection of coins and bills. Give the rest of the participants a hundred-dollar bill and have them purchase one item at a time, checking to make sure that the cashier gives the correct change when they do not give an exact amount.
  Variation: After Lesson 3, have participants buy several items at a time. They have to add to find the total cost to make sure they have enough money. You can either have the cashier then also find the total cost, or check what the buyer claims to be the total cost.

Games

- After Lesson 4
  Materials: Store cards, paper and pencil
  Purpose: Subtract money amounts.
  Goal: Buy the most amount of items.
  Procedure: Shuffle the cards and place them face down. Players each start with a total of $100.00, which they write down. They turn over one card at a time and subtract the amount from their total each time, "buying" the item. The first player to use up all their money or not have enough to pay for the next item wins.

Chapter Opener (p. 209)

This Chapter Opener is primarily a review of calculations involving money that students learned in earlier levels. If your student did not use Dimensions Math® 2B, and has not worked with money when the amount is both dollars and cents, you can skip it for now, do Lesson 1, which is a review, spending as much time as needed with Lesson 1, and then come back to it, if you want.

Dion is thinking of the equation he would use to find the change Mei will get after buying the apple. Have your student find the answer. They should use mental math strategies for subtracting from 100, which they have learned previously in this level.

Have your student write an expression for the change Alex would get after buying the watermelon. They can write $5 – $2.79 or $5.00 – $2.79 (with or without the cents for five dollars). Have them find the answer any way they want. Discuss Sofia's solution. She is finding the change as if "making change," that is, counting up the cents to the next whole number of dollars, then counting up the dollars to the total of $5.

If your student needs practice making change (as well as counting money), you can do that during Lesson 1, spending more than a day with the review. Give them some coins and bills, then tell them you are buying a item that costs an amount within $10.00 and paying with a ten-dollar bill. They need to give you exact change. You can use the store cards if you made them (see Materials).

Lesson 1 Dollars and Cents (pp. 210–213)

Think (p. 210)

Have your student find the answers. They should be able to count the money using the pictures (they could cross out coins as they count them), or you can give them actual coins and bills to count.

Learn (p. 211)

This shows one strategy for counting the amount of money in coins: finding combinations that make a quarter where possible. Four quarters make another dollar. Other strategies are possible, such as simply counting on, starting with the coins of the highest denomination, and remembering that 100¢ is \$1. It will not always be possible to set aside exactly \$1 in coins, such as if there were 3 quarters and 3 dimes only.

This also reviews how to write the total amount of money in dollars, even when there is more than \$1 in cents, and to convert from dollars (dollars and cents written with a decimal point or dot) to cents only.

Answers

\$17.12

1. 245¢

2. \$4.60

3. (a) \$21.30 2,130¢
   (b) \$62.05 6,025¢

4. (a) 2,305¢
   (b) 1,299¢
   (c) 4,090¢
   (d) 31¢
   (e) 3,100¢

5. (a) \$15.43
   (b) \$8.20
   (c) \$20.06
   (d) \$0.42
   (e) \$0.03

6. (a) 15¢ (b) 75¢
   (c) 57¢ (d) 29¢
   (e) \$0.40 (f) \$0.65
   (g) \$0.96 (h) \$0.09

Do (pp. 212–213)

3. If necessary, remind your student that we write a 0 after the dot if the amount of cents is less than 10 (we don't write \$62.5 for 62 dollars and 5 cents).

4. If necessary, for (d), remind your student that we can write cents as dollars even when the total amount of money is less than a dollar; we write 0 before the dot. For (e), remind them that we do not have to write a dot and two zeros if there are no cents (we can write \$31 instead of \$31.00), but do have to remember to include the two zeros when writing the amount as cents (\$31 = 3,100¢).

6. This problem reviews "making \$1," which is essentially the same as "making 100," something students have learned to do previously.

Lesson 2 Making $10 (pp. 214–215)

Think (p. 214)

Ask your student to find the answer. They can use any method they want.

Learn (p. 214)

This shows some mental math strategies for "making $10."

Method 1: Make 100, or $1, with the cents, and $9 with the dollars. $1 and $9 is $10 in all.

Method 2: Think of "making the next dollar," (which is still essentially making a dollar with the cents, as in the first method, but there is now a total of $8.) That is the cents needed. Then the dollars needed is just the difference between $10 and $8.

Since $10 is 1,000¢, we could also "make 1,000" with the total cents, as suggested by Dion's thought bubble. $7.65 is 765¢. Then 2 more hundreds makes 9 hundreds, 3 more tens make 9 tens, and 5 more ones make 10 ones, so the answer is 235¢, or $2.35.

Do (p. 215)

1. Some students might realize that in cases where there is only one price with a given dollar amount, they just need to match it with a price where the dollar amounts add to $9. If so, the only ones where they need to look at the cents are the ones with 5 and 4 as dollar amounts.

Answers

$2.35

1.

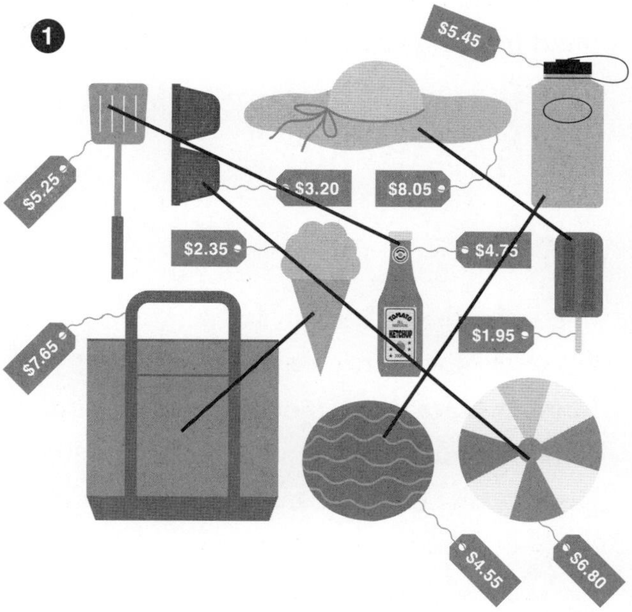

2. (a) $9.99 (b) $9.15 (c) $3.57
(d) $9.40 (e) $0.75 (f) $2.65
(g) $4.29 (h) $3.96 (i) $5.09

Lesson 3 Adding Money (pp. 216–219)

Think (p. 216)

Have your students write the addition expression, find the value, and then finish the equation. They can use any method they want.

Learn (pp. 216–217)

This shows a variety of methods for adding the two amounts. Make sure your student understands the reasoning behind each. Other strategies are possible. The first three strategies are mental math strategies, with the thought process indicated by the expressions or words in the thought bubbles.

Method 1: First add the dollars, then the cents. In this case, the cents are added using the strategy of "make $1."

Method 2: This also essentially uses the strategy of "make $1" to add cents. Another 60¢ makes the next whole number of dollars with $29.40. Split $9.80 into 60¢ and $9.20.

Method 3: $9.80 is almost $10. We can add the next whole number of dollars and subtract the excess. This method would also work well in situations such as 35.35 + 6.98, where the cents are close to $1.

Method 4: This method uses the addition algorithm. It can be used at any time when a mental math strategy is not quickly obvious or when it looks like there will be a lot of regrouping, such as $59.76 + $67.84.

Answers

$39.20
$39.20
$39.20
3,920¢ $39.20
$39.20 39.20

1 (a) 90¢ $1.00 $1.20
(b) $7.00 $7.20 $47.20
(c) $3.00 $3.25 $33.25

2 (a) $24.50 ⟶ $25.25
(b) $21.00 ⟶ $36.25
(c) $37.50 ⟶ $37.45
(d) $54.55

3 (a) $51.10 (b) $31.30
(c) $22.00 (d) $22.05
(e) $26.75 (f) $27.05
(g) $13.30 (h) $18.15
(i) $61.35 (j) $6.01
(k) $21.81 (l) $49.03

Do (pp. 218–219)

1 Students are encouraged to use the strategy involving making $1.

2 Discuss the strategy shown for each of these. It might be helpful to first write the addition expression. You can ask your student to speculate why each friend might have chosen a particular strategy for that specific problem.

3 You may want to assign only some of these. The later problems are a bit more challenging than the earlier problems.

Lesson 4 Subtracting Money (pp. 220–223)

Think (p. 220)

Have your students write an expression, find the value, and then finish the equation. They can use any method they want.

Learn (pp. 220–221)

This shows a variety of methods for adding the two amounts. Make sure your student understands the reasoning behind each. Other strategies are possible.

Method 1: First subtract the dollars, then the cents. The number bond indicates that the second step is done by splitting the 85¢ into 50¢ and 34¢ so that 50¢ is subtracted first, then 35¢ is subtracted from $12.

Method 2: This is similar to Method 1, but the cents are subtracted first to make a whole number of dollars. The second step is not explained. $6 and 35¢ could be subtracted in either order.

Method 3: Dion notices that $6.85 is almost $7. This method of subtracting a whole number of dollars and adding the excess is easier if the number subtracted is a multiple of 10 or 5 than if it is not, but would also work well in situations such as $35.35 – $6.98, where the cents are close to $1.

Method 4: This method uses the subtraction algorithm. It can be used at any time when a mental math strategy is not quickly obvious or when it looks like there will be a lot of regrouping, such as $82.17 – $67.84.

Answers

$11.65
$11.65
$11.65
11.65 1,165
$11.65

1. (a) 60¢ $7.60
   (b) 60¢ $7.75

2. (a) $3.25 (b) $3.75
   (c) $12.65 (d) $26.85
   (e) $34.15 (f) $49.95

3. (a) $8.50 ⟶ $7.75
   (b) $5.00 ⟶ $4.95
   (c) $11.50 ⟶ $11.55
   (d) $16.81

4. (a) $60.40 (b) $85.15
   (c) $23.30 (d) $59.25
   (e) $48.25 (f) $28.26
   (g) $35.83 (h) $31.45

Do (pp. 222–223)

1. 2. Students are encouraged to use a strategy involving subtracting cents from a whole number of dollars.

3. It could be helpful to first write the subtraction expression before discussing the strategies shown here.

4. You may want to assign only some of these. The later problems are a bit more challenging.

Lesson 5 Word Problems (pp. 224–226)

Think (p. 224)

Have your student solve the word problem. It is a relatively simple two-step problem, and students who have mastered previous content should not need to draw a bar model to be able to solve this.

Learn (p. 224)

Discuss the solution shown here, as well as Dion's alternate solution, which is simply doing the operations in a different order.

Do (pp. 225–226)

The problems here are similar in type to ones students have seen before, except that the values are now dollars and cents, rather than whole numbers. In general, encourage your student to draw models (when one is not provided) if they have any doubt whatsoever of what steps to take to solve these types of problems.

1 The bar model shows why this is an addition problem and not a subtraction problem, which some students might assume from a quick reading of the problem.

3 You may want to have your student also label what they need to find in some way. This is not a particularly challenging problem, but drawing a model can help keep track of the numbers, particularly since Carlos' amount is given in the last sentence.

Answers

$33.40
$40 – **$33.40** = **$6.60**
6.60

1 **$27.95**
$15.65 + $12.30 = $27.95

2 **$34.45**
$24.65 – $14.85 = $9.80
$24.65 + $9.80 = $34.45

3

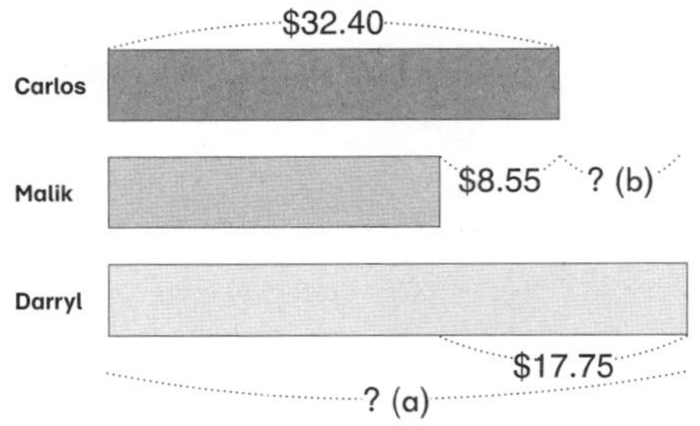

(a) **$41.60**
$32.40 – $8.55 = $23.85
$23.85 + $27.75 = $41.60

(b) **$9.20 more**
$41.60 – $32.40 = $9.20

4

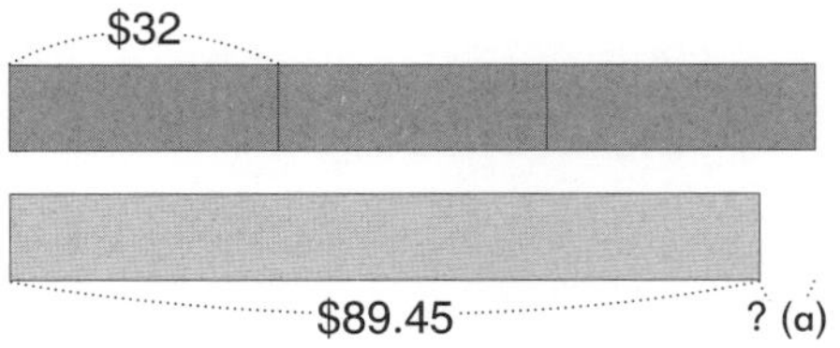

(a) **$6.55**
3 × $32 = $96
$96.00 – $89.45 = $6.55

(b) **$13.43 more**
$9.99 + $9.99 = $19.98
$19.98 – $6.55 = $13.43

4 Although a model is provided, most students should be able to solve this type of problem by now without one.

6 At this level, your students might still need to draw a bar model for this type of problem in order to see a method of solution, even though they have seen similar problems often. Students might also start a model and then not actually have to complete it to see that the solution is straightforward. Drawing a model is a tool, not the solution.

Answers (continued)

5 (a) **\$15.25**

\$6.80 + \$3.20 = \$10.00

\$10.00 + \$5.25 = \$15.25

(b) **\$4.75**

\$20.00 – \$15.25 = \$4.75

6 **\$36.15**

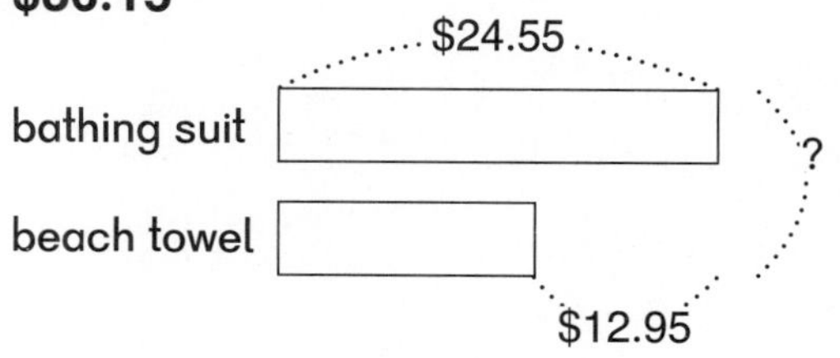

\$24.55 – \$12.95 = \$11.60

\$24.55 + \$11.60 = \$36.15

Lesson 6 Practice (pp. 227–228)

This practice is straightforward and the word problems are not particularly challenging. Your student should be able to do it independently.

Enrichment

Students have learned to multiply a three-digit number by a one-digit number. You can point out that they can easily multiply money amounts (less than $10) by converting to all cents and then multiplying or dividing as with whole numbers.

$5.69 × 6 = 569¢ × 6
= 3,414¢ = $34.14

Students have not formally learned to multiply and divide four-digit numbers by a one-digit number; however, they can multiply a dollar amount between $10 and $100 by multiplying the dollars separately from the cents, and then adding the two products together. (This is actually a good mental math strategy for 4-digit numbers, particularly when the tens and ones are easy to multiply by the one-digit number.)

$35.25 × 6
$35 × 6 = $210   25¢ × 6 = 150¢
$210 + $1.50 = $211.50

You can explain these strategies to your student and give them a few problems as a review of multiplication.

Answers

1. $12.38
   1,238¢

2. (a) 705¢   (b) $1,887¢
   (c) 2,852¢   (d) 3,020¢

3. (a) $5.10   (b) $12.04
   (c) $27.10   (d) $35.50

4. (a) $71.70   (b) $50.05
   (c) $46.90   (d) $47.95
   (e) $19.78   (f) $33.10
   (g) $8.35   (h) $12.34

5. **$16.50**
   $45.00 – $28.50 = $16.50

6. **$12.80**
   $52.75 – $39.95 = $12.80

7. **$12.65**
   $25.60 – $12.95 = $12.65

8. **$2.20**
   5.45 + 2.35 = $7.80
   $10.00 – $7.80 = $2.20

9. **$40**
   $23.35 + $8.75 = $32.10
   $32.10 + $7.90 = $40.00

10. **$13**

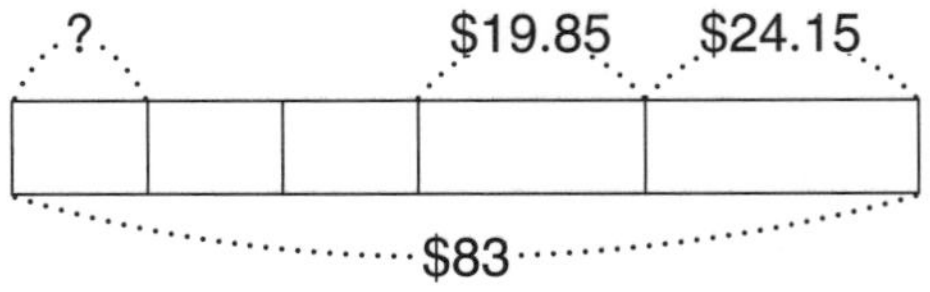

   $19.85 + 24.15 = $44.00
   $83 – $44 = $39
   $39 ÷ 3 = $13

Review 4 (pp. 229–232)

The two reviews together cover topics from both Dimensions Math® 3A and 3B. You might want to allow more than 2 days for both reviews, since the workbook reviews are also long.

5 This problem reviews not only bar graphs, but also calculation and solving simple word problems. Students should know which problems are easier to answer using the graph, and which ones require the data in the table. Students might use a different method for (j) and (l) than that shown in the answers here, multiplying or dividing the sales for each time period separately, then subtracting.

Answers

1 763
59

2 8,734

3 (a) P: $\frac{1}{3}$ Q: $\frac{1}{2}$ R: $\frac{5}{6}$

(b) $\frac{10}{12}$

(c) 4

4 (a) $\frac{5}{6}$, $\frac{3}{5}$, $\frac{8}{9}$, $\frac{9}{8}$

(b) $\frac{3}{10}$, $\frac{3}{8}$, $\frac{3}{5}$, $\frac{5}{6}$, $\frac{8}{9}$, $\frac{9}{8}$

5 (a) 100
(b) 10
(c) 50
(d) Saturday
(e) Tuesday
(f) **125 more people**
567 – 442 = 125
(g) **about 1,600 people**
300 + 200 + 500 + 200 + 400 = 1,600
(h) **$4,536**
567 × $8 = $4,536
(i) **$2,445**
489 × $5 = $2,445
(j) **$816 less**
$308 – $172 = $136
136 × $6 = $816
(k) **49 people**
$294 ÷ $6 = 49
(l) **57 more people**
$928 – $472 = $456
$456 ÷ $8 = 57

❻ Methods of solution can vary. For the problems involving elapsed time, students might draw time lines, use arrow diagrams, or mentally count on. If your students solves the problem mentally and gets an incorrect answer, ask them to justify their answer.

Answers (continued)

❻ (a) **6 h 30 min**
12 h – 10 h = 2 h
2 h + 4 h 30 min = 6 h 30 min

(b) **9 h 30 min**
6 h – 4 h 30 min = 1 h 30 min
6 h 30 min + 1 h 30 min
+ 1 h 30 min = 9 h 30 min

(c) **$8.65**
$12.40 + $18.95 = $31.35
$40 – $31.35 = $8.65

(d) **10:15 a.m.**
5 h 30 min – 3 h 45 min
= 1 h 45 min
12 h – 1 h 45 min = 10 h 15 min

❼ (a) **1 kg**
$\frac{5}{8} + \frac{3}{8} = \frac{8}{8} = 1$

(b) **$\frac{1}{4}$ kg**
$\frac{5}{8} - \frac{3}{8} = \frac{2}{8} = \frac{1}{4}$

❽ **67 L 500 mL**
95 L – 27 L 500 mL = 67 L 500 mL

Review 5 (pp. 233–236)

❸ Students may draw time lines or use arrow diagrams for problems involving time.

Answers

❶

	Perimeter	Area
K	18 units	9 units²
L	18 units	10 units²
M	18 units	10 units²
N	14 units	10 units²

(a) N

(b) K

❷ (a) **1 m 92 cm**

Side length for triangle:

72 cm ÷ 3 = 24 cm

Perimeter:

8 × 24 cm = 192 cm

(b) Yes, it is a quadrilateral with 4 equal sides.

(c) $\frac{1}{4}$

2 out of 8 triangles are green.

$\frac{2}{8} = \frac{1}{4}$

(d) s and t

(e) r and u

❸ (a) **8 h 15 min**

4 h 55 min + 3 h 20 min

= 8 h 15 min

(b) **7:15 a.m.**

8 h 15 min + 15 min + 15 min

= 8 h 45 min

12 h – 10 h 30 min = 1 h 30 min

8 h 45 min – 1 h 30 min

= 7 h 15 min

Or:

10:30 p.m. $\xrightarrow{\text{15 min}}$ 10:45 p.m. $\xrightarrow{\text{8 h}}$ 6:45 a.m. $\xrightarrow{\text{15 min}}$ 7:00 a.m. $\xrightarrow{\text{15 min}}$ 7:15 a.m.

4. Methods can vary; two are shown here.

7. This is a three-step problem. Students may want to draw a bar model. Since the division involves grouping, rather than sharing, the model may look somewhat like this:

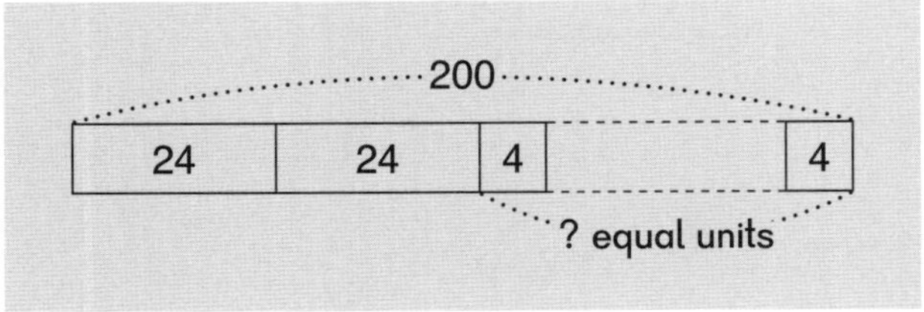

8. Students can use a set square, or corner of an index card, if needed.

9. Students can use a set square, or corner of an index card, to determine which angles are right angles, and a compass or a ruler to determine which sides are equal.

Answers (continued)

4. **10:15 a.m.**

   4 h 15 min – 2 h 30 min = 1 h 45 min

   12 h – 1 h 45 min = 10 h 15 min

   Or:

   2:30 p.m. $\xrightarrow{-4\text{ h}}$ 10:30 a.m.

   $\xrightarrow{-15\text{ min}}$ 10:15 a.m.

5. **2 km 460 m**

   120 m + 85 m = 205 m

   2 × 205 m = 410 m

   6 × 410 m = 2,460 m

6. **48 cm**

   2 × 10 cm = 20 cm

   20 cm + 12 cm + 16 cm = 48 cm

7. **38 baseballs**

   Cost of bats: 2 × \$24 = \$48

   \$200 – \$48 = \$152

   \$152 ÷ \$4 = 38

8. C

9. (a) V and W

   (b) X

   (c) W and X

   (d) V

   (e) V: 4 square units

   W: 6 square units

   X: 4 square units

   Y: 8 square units

   Z: 6 square units

10. **Diameter: 56 cm**

    112 cm ÷ 2 = 56 cm

    Radius: 28 cm

    56 cm ÷ 2 = 28 cm

11 Students may realize that the hour hand will point a little past 12. If necessary, they can use a clock and imagine that the hands form a straight line from the center to the tip of the hand.

12 Methods can vary for finding the area. One method is to find the area of a large rectangle (144 m^2) and subtract the area of two small rectangles (18 m^2 and 4 m^2).

13 Students should realize that the figure is made up of 9 squares all the same size.

14 This problem is challenging. Discuss it with your student, if they are struggling. Let the side of the small square be 1 unit. The larger squares are made up of 4 of the small squares, so the total perimeter is 20 units, and the figure has the same area as 9 squares. The larger squares are 1 small square apart from each other, so the total length of the decoration is 5 units.

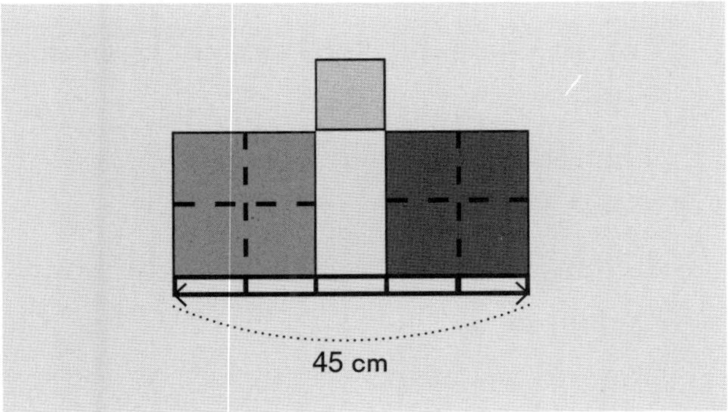

Answers (continued)

11 No

12 **\$976**

Area: 122 m^2

$122 \times \$8 = \$976$

13 (a) $\mathbf{\frac{2}{3}}$

6 of the 9 squares are blue.

$\frac{6}{9} = \frac{2}{3}$

(b) **96 cm**

16×6 cm = 96 cm

(c) **324 cm²**

6 cm × 6 cm = 36 cm^2

9 × 36 cm^2 = 324 cm^2

14 (a) **1 m 20 cm**

5 units ⟶ 45 cm

1 unit ⟶ 45 cm ÷ 5 = 9 cm

20 × 9 cm = 180 cm

3 m − 1 m 80 cm = 1 m 20 cm

(b) **729 cm²**

9 cm × 9 cm = 81 cm^2

9 × 81 cm^2 = 729 cm^2

Chapter 15 Workbook Answers

Exercise 1 pp. 199–201

1 (a) Ada: $2.02 202¢
Cora: $6.60 660¢
Lily: $3.00 300¢
(b) $0.98
(c) $3.27
(d) Cora

2 $0.82 82¢
$1.23 123¢
$6.83 683¢
$12.33 1,233¢
$46.05 4,605¢

3 (a) 65¢ (b) $0.58
(c) 29¢ (d) $0.08

4 (a) 1,468¢ (b) $61.25
(c) 1,808¢ (d) $30.04

5 (a) 42
(b) 85
Students are not expected to multiply 2.10 by 20 or 8.50 by 10, but rather to determine the number of nickels or dimes first in each dollar, then in the cents, and add.

Since this chapter is mostly review, the next four problems involve thinking of a strategy using known skills to solve problems involving the denominations of bills and coins, and so could be optional. Solutions can vary.

6 **1 ten-dollar bill**
The only way to have 4 bills is to have 1 ten-dollar bill and 3 five-dollar bills.

7 **4 quarters**
4 quarters = $1
4 nickels = 20¢
If your student does not immediately see that the answer must be 4 quarters, they can use coins, counting out 1 quarter and 1 nickel at a time until they have $1.20.

8 **49 nickels**
5 quarters = 1 dollar and 1 quarter, so there are 2 dollars total, as well as 1 quarter and 2 dimes.
$2 = 40 nickels
2 dimes = 4 nickels
1 quarter = 5 nickels
40 + 4 + 5 = 49

9 **$3.75**
1 quarter is 25¢.
Jamal has twice as much money (not twice as many coins) in dimes than quarters, so for every quarter he has 50¢ in dimes, or 5 dimes. For every 6 coins, 1 of them is a quarter, and 5 of them are dimes.
Number of sets of these 6 coins:
30 ÷ 6 = 5
He has 5 sets, so he has 5 quarters and 25 dimes.
5 quarters = $1.25
25 dimes = $2.50
$1.25 + $2.50 = $3.75

Chapter 15 Workbook Answers

Exercise 2 pp. 202–203

1. (a) $6.62
   (b) $3
   (c) 38¢
   (d) $3.38

2. (a) 65¢ (b) 65¢
   (c) 65¢ (d) 65¢

3. (a) $6 (b) $0.55
   (c) $6.55

4. (a) $1 (b) $0.48
   (c) $1.48

5.

O	N	E		H	U	N	D	R	E	D
$7.54	$3.50	$8.86	$1.25	$3.95	$7.85	$0.30	$5.05	$4.90	$5.80	$2.00

	P	E	N	N	I	E	S	
$4.37	$4.75	$6.68	$2.09	$8.60	$2.73	$0.71	$6.29	$1.12

6. (a) $5.54
   (b) Answers can vary. The fewest number of bills and coins would be 1 five-dollar bill, 2 quarters, and 4 pennies.

Exercise 3 pp. 204–206

1. (a) 25¢, $1.25 (b) 35¢, $1.35
   (c) 15¢, $4.15 (d) $5.80, $6.80

2. (a) $41.35 $42.00
   $42.00
   (b) $18.00 $29.25
   $29.25
   (c) $51.45 $51.40
   $51.40

3. 1 5 7 4
   6 3 2 2
   $63.22

4. A $74.10 B $42.45 G $69.35
   N $40.75 R $75.55 E $75.20
   S $63.30 C $41.28 K $24.77
   GREENBACKS

5. **$53.45**
   $21.60 + $31.85 = $53.45

6. **$52.19**
   $37.99 + $14.20 = $52.19

7. **$78.03**
   $39.98 + $21.56 + $16.49 = $78.03

Exercise 4 pp. 207–209

1. (a) 20¢, $0.20 (b) $1.00, $0.75
   (c) 45¢, $0.45 (d) $1.00, $4.60

2. (a) $8.35 $7.70
   $7.70
   (b) $17.00 $5.55
   $5.55
   (c) $21.45 $21.50
   $21.50

3. 1 5 7 8
   2 6 6 8
   $26.68

4. A $42.80 N $40.55 O $17.75
   I $3.85 R $17.85 G $19.35
   I $18.95 O $44.44 L $38.39
   A ROARING LION

Chapter 15 Workbook Answers

5 Fernando, 30¢ more

Liam has $32.55.

$32.85 – $32.55 = $0.30

6 $11.13

$80.00 – $68.87 = $11.13

7 $61.47

$79.27 – $17.80 = $61.47

Exercise 5 pp. 210–212

1 $98.95

shirt: $34.65 – $12.80 = $21.85

jacket: $21.85 + $20.60 + $42.45

$34.65 + $21.85 + $42.45 = $98.95

2 $95.20

1 shirt: $45 ÷ 3 = $15

6 shirts: 6 × $15 = $90

$90 + $5.20 = $95.20

Or:

There are 6 units plus $5.20. 3 units is $45, so 6 units is twice that.

2 × $45 = $90

$90 + $5.20 = $95.20

3 $7.25

Money spent: $9.95 + $2.80 = $12.75

$20.00 – $12.75 = $7.25

4 $27.88

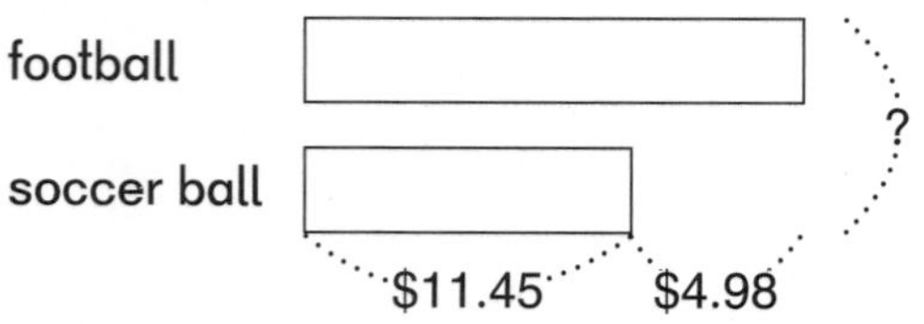

football: $11.45 + $4.98 = $16.43

$11.45 + $16.43 = $27.88

5 $12.50

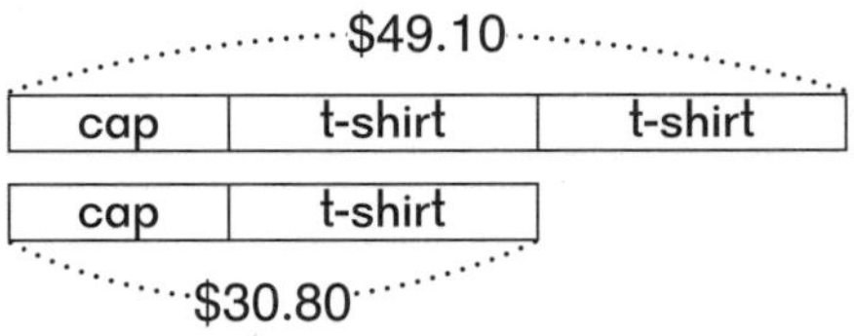

t-shirt: $49.10 – $30.80 = $18.30

cap: $30.80 – $18.30 = $12.50

6 $46.15

speakers: $29.50 – $2 = $27.50

headphones: $19.15 – $0.50 = $18.65

$27.50 + $18.65 = $46.15

7 $276.75

9 × $38 = $342

$49.50 + $15.75 = $65.25

$342 – $65.25 = 276.75

Students can subtract $65 and then another 25¢, and may be able to use mental math to do so. If they convert to cents and subtract, they will have a 5-digit number.

8 $12

$51 + $33 = $84

7 vases and 7 placemats cost $84

$84 ÷ 7 = $12

Students may automatically draw a bar model, such as the one below, if they did for 5, and then not see how to proceed.

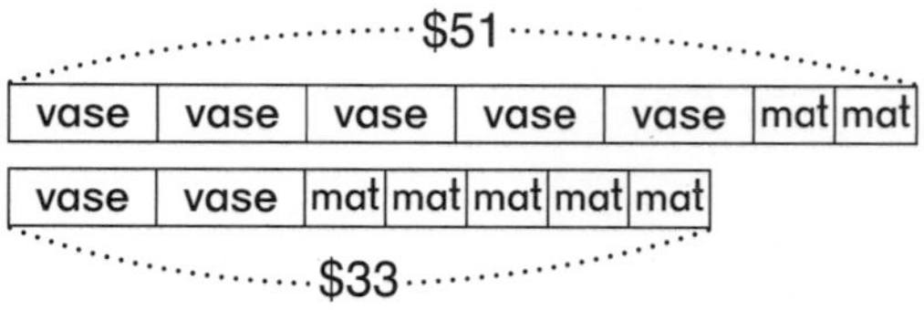

Point out that the problem is asking for the total cost of a vase and a placemat, and suggest they consider how many "vase-mat units" they have.

Chapter 15 Workbook Answers

Exercise 6 pp. 213–216

1 (a) $43.05   4,305¢
(b) $56.95

2 (a) **2 quarters**
26 ÷ 4 is 6 with a remainder of 2
(b) **65 dimes**
24 quarters is $6, which is 60 dimes. The remaining 2 quarters is 50¢, which is 5 dimes.

3 (a) $0.11   (b) $5.56
(c) $3.79   (d) $5.25
Students should solve these mentally. For (d), they are expected to split $20 into $10 and $10 in order to subtract from a $10, and not necessarily use the algorithm.

4 (a) **$17.55 more**
$39.50 – $21.95 = $17.55

(b) **$3.84**
She paid with $90 in bills
$62.16 + $24.00 = $86.16
$90.00 – $86.16 = $3.84

(c) **$142.80**
$79.45 + $23.85 + $39.50
= $142.80

(d) **Helmet and skateboard**
Students should realize that the items could not be the bicycle or racket. It would have to be the helmet and one of the other three items.

(e) **$36**
18 tennis balls is 2 more cans of balls.
2 cans: $24 ÷ 2 = $12
6 cans: 3 × $12 = $36
Or:
1 can: $24 ÷ 4 = $6
6 cans: 6 × $6 = $36

(f) **$18.21**
Racket: $62.16 + $10.85 = 73.01
Shipping: $4.10 + $4.10 = $8.20
$73.01 + $8.20 = $81.21
Explain to your student that Sharon would get her money back for the first tennis racket, but not for the shipping cost.

5 **$125**

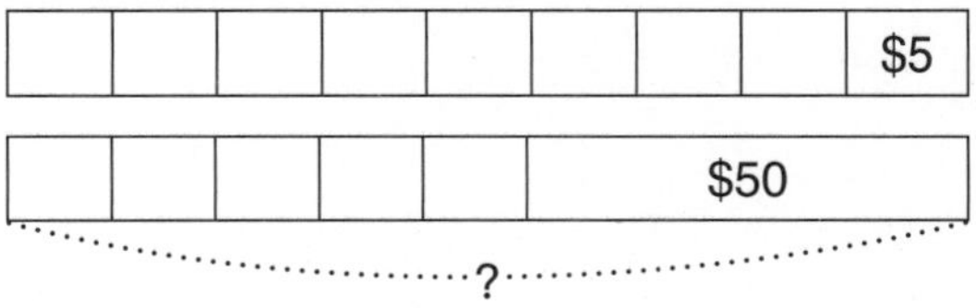

3 units ⟶ $50 – $5 = $45
1 unit ⟶ $45 ÷ 3 = $15
5 × $15 = $75
$75 + $50 = $125

6 **1 twenty-dollar bill,**
3 ten-dollar bills,
1 five-dollar bill
1 one-dollar bill
There are only two possible combinations of 6 bills that make $56. The other is:
2 twenty-dollar bills
3 five-dollar bills
1 one-dollar bill
This must be what John has, since he has 2 more five-dollar bills than Logan.

Chapter 15 Workbook Answers

7 **ball: $13, tiger: $18, car: $22**

Students could draw bar models, aligning like ones, even if they do not know the relative lengths of the bars to show each total. They could also think of the toys aligned similar to bar models, or draw them that way. If necessary, suggest they start by comparing sets where the difference is only one type of object.

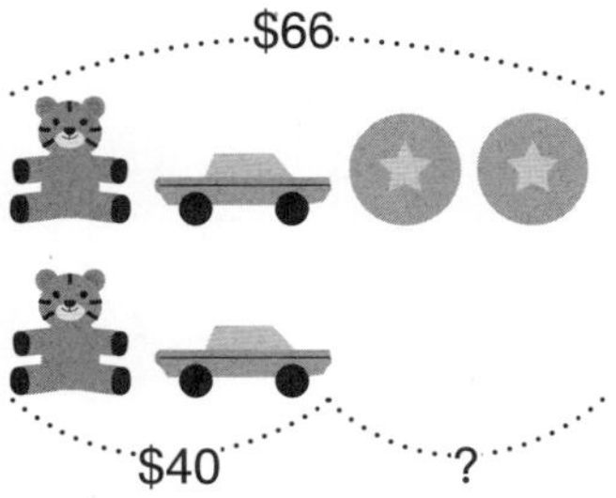

2 balls ⟶ $66 – $40 = $26

1 ball ⟶ $26 ÷ 2 = $13

2 tigers ⟶ $49 – $13 = $36

1 tiger ⟶ $36 ÷ 2 = $18

1 car ⟶ $40 – $18 = $22

Exercise 7 pp. 217–221

1 $4,209

2 Quotient: 85

Remainder: 7

3 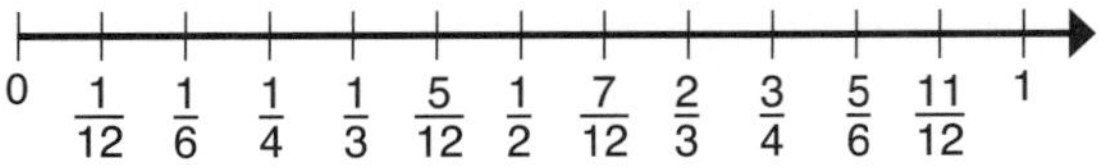

4 **3 L 160 mL**

bottle: 2,250 mL – 1,340 mL = 910 mL

both: 910 mL + 2,250 mL = 3,160 mL

5 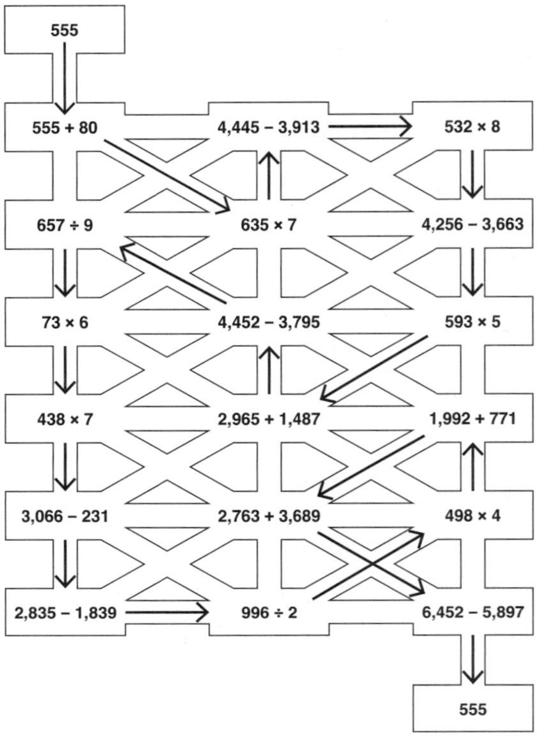

6 (a) $\frac{1}{2}$

(b) 32 square units

7 16

8 (a) **about 13 miles**

66 ÷ 5 is 13 R 1

(b) **about 3 km 60 m**

9 × 340 m = 3,060 m

Chapter 15 Workbook Answers

9 (a) **26 cm**
7 cm + 7 cm + 12 cm = 26 cm
(b) 2
(c) 2
(d) **rhombus, 28 cm**
4 × 7 cm = 28 cm

10 (a) **2 min 8 s longer**
10 min 11 s – 8 min 3 s = 2 min 8 s
(b) **12 h 22 min 59 s**
April 8 is 6 days after April 2
There will be a gain of 6 times as many minutes and seconds.
6 × 2 min = 12 min
6 × 8 s = 48 s
12 h 10 min 11 s + 12 min 48 s
= 12 h 22 min 59 s

11 **At least 3 times**
120 m + 60 m = 180 m
2 × 180 m = 360 m
Perimeter: 360 m
2 × 360 m = 720 m, less than 1 km
3 × 360 m = 1,080 m, more than 1 km

12 **148 cm**
The perimeter is 24 sides.
6 sides = 37 cm
24 ÷ 6 = 4
There are 4 groups of 6 sides.
4 × 37 cm = 148 cm
If your student first tries to find the length of a side and divide 37 by 6, and then does not know how to proceed since there is a remainder, suggest they think about "flattening" out a hexagon and laying its perimeter along the perimeter of the whole figure.

13 **$305**

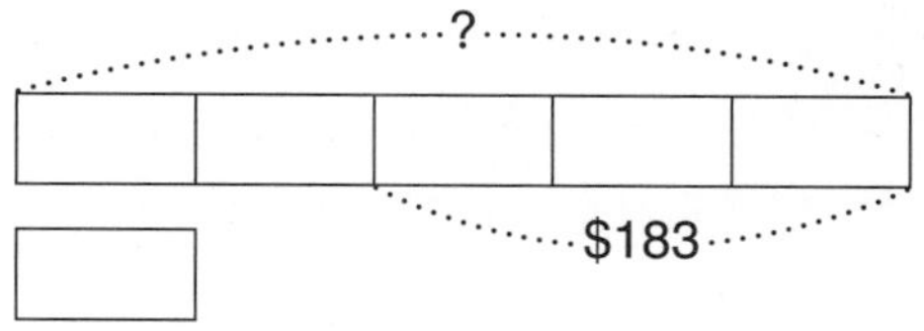

1 unit ⟶ $183 ÷ 3 = $61
5 units ⟶ 5 × $61 = $305
Drawing a bar model makes this problem relatively easy.

Exercise 8 pp. 222–226

1 (a) 280
(b) 36
(c) 5
(d) 9

2 **19 lollipops**
$4 = 16 quarters
80¢ = 3 quarters and 1 nickel
Total quarters = 19

3 $\frac{8}{10} = \frac{4}{5}$ $\frac{5}{10} = \frac{1}{2}$ $\frac{6}{8} = \frac{3}{4}$
$\frac{3}{7}, \frac{1}{2}, \frac{3}{4}, \frac{4}{5}$

4 (a) A 152 cm
B 3 m 48 cm
C 370 cm
D 1 m 58 cm
(b) C

5 **A, $\frac{1}{3}$ m**
Pole A: $1 - \frac{4}{9} = \frac{5}{9}$
Pole B: $1 - \frac{7}{9} = \frac{2}{9}$
$\frac{5}{9} - \frac{2}{9} = \frac{3}{9} = \frac{1}{3}$
Students may simply draw a picture or even a number line.

Chapter 15 Workbook Answers

6 **3:10 p.m.**

Time to noon:

12 h – 10 h 45 min = 1 h 15 min

Total time – time to noon:

4 h 25 min – 1 h 15 min = 3 h 10 min

7 **13 h 15 min**

Time to noon:

12 h – 6 h 30 min = 5 h 30 min

Total time:

5 h 30 min + 7 h 45 min = 13 h 15 min

8 (a) 2 min 55 s

(b)

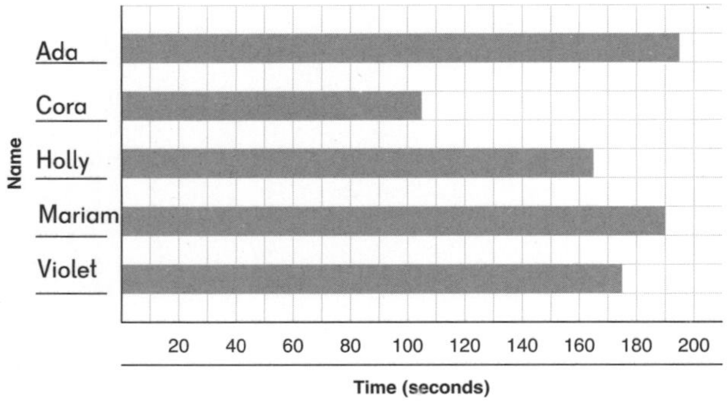

(c) 105 s, 2 min 45 s, 2 min 55 s, 3 min 10 s, 195 s

(d) **1 min 30 s**

195 s – 105 s = 90 s

9 **Perimeter: 38 cm**

Area: 44 cm²

There is a 8 cm by 7 cm rectangle with a 4 cm by 2 cm rectangle and a 2 cm by 2 cm rectangle cut out from it. Methods can vary.

10

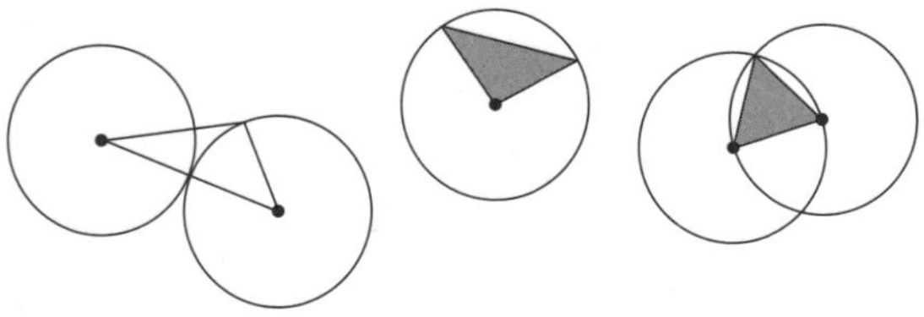

11 **224 eggs**

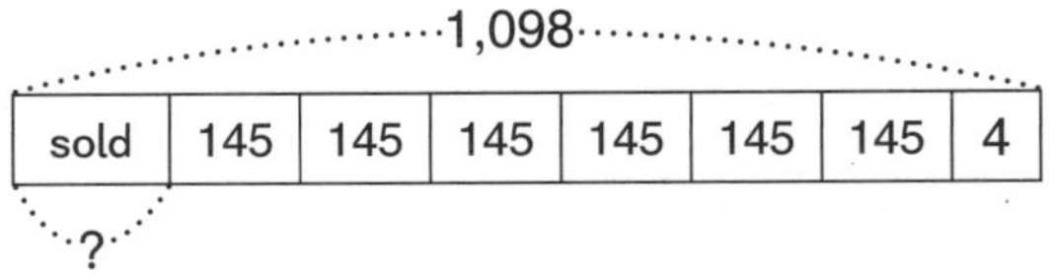

6 × 145 = 870

870 + 4 = 874

1,098 – 874 = 224

12 **1 kg 750 g**

200 pennies ⟶ 500 g

100 pennies ⟶ 500 g ÷ 2 = 250 g

700 pennies ⟶ 7 × 250 g = 1,750 g

If your student starts out by trying to divide 500 by 200 to find the weight of one penny and does not know how to proceed, suggest they think in terms of groups of 100 pennies.

13 **17 cm**

The third side must be 7 cm. The sum of the length of every two sides has to be longer than the third side.

7 cm + 7 cm + 3 cm = 17 cm

14 **14 cm²**

Total length of both widths:

18 cm – 14 cm = 4 cm

Width: 4 cm ÷ 2 = 2 cm

2 cm × 7 cm = 14 cm²

If your student struggles, suggest they use graph paper and try to draw the rectangle.

15 **1 unit**

The only whole numbers with a product of 11 are 1 and 11.

